Dear Graduating Tufts Senior,

Congratulations! On behalf of the Tufts University Alumni Association (TUAA), I welcome you to a prestigious group of over 96,000 men and women—the alumni of Tufts University! We at TUAA share your sense of accomplishment and excitement as you graduate and prepare to face a future full of possibility and promise. This book, "Gradspot.com's Guide to Life After College," is one way we hope to assist you in this important transition from student to professional life. I'd like to thank our partner, Tufts University Career Services, and our generous sponsor, Ringware, for working with us to make this book available to you.

Tufts University Alumni Association strives to promote Tufts' spirit and traditions, and to strengthen the links between our various constituencies and their alma mater.

Stay in touch!
Your Tufts experience doesn't end with commencement. As you embark on the next chapter of your life – whether in graduate school, employment, or both—we encourage you to stay connected to Tufts' network of dynamic and accomplished alumni.

We're pleased to offer you a variety of opportunities to do this. Our Web site, www.tufts. edu/alumni, is your gateway to a global network of alumni. By registering as a Tufts alumnus/ae, you can take advantage of a variety of tools to help you foster connections among friends old and new, cultivate your career and personal interests, maintain your relationship with Tufts, and create new relationships with other alumni.

The online community offers many electronic tools to help you get the most out of your Tufts connection, including:

- **Alumni Directory**—Find friends; update your contact information; and network with alumni from around the globe.

- **Career Center**—As a Tufts alumnus/ae, the Career Center is always an available resource for you! Post your resume and search career opportunities submitted by fellow alumni – and as you grow in your career, post job openings and browse resumes for the perfect Tufts candidate for a position you may have open.

- **Library Databases**—Tufts libraries offer alumni access to the same databases you used as a student: ABI/Inform, Expanded Academic, and Ovid MEDLINE.

- **@alumni.tufts.edu**—By getting a Tufts forwarding address, you can avoid having to notify everyone the next time your email address changes. Update your alumni email account, and your friends will always be able to reach you.

- **Classnotes**—A place to share your news or catch up with classmates online.

- **Social Networking**—Showcase and link up with your circle of friends. In addition to networking opportunities available on our Web site, Tufts Alumni groups can be found on Facebook, LinkedIn, and individual chapter or shared interest group Web sites.

- **Discussion Groups**—Share ideas and get advice from fellow alumni.

- **Alumni Web pages**—We provide easy-to-use templates and tools for classes, clubs, and other alumni chapters to create and maintain their own Web sites.

- **Yellow Pages**—A great place for business owners to promote their services and for alumni to seek out alumni-owned businesses in their area.

Join Regional Chapters and Shared Interest Groups

TUAA provides alumni regional chapters in major cities across the globe. There are currently over 50 chapters in cities worldwide from London, to Hong Kong, to San Francisco. If there's not a chapter in your area, continue to check our Web site for updates — alumni are continually coming forward to organize groups and activities. Or connect with TUAA to start your own regional group; our experienced staff is available and ready to help!

TUAA also offers groups centered on shared interests. Shared interest groups are organized around cultural background, major, profession, or other Tufts-related interests—including Tufts Lawyers Association, Tufts Association of Black Alumni, and the TCU Senate Alumni organization. Each of these groups encourages its members to enhance their connection to Tufts and to other alumni through continued exploration of shared experiences.

Volunteer

As a Tufts grad, you're now able to shape and sustain the institution that shaped you. Continue Tufts' spirit of community involvement by volunteering for alumni groups and events. Whether participating in a one-day event, or on a long-term committee, you have the opportunity to lead individuals, groups, and communities to make a difference.

Sustained volunteering opportunities:
Join a steering committee for your regional chapter, class year, or shared interest group; assist in creating or maintaining Web sites for your chapter or shared interest group; or plan reunions, homecoming or local events.

One-day volunteering opportunities:
Sit on a career panel during career day; offer resume critiques or mock interviews; help recruit the next generation of Tufts students as an interviewer, host or outreach volunteer; join in our fundraising program; or nominate and vote for alumni council members and trustees.

Enjoy Alumni Events

Our staff of dedicated professionals at the TUAA works collaboratively with alumni committees to organize a variety of events year round. From class reunions and homecoming, to Third Thursdays and Travel-Learn programs, there are constantly on-campus and regional events available to you!

No matter how you choose to continue your relationship with Tufts, we welcome your involvement. We take pleasure in making all our alumni feel welcome to participate in all activities and events, and in fostering strong connections between alumni and their alma mater. Please don't hesitate to contact any of our staff members to assist you with anything you might need from Tufts. We are here to help and serve you!

Please keep alive the spirit of Tufts University and the special experience that you and others value so deeply. In 2010 the TUAA will have its 150th anniversary. Join with us in celebrating, preserving and in enhancing our unique heritage and our great university.

On behalf of the Tufts Alumni Council and the entire Tufts University Alumni Association, congratulations, best of luck, and stay in touch!

Mark D. Alpert, A70
President
Tufts University Alumni Association

Gradspot.com's
Guide to Life After College

Written and Edited by
Chris Schonberger with Stuart Schultz

Copy Edited by Evan Benn and Mary Falls

We would like to extend a very special thanks to our amazing team of writers,
whose research and writing were invaluable in the process of making this book:
Julie Fishman, David Pekema, Rachel Solomon, Arielle Sachar, Karen Keller, Aryeh Cohen-Wade,
Theodore Bressman, Christine Margiotta, Rebecca Shore, Jennifer Pollock, Mandy Erickson,
Jenny Williams, Lauren Levinson, Josie Swindler, Julia Bonnheim, Erin Hartigan, Erin Kandel,
Orli Van Mourik, Jennifer Cunningham, Jake Tuck, Sean McManus, Stephanie Berger,
Molly Martin, Richard Koss, Christopher Stella, Nick Schonberger, and Courtney McClellan.

We would also like to thank the following people for their contributions and support:
Antony Clavel, Matthew Demmer, Randi Hazan, Rachel Kinrot, Chris Nakamura, Sarah Reidy,
Andy Heidel, Lily Kosner, Matty Marcus, Naledge, Dr. Valerie Young, Neilesh Mutyala,
Steve Rosengard, Nate Houghteling, Kyle Berkman, Greg Konover, Seth Robinson,
Ben Herzberger, Davina Pike, and everyone who gave us feedback or commented on our site.

To order additional copies of this book, please visit:
www.gradspot.com/book

Book design by Hazan and Company

Acknowledgements

Chris Thanks

Mom, Dad, and Brother (in no particular order!); Grandma and Granddad; Sarah, for consistently overrating me; Cheddar and T.Wise, my muses; Trevor and Charlie, my diamond Gchat geezers; Tony, for keeping it real with your boy; Stu, for helping me maintain a "positive" disposition; the Greek, for textbook punditry; Shinjo, for always repping the cause; the Bressman clan; all the heads who let me sleep at their crib; and the whole Gradspot.com team, without whom I could never have pulled this off.

Stuart Thanks

Dad and Mom for being so supportive (have to be equitable with the order considering Chris' above); Antony Clavel and Matthew Demmer for helping me get Gradspot.com off the ground; John Saroff for always pushing me along; T.R. Newcomb for sharing your eureka moments; Pat Shah for your pearls of wisdom; David Politis for always lending an ear and giving me your insights; Andrew Jacobs for being the eternal entrepreneur; Spencer Gellman for your Facebook prowess; Jessica Mimi Beck for spreading the Gradspot Gospel; Omar Isani and Salima Vahabzadeh for your business acumen; Justin Pollak for the game of "soccer"; and everyone, including the Gradspot.com community, who passed along tips, tricks, and everything else that made this book a possibility and Gradspot.com a huge success.

Table of Contents

Preface

About This Book

Why We Made This Book

A few months after launching our website, Gradspot.com, we received an e-mail from one of our users who was looking for help improving her living situation. After we pointed her to content on our site and answered some questions, she said something we haven't forgotten since: "If only you guys had been around when I graduated last summer. Then I probably wouldn't have ended up in Newark!" Now, no offense to Newark, but we fully understand her sentiment. After all, it was just a short time ago that we were leaving school and feeling completely unprepared to deal with issues like 401(k)s, sheisty landlords, and office politics.

Time and again, our peers echoed our concerns about being sent out to sea without a life vest, as have the graduating classes that followed after them. Some didn't have any clue what to expect, while those who were actually proactive enough to seek out resources found that they were either out of date or out of touch. Thus, we figured there was no better time to create a resource that could fill that void—first Gradspot.com and now this book. Ultimately, **our goal in these pages is to expose you to the issues that are most likely to arise in your first year out of school and to share the methods we and others have used to successfully navigate them.**

On top of all of the insights we picked up from our own experiences and included in this book, we've also called upon other recent grads and college students to share tips, reached out to a wide range of topic experts for their input, and trolled every other resource out there that is pertinent. We even set up a "Life After College" laboratory to test out high-pressure showerheads, budgeting tools, and anything else that might make the transition a little bit easier.

Being twentysomethings ourselves, we understand what it's like to be a graduate today rather than in 1965. Times have changed, and we wrote this book to reflect the experience of a recent grad now. We hope you'll find it helpful and that it will ease the exciting, yet intimidating transition to life after college.

How to Use This Book

Gradspot.com's Guide to Life After College has many uses. You can prop up a wobbly chair with it, burn it for warmth when your parents kick you out the house, or "donate" it to your alma mater instead of making an actual monetary contribution.

Before you do all those things, however, we hope that you'll read it. While there is no set chronology to life after college, we've laid out the chapters in a way that approximates the general order in which you're likely to encounter different issues, from moving back home to coping with the pressures of a "one-year rut." To help you browse the book, we've created a very thorough table of contents and an easy-to-use cross-referencing system that will allow you to navigate between topics quickly. We hope each chapter will provide a solid foundation for overcoming a range of obstacles along the post-college road.

While we can help you understand the basics, share tips and tricks about how to take the next step, and give you the tools to make informed choices, many of the decisions that need to be made are based on your unique situation and may require extra research. We created Gradspot.com as a place to learn more about the issues you'll confront, to interact with peers, and to find useful tools. We even built a landing page specifically for readers of this book (gradspot.com/book) so that you can easily take your research to the next level where necessary. Yet even with all the acumen you'll pick up here and online, we encourage you to be careful when dealing with major issues. Whether you're filing a tax return, choosing a dental plan, consolidating student debt, or doing anything else that we discuss in this book or on our website, always consult a professional for help. Remember, many of your choices now will affect you for years to come.

Visit Us Online!
Needless to say, no matter how long we make this book, there will always be more to discuss. If anything else comes up that you can't find in these pages, never hesitate to visit us at the online destination for life after college: Gradspot.com. Enjoy the read, and good luck!

Author's Forward

No matter how hard I try, I can't remember who spoke at my graduation. It's weird, because it's not like the whole day is a blank: I remember that it was raining and that I wanted a coffee from Dunkin' Donuts. I remember getting my diploma, massacring an hors d'oeuvres spread, and taking some pictures with the family of this guy I didn't really know. And I vividly remember telling a friend's mother that I was now "an incomparable Lord of Academia," a declaration that was met with an uncomfortable move away from me and toward the canapés. But what about those sage words that were meant to usher me into the "real world" with a sense of direction and purpose? The speech that my school probably paid $100,000 for me to enjoy on the most momentous day of my young life? No recollection whatsoever.

I guess there are two possible lessons here: 1) I have an extremely accelerated form of Alzheimer's, or 2) Inspirational words are nice and all, but they fade into oblivion once you've been sleeping on your friend's trundle bed for two months because the best job you can get is as an assistant lacrosse coach at a middle school. Essentially, this book is about avoiding these sorts of situations, or at least navigating them more seamlessly than I did. But if you'll humor me, I've got a few philosophical nuggets of my own to share before we get going. I would say "write this down" so you don't forget, but we've already done that for you.

Let's start with a quotation, as is customary on these occasions. Here's one from Eric Butterworth: "Don't go through life, grow through life." Probably my favorite quote from Mr. Butterworth, whose M.O. is flipping the script on conventional wisdom. But as much as we all feel the urge to put s—t like that on our Facebook profiles once in a while, I don't want to defer to truisms. The ones I heard before college turned out to be pretty off the mark, so why would I rely on any now?

For example, I'm sure a lot of people told you the same thing they told me before I arrived on campus: "Get ready for the best four years of your life." Well, that probably seemed like an exciting prospect four years ago, but what now? Does life really peak with Pimps 'n' Hos parties, dining hall dinners, and feigned enthusiasm for community service? Is studying for pointless exams really as good as it gets? Maybe it's time to reassess this "wisdom."

Don't get me wrong—there were definitely some times when I yearned to crawl back into the womb of university life in the first year after I graduated. Not only because the notion that your "best years are behind you" is incredibly depressing, but also because the simplicity of college life was tough to leave behind. As time has gone on, however, I've realized that life only improves after graduation. Whenever I want, I can cycle through my Facebook photos and Microsoft Word documents and pretty much relive college in 45 minutes. Great, I drank hundreds of beers and wrote some incredibly sick papers. Next!

For you, "next" is a scary word right now because everyone keeps badgering you about the "next step." Where are you gonna live *next*? What are you gonna do *next*? How many episodes of *Next* are you gonna watch on MTV while you're unemployed? After the clear-cut expectations of college, it's tough to encounter so many question marks and not know how to proceed. But trust me—soon you'll be checking your "Acapulco-lypse Now" album and thinking, "Yeah, those were the days in a way, but these days are more fulfilling in a broader sense."

In school, the best you can do is be considered cool and get As. That's pretty great, but here are two more lessons from post-college life: 1) *Sic transit coolness* (translation: coolness fades), and 2) Except for when you're slyly fudging your GPA on your résumé, grades are yesterday's news. After college, by contrast, you can accrue legitimate respect from others. More importantly, you can go out on a limb and achieve something truly remarkable—something with a value that transcends letter grades. Get rich, cure eczema, create something beautiful... whatever. The sky is not the limit. That part of the atmosphere above the sky is.

And it is in this realization that we encounter the true meat and potatoes of life after college: opportunity and fulfillment. When you make your own opportunities outside of the predictable structures of school life, you will experience a more intense sense of accomplishment than you ever knew existed. No matter how you slice it, a victory in the real world will always feel better than an academic victory—the odds are tougher, fewer people are genuinely pulling for you, and the formula for success is less obvious. Navigate that unholy trinity and you are going to feel pretty good about yourself. And you should.

But honestly, I see no reason to worry about you guys. I mean, look at you—you're a new breed carrying an extremely valuable asset in spades: potential. You are tech-savvy and completely "wireless." You were all born in the 80s, except for a few degenerates and some people who went to "German school." You have literally burned so much "midnight oil" that you have caused a massive war. And statistically, 10 percent of you are gay. Combine those last two facts, and you've successfully historicized the "don't ask, don't tell" policy.

So, at this moment, I urge each and every one of you to expand your conception of life after college to include a little thing called "dreams." Because as Ryan Seacrest put it, "You are America's Idol." Was he talking about Kelly Clarkson at the time? Sure, but right now you are all American idols. And just like Kelly back in the day, all you really lack is a little experience. That's where we can help. As you set forth into the world, let this book be your crib sheet to the Book of Life. *The Merriam-Webster's Spanish-English Dictionary* to your *Cien Años de Soledad*. The strategy guide to your own *World of Warcraft*.

Whenever you are feeling confused, just remember that those same idiots who said "college is the best four years of your life" are now saying "life starts at 50." As Eric Butterworth would probably say to these people, "Make up your own mind before you try to make up mine." It's time to flip the script—life after college is where the fun really begins.

—Chris Schonberger

Chapter I: Holy $*%#, I Just Graduated!

Holy $*%#, I Just Graduated!

The last couple months of school are jam-packed with finals, parties, farewells, and finally... graduation. With so many things going on, this time can fly by in a disorienting haze of sadness and joy. But when you grab your diploma, drink your champagne, and walk out the gates, be prepared for a Jaromir Jagr-style reality check to the boards. The following questions will undoubtedly consume your mind:

What just happened? You graduated, homey! Well played.

Am I still alive? Yes, you made it. Well done! Staying alive is half the battle.

Did I have sex? Hmmm. Really only you can answer that question.

What now? Up to you. Have an ice cream sandwich and calm down. We have plenty of time to answer that question.

Unless you are one of those precocious children who gets a degree before he hits puberty, you've just spent the last 18-odd years of your life going to school. Moreover, it may be many moons before you get to mess around for three uninterrupted months without risking a divorce or an eviction. So don't ruin this time by stressing too much about the rest of your life. What do you have to worry about anyway? Let's assess the damage...

If you didn't graduate with a job offer in hand, you probably feel like there is a massive void in front of you marked "the rest of your life." Up until now, everything has been decided for you and served up on a platter—or at least force-fed. You went to high school. You did your homework sometimes. You went to college, chose a major, and, if you were lucky, that basically accounted for all the big decisions you had to deal with for four years. But now, maybe for the first time ever, it feels like the "next step" is not completely obvious. And worst of all, you feel like you need to decide what you want to do for the rest of your life *right now!*

This is a pervasive fear that the vast majority of recent graduates faces, but it is basically irrational. Sure, the educational system is no longer there to break your life into easily measurable blocks of time that are concurrent with the progress of the majority of your peers. But who cares? Statistics overwhelmingly suggest that you will spend less time at your first job than you did attending college. And while that job may either launch a career or help you find another one, it's important to realize that there are still more life phases to come that are both manageable and malleable. It's not just college and then "the rest of your life." You now have more freedom to set your own time frames. Give yourself a year to decide if you're interested in finance, or take a six-month internship to see if publishing is right for you. Remember, you've got a lifetime of work ahead of you—there's no need to rush into anything.

Of course, career issues and job-related decisions are not the only source of concern, and we don't mean to downplay the many issues lurking on the horizon. Along with finding employment, you are eventually going to have to figure out where to live, which may require a stopover at your parents' house (for most it does). Maybe you were in a relationship when you graduated and are trying to figure out how it will factor into your post-college plans. Life isn't simple, we know. But while graduating college can seem like an overwhelming transition, it's also a time of unprecedented freedom. As a great man probably said ages ago, "Don't fetter yourself with the shackles of indecision."

The first thing you should really be thinking about after grabbing your diploma is this: how much time do I have to screw around, and how much money can I legitimately afford to spend before I have to get a job? Even if you landed one already, we hope you at least have a couple months of summer to call your own.

In this chapter, we'll help you ease into life after college, celebrate your educational achievements, and figure out viable ways to avoid jumping straight into a job that you don't really want. We'll also navigate the slippery slope of living at home and help you plan the perfect post-college trip. This is the time when you want to set the tone for your new life as a college grad. Whenever things are getting you down, just think about these two words: no homework!

The First Summer

When I graduated, my friend and I urinated on our dorm room, packed my Ford Escort so tight that I could not see anything behind me or peripherally, and then took the least efficient route back to my dad's house while listening to rap music. Next, we each ate approximately 20,000 calories worth of food and went to a driving range attached to a bar. We ordered two Stellas and a plate of fried calamari, looked into each others' bloodshot eyes, and said, "End me?"

Upon leaving campus, it may take over a fortnight of non-stop gluttony and sleep to get you back to full strength. But after that, you owe yourself a proper celebration. The family-and-friends gathering is nice, but it can only take you so far. The real post-grad celebration is not so much about one blow-out party as it is about taking some time for yourself—get your middle-aged woman on and engage in a bit of pampering! That doesn't have to involve shopping sprees and Swedish massages with men who are manlier than your husband (but, hey, if that's what you're into...). The point is, if you thought it was hard to get everything done in college, you're in for a shock to the system. Life only gets busier, so take full advantage of this down time.

One of the hardest parts about adapting to working life is that it's no longer assumed that a quarter of the calendar year is completely open for you to do what you want. Of course, if you've been counting down to the day when you can move to the city of your dreams and start stacking paychecks, then get out there and do your thing. But for those who aren't quite as gung-ho about what lies ahead, take advantage of this final installment of the "academic calendar."

The best way to postpone (if not avoid) the feeling of post-grad dread is to take a step back and give yourself some time to decompress. For all the tomfoolery that goes on, college is a tough gig, and you wouldn't be the first person to feel burnt out on commencement day. Whether it's a week or the whole summer, set yourself a realistic timeframe for how long you can relax before you start seriously job-hunting. Creating this buffer zone between college and the "real world" will pay off in the long run because it will put you in a better place mentally to decide what to do.

Top 10 Things to Do After Graduating

1) **Go skydiving.** Not my cup of tea, but if you want to act like the second coming of Dan Cortez, more power to you. I mean, that dude was pretty cool.

2) **Apply to a reality TV show.** Ever since they green-lit the return of *American Gladiators*, those "15 minutes of fame" are being handed out like hot cakes. What do you have to lose (except dignity and the support of your family)?

3) **Read.** College is all about books you have to read, whereas post-college is about reading what you want. Who knows, you might even make it past page 50 this time.

4) **Travel.** The post-gradation trip is a classic move for those who can afford it, and even grads on a tight budget have plenty of options close to home. Read more on page 28.

5) **Learn to cook.** Once you're living alone sans a meal plan, the ability to whip up a fricassee will save big bucks and impress potential mates like the plumage of a peacock. Read more on page 211.

6) **Spend time with your family.** Take advantage of the time you can spend with your loved ones now, because tomorrow you might be busy. Or they might be dead. (Only joking.)

Top 10 Things to Do After Graduating Continued...

7) **Be a kid again.** Go home and rekindle all those old feelings you had as a child. Dust off your old Nintendo console. Hit a tennis ball against a wall and pretend it's Monica Seles. Whatever it takes to get that spring back in your step.

8) **Get in ridiculous shape.** Hitting the gym hard is sort of a chach college maneuver favored by dudes who exclusively do upper body and can barely run a mile, but exercise is an easy way to feel better, look better, and motivate yourself to take the next step.

9) **Volunteer.** Before you become too "busy" making money for yourself, demonstrate a little of the philanthropic spirit for which you may or may not be famous. Find something that appeals to you personally and get involved.

10) **Write a book.** Or if writing's not your thing, pursue anything that you're passionate about. Record songs, paint pictures, or write the screenplay you've been talking about for three years. Now is the time.

 Get a tattoo: My brother claims this is an awesome idea.

Moving Home

One of the most immediate issues facing the recent graduate is where to seek shelter after getting kicked out of the dormitory. If you're like most of your contemporaries (about 60%, according to a Monster.com survey), the default answer is the parents' house. And why not? Home provides many creature comforts, the rent is extremely competitive (i.e., $0), and cable is free. But apparently, not everyone thinks it's such a no-brainer.

If you believe the Baby Boomer-biased media, you'd think America had an epidemic on its hands. Yes, it's true—more and more college grads are moving home after graduation than ever before. As the naysayers like to point out, young people are making financial sacrifices early on in their adult lives while forcing their parents to postpone retirement to support them. In her book *Generation Me*, sociologist Jean Twenge even goes so far as to suggest the underlying motivation for this trend is selfishness: We are a generation of narcissistic daydreamers who would rather lounge at mom and dad's house thinking about our passions than worry about a mortgage. Sounds like the end of the world!

Ms. Twenge is entitled to her opinion, but the rulebook has changed since our parents first left college. The old paradigm of "graduate college, move out, start a career, get married, have some kids" no longer holds. Career paths are more varied but also more complicated than they once were, and it takes the average graduate several months to find a job. Anyway, if you want to talk about a real "mooching off the 'rents" epidemic, look no further than Italian men—those mama's boys have gotten so hooked on homemade pasta and meatballs that an economic minister proposed tax breaks for young people who rent in Italy! (True story.)

If you're 35 and still getting yelled at by your mom for leaving the toilet seat up, then you might have cause for concern. But for now, don't beat yourself up about settling back into the nest, whether it's for a summer or a year. As long as you treat it as a temporary solution and show a little initiative to do *something* other than sit around reading the collected works of J.K. Rowling, things will eventually work out. Here are some tips for navigating a potentially thorny situation.

Don't Fall Back into Bad Habits. Presumably, at least four years have passed since you really lived with the 'rents. They got used to daily life without you, and (no offense) they probably liked it. Even if you have younger siblings, your departure to college meant one less mouth to feed, one less load of laundry each week, and far fewer ornery teenagers displaying horrible posture throughout the house. You'll do yourself a favor by seeing their side of the story and easing your way back into the Matrix. It's amazing how quickly that feeling of youthful entitlement can creep back into your psyche when you enter the house, but you don't want your selfish demands to come crashing down on your parents like a ton of bricks. Clean your clothes, wash the dishes, offer to buy groceries, and do some cooking. You can annoy them all you want and make them worry day and night, but don't make your return to the house feel like more *work*.

Make the Most of the Time with Your Family. Tempers fray easily in the pressure cooker of post-college life. As if job-hunting wasn't aggravating enough, being forced to give Ma Dukes a nightly recap of your progress can become extremely irksome. And ironically, it can be even harder if you've got a job. The last thing you want to do when you come home tired at the end of the day is tell your mom all about the papers you filed and copies you made—it salts the wound liberally. That said, it's wise to fight past the feeling of being smothered by your parents. Whether it's two weeks, six months, or a year from now, eventually you'll be off on your own. Careers will force you to move around, girlfriends will demand that you go to their house for Thanksgiving—all sorts of things will ensure that you see your parents less frequently. Have dinner together, hang out with younger siblings, and plan activities that you all can enjoy. Trust us, you'll feel better for it in the long-run. And if peace of mind doesn't motivate you, then just think of your civil behavior as remuneration for your room and board.

Dad-juation (and Mom-juation). Parents also go through a transition after you graduate, so it's important to keep their interests in mind when you re-infiltrate their home. If they helped finance your education, they are probably pretty pleased about not having to pay another semester's tuition. Don't rain on the parade by finding new and less justifiable ways to be a financial burden. Give them space when they want to have friends over instead of sitting in the living room playing Xbox Live with headphones on—that's embarrassing for everyone. Overall, try to avoid giving the impression that your college career was a complete waste of time and money.

Save As Much Money As Possible. Moving back home is usually motivated in part by financial reasons. Whether you're jobless, interning, or stuck at a starting salary that can't support you month to month, the luxury of not paying for rent, utilities, or food can make a huge difference. However, if you go and blow any loot that does come into your hands on unnecessary extravagances, you will be doing yourself a huge disservice for the day when you do actually need to pay for things. Adopting a frugal lifestyle should not be that difficult, because let's be honest, living "la vida loca" (whatever that means) and staying with your parents don't necessarily vibe. Do you really want to be hitting the bar and getting it cracking in your childhood bed? Save the money for a time and place when you can ball out more freely. Who knows—the good budgeting and saving habits you start now might even translate to life beyond the nest.

Set a Schedule. Being semi-productive every day—or at least constructing an elaborate façade of industriousness—will help to get your parents off your back and make you feel more motivated. If you are already working, this shouldn't be too difficult. If not, wake up at the same time every day, and try to make sure that it's before noon. After that, try to do something useful. In *The Quarterlifer's Companion*, Abby Wilner and Catherine Stocker suggest scheduling at least one activity each day to help you on your job search: "It can be an interview, a trip to the library to do research, a trip to Kinkos to copy résumés, anything." It doesn't really matter what activity you choose to schedule as long as loafing around and being cantankerous does not become your *modus operandi*.

Enjoy the Fairies. Sometimes you will leave your room covered in soiled clothing, only to return later in the day and find it neatly ironed and folded on your bed. That, my friends, is the Laundry Fairy. Or maybe one day you will be watching reruns of *Who Wants to Be a Millionaire* and suddenly dinner will magically appear in front of you.

Thank you, Dinner Fairy! Some of us are lucky enough to have parents who, in spite of their better judgment, can't help but spoil us when we are around. Maybe your moving home is not cause for celebration, but you've still been gone long enough for your parents to miss you a little bit, and you also just achieved a great milestone by graduating. In other words, you are in good standing! Milk this situation as much as your conscience will allow you to, because when you move into your own place, those fairies will be slaughtered and subsequently resurrected as ruthless demons that will make your life infinitely more difficult.

Making It Long Term. Some people end up working or going to graduate school in the city their parents live in, and financially it might make sense to create a long-term arrangement that could span several years. This is a trickier situation that depends a lot on your relationship with your parents. If they let you do the things that you need to do to feel sane and you don't step on their toes too much, it can work out nicely and allow you to save money that you would otherwise be pouring down the drain unnecessarily.

At the end of the day, you need to be honest with yourself and make sure you are not stifling your potential by staying shacked up in the house. If you really feel that you need to get out, you'll find a way to make it work.

Will Work to Buy Time

If your parents aren't thrilled by the prospect of you weezing off their grindage for an indeterminate amount of time, you may have to start bringing in some *dinero*, stat. It's sort of a bummer, but there are plenty of ways to buy yourself some time so that you can weigh your options before jumping into a full-time gig. One way is to sell some of your belongings, but there are also one-off and part-time jobs that can help get you through the summer without sacrificing the opportunity to watch every *Martin* marathon that comes on. The best advice we can give is to swallow your pride (you're going to need a few punch-lines for your memoir, right?), but also to **be careful and don't take unnecessary risks.** It's advisable to pack an industrial-sized can of common sense before venturing out into the world of random employment.

Auction Off Your Zubaz. Between the remnants of your college dorm and the ridiculously small sweaters taking up closet space at your parents' house, you are sitting on a cash cow of used stuff. In the age of eBay and Craigslist, unloading it is as easy as ever—you don't even need a garage. Ask the rest of your family if they want to get rid of anything as well, because they'll probably be happy just to get it out the way. If you've got a lot of clothing in decent condition, Buffalo Exchange has locations across the country and will pay cash for your garments. Second-hand CD stores will take all your Nickel-back albums (after you've uploaded them onto your laptop!), as will SecondSpin.com and CashforCDs.com. Try Half.com or your school's network in Facebook Marketplace for textbooks, or head to Amazon to sell niche titles. Anyway, you get the point. Whatever you've got, someone somewhere probably wants it. You just have to be willing to put in some effort to make it happen.

The Tutors. There's a pretty penny to be had from helping kids write social studies essays and pass the LSAT. Even without a teaching certification, college graduates can make anywhere from $10-200 an hour tutoring. Check out the "education" section of Craigslist, or try going through an established tutoring company like Kaplan.

Freelance Like It's Your Job. Freelancing, despite what some embittered journalists will tell you, is not a sucker's game. Sure, in the long run it's a bit of a shaky existence (especially with no health insurance), but for a quick buck and some exposure it's definitely a viable option. In the age of online content, finding freelance gigs is easier than ever, though the pay has suffered as a result. Moreover, you don't have to be a writer to freelance—web designers, artists, programmers, and copy editors can all pawn off their services. Along with Craigslist, check out Indeed.com, MyJambi.com, Solo-Gig.com, and Mandy.com. (Writers and editors should also look at Ed2010.com and MediaBistro.com.)

Start a Blog. If you're too proud to work for others and think you've got what it take to hack it on your own, start a blog (Blogger and Wordpress are good platforms), then

sell ad space via Google's free AdSense service. You will get paid every time someone clicks on an ad, so if you drive enough traffic the revenue might not be negligible. Plus, you get to build a body of work and write about whatever you want (though bear in mind it will be easier to attract visitors if you target a wider audience than "people who think I'm hilarious"). Become a regular reader of ProBlogger.com to stay on top of ways to expand your audience and make money from your blog.

Walk It Out like an Usher. In cities full of lazy pet owners (e.g., New York), pet-sitting and dog-walking can be an amazing way to chill with animals while stacking loot. You can offer your services independently on Craigslist and MyJambi, or find a local business that provides pet care services. "Cash-in-hand" may not be a phrase the IRS likes, but who can resist a lil' pup who needs to urinate?

Whore Yourself Out (Not Literally). We don't encourage prostitution, but now we're getting into the realm of all-out, no-holds-barred, Matthew-Lesko-in-a-question-mark-suit insanity. Become an extra in a movie that doesn't involve showing off your "best bits" by checking the local paper or visiting Mandy.com, Backstage.com, and EntertainmentCareers.net. Most large move studios pay the SAG union rate of $115/day plus snacks and a meal every six hours. If "acting" is not your style, scan Craigslist for other wacky jobs, like foot modeling, flyering, or dressing up as a giant burrito. Got a car? Check out FreeCarMedia.com to see how you can give your whip the NASCAR treatment and make anywhere from $50-500 a month "renting out" space on your vehicle.

Get Paid to Shop. If that sounds like a dream come true, you might want to look into a job as a "mystery shopper" (aka spotters, secret shoppers, anonymous audits, experience evaluators, virtual customers, etc.). Companies pay mystery shoppers to go to stores and provide feedback on the service that they receive—sometimes they even provide a script to follow. Pretend you are dehydrated and faint next to the board shorts. Inquire about gift-wrapping a 60-inch flat-screen TV. Who needs drama school? Generally, shoppers are rewarded with some combination of money, store credit, or merchandise—being Big Brother's little helper has perks. However, beware of online scams. If it seems shady, check in with the Better Business Bureau before proceeding.

From Grad to Guinea Pig. Usually you have to pay exorbitant fees to get medication. So why would anyone pay you to take it? Well, they can't sell it until they figure out if it f—ks people up—that's where you come into play. Be careful and don't jeopardize your health or sanity for a few hundred bucks. However, if you feel comfortable with the risks, there are many ways to pawn your body for financial reward within the medical world. Labs, universities, and hospitals nationwide are always looking for volunteers for scientific studies. Try a new flu vaccine, get a psychiatric evaluation, or get paid to sleep (though beware that sleep studies can be insane). The best approach is to contact a college or university in the area to inquire about research and testing volunteers—psych departments and med schools are good places to start. Also scan the local newspaper and check the volunteer and "ETC" sections on Craigslist.

Medical "Donations." Who would have thought you could get paid to have a wank? Compensation for a vial of semen (about .7ml) in the U.S. ranges between $200-3,000, but be prepared to feel emasculated if your seed doesn't make the cut. Thanks to "equal rights," women can also donate their eggs now, bringing home a fat check that can range anywhere from a few hundred to thousands. However, depositing some ovum isn't as simple as knocking one off the wrist into a plastic cup—no surprise that men have it easier again! The whole process involves extensive medical testing, injections of fertility drugs, and a surgical procedure. For those who are a bit squeamish about "sex things," there's a more standard approach—the Red Cross no longer pays for blood donations, but plasma still earns a pretty penny. If you meet the donor criteria (healthy, 17+, over 110 pounds—what are we talking about again?) then you can get $20-30 per visit. Visits are limited to two a week with at least 48 hours between each one; check online for donation centers or call 1-800-GIVE-LIFE.

Holy S*%#, I Just Graduated!

Travel Like Dikembe Mutumbo

Traveling after graduation is a time-honored tradition because, let's face it—it's the perfect time to travel. You've been married to the books (or the booze) for four years now, so it's time for a belated honeymoon. Moreover, the chances of taking a two-month backpacking trip grow slimmer by the day once you're a working cog. We don't want to suggest that the clock is ticking on fun and exploration, but if you've got the money (and we understand that's a big "if"), all of the pieces are in place for a great trip—youth, health, and a celebratory subtext. So why not get cracking on that "places to visit before I die" list? (Note: Even if you are broke, there are still plenty of ways to travel on the cheap domestically.)

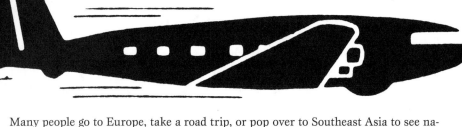

Many people go to Europe, take a road trip, or pop over to Southeast Asia to see nature's greatest mystery: the "ladyboys." Some go with their parents because A) they love them, or B) it is the only way to finance the trip. Others go with friends with the intention of having "one last hurrah." As long as everyone's expectations are in sync, taking a graduation trip with friends is an almost unconditionally good idea. But it's not always as smooth as expected. At the risk of sounding like curmudgeons, let us fly a quick cautionary flag.

Traveling is a lot different from casually hanging out, and even lovers can make bad travel buddies. Haggling over Euros, getting jacked up by Grecian purse-snatchers, and arguing about train schedules can drive a stake between you and your friend that could take months or years to decompose. So before you book a hostel, take a few moments to decide whether you and your "BFF" are travel-compatible. Here are a few red flags that could turn the post-grad honeymoon into *Turistas 2* (aka *Hostel 4*):

- One of you is on a travel grant budget and the other is on a trust fund budget.
- One of you likes foreign men and the other thinks they are criminals.
- One of you is an adventurous eater and the other is a McDonald's junkie.
- One of you likes to sight-see and the other likes to beach-bum and party.
- Neither of you enjoys handling "logistics."
- Traveler's diarrhea.

If one or more of these situations gave you pause, it doesn't mean you have to throw the whole idea out the window. However, thinking about these issues before setting sail can help diffuse some potentially frustrating arguments down the line. Ask your rich friend if he's willing to steer clear of the Four Seasons and see how the other half lives (or travels, as the case may be). Plan an itinerary that balances culture and clubbing if that will make all parties happy. A stitch in time will invariably save nine (of what I'm not sure).

Brainstorming Trips

The main factors that go into planning the perfect summer trip are budget, duration, and companionship. But once those are settled, the fun part can begin—what do you really want to do? There are countless places to get your post-college groove on. Here are just a few ideas to get you started. **Note: Before you set out for a foreign country, get your passport straight (see p. 30) and be sure to check if you need a visa or any vaccinations (see p. 35).**

The "Generic European Backpackers" Trip. It's a well-trod path, but everyone's got to do it once. Whether you focus your efforts on the capitals of the West or the increasingly popular cities of the East, the classic European vacay rarely disappoints. Culture by day, booze by night, and an endless string of hostels packed with German ravers and cool but slightly arrogant Aussies. Places like London, Paris, and Vienna are not cheap, but the summer is rife with music and art festivals, and you can save money by purchasing food and drinks at grocery stores and traveling by train with a Eurail pass (see p. 35). For some fun in the sun, hit up Croatia's Dalmatian Coast or don some Capri pants for a jaunt through southern Italy. If you're a smooth operator, you might be able to locate a nude beach or two. Who packed the binoculars!? **Book to Bring:** *Neither Here Nor There: Travels in Europe,* by Bill Bryson (and watch *Eurotrip,* one of the most underrated films of the past five years).

Holy S*°%#, I Just Graduated!

Tips & Tricks: Passports

Before you can get enough stamps in your passport to compete with Bono, you need to actually have a passport. Be warned: nothing sets a worse tone for a trip than the bro who shows up without the necessary identification documents. If your passport has expired, check the State Department website to find out where you need to send it for renewal. If you don't have your old passport, have never had a passport, or were under 16 when you received your most recent passport, you've got to trek down to the Post Office or your local City Hall and apply in person. You'll need a valid ID, two passport photos, and proof of U.S. citizenship (e.g., a birth certificate). Generally, passports take about 4-6 weeks to arrive, but you can pay an extra $60 to get the expedited service (about 3 weeks). If you're really in a bind (way to plan ahead!), non-governmental agencies like PassportsAndVisas.com can handle business Mafia-style—it's around $59 for 8-20 business days and $169 for the 24-hour service.

The "Getting Plastered like an Irishman" Trip. Ireland ain't cheap, but for rugged terrain, intriguing history, and unbeatable *craic*, a trip to the Emerald Isle delivers almost anything you could ask for (except good weather). Try to get beyond Dublin, which has plenty to see but may feel generically cosmopolitan to more seasoned travelers. (Go to a pub in the famous Temple Bar district and you're more likely to be served your Guinness by an Eastern European student than a true Irishman.) For the authentic experience, rent a car or hop on a bike and make your way from town to town. While the southern tourist trail is most popular, Northern Ireland mixes the fascinating political history of Belfast and Derry with beautiful scenery along the Causeway Coast. And, believe it or not, some of the best surfing in Europe can be found on the west coast of Ireland around towns like Bundoran and Sligo. **Book to Bring:** *Round Ireland with a Fridge*, by Tony Hawks (not to be confused with Tony Hawk).

The "From Russia with Love" Trip. While visiting Russia in winter may lead you to drink vodka mixed with airplane fluid just to stay warm, the summer will allow you to see the sights in comfort and imbibe spirits for pleasure rather than survival. Moscow is architecturally stunning, combining the antique stylings of the Kremlin with the surreal domes of Saint Basil's Cathedral and the many imposing Stalin-era constructions. (When you visit Lenin's tomb, start singing "Imagine" and you'll surely win over a few tour groups in the process.) History buffs should also make a point of visiting Saint Petersburg, which has palaces galore and the majestic feel of an old European capital. Beyond the major cities, Siberia is apparently a pretty big place—grab your rucksack and start exploring. **Book to Bring:** *Notes from the Underground*, by Fyodor Dostoevsky.

The "Beach Rental with Friends" Trip. If you live on the coasts, you don't have to travel halfway around the world for a beach-bumming bender. Nantucket and Martha's Vineyard are popular destinations for East Coast grads, particularly those who favor ribbon belts and pants embroidered with pheasants. Out in Cali, those who can't afford Malibu still have hundreds of miles of beaches to explore. The key to making a beach week affordable is to share the rental with as many people as possible, cook your own food, and exclusively drink MGD (aka Mad Gangster Dancing). **Book to Bring:** Just wait until the end of the day and the beach will be littered with discarded bestsellers.

The "Superpowers of Tomorrow" Trip. Touted as rising superpowers (mostly by other, slightly condescending superpowers), China and India have dominated the press over the past few years. Pundits cast the growth of the two "Asian giants" as the ultimate articulation of globalization, spawning constant debate about which country will outpace the other as the next great industrial force. That means one thing for you: get there before they both look exactly like America! We're joking (sort of), but now is certainly a good time to explore these enormous, culturally diverse countries. From major cities like Beijing and Delhi to tourist destinations like the Great Wall and the Taj Mahal, the options are pretty much unlimited, and you can do it 5-star all the way or dirt cheap depending on your preferences. However, it's important to do some research beforehand, because both of these countries can be overwhelming without at least a vague plan of action. **Book to Bring:** *Siddhartha*, by Herman Hesse; *River Town: Two Years on the Yangtze*, by Peter Hessler.

The "Soul-Searching in Southeast Asia" Trip. Have you seen *The Beach*? Dude, it's gonna be exactly like that! Let your inhibitions slip away as you eat a still-beating snake heart and feel its warm blood coat your esophagus. Live on a beach for a dollar a day and grow disgusting dreads. Shack up with a "ladyboy" and realize gender is just a state of mind. All jokes aside, Southeast Asia is a wonderful and extremely cheap place to visit, but from the food to the accommodations, its pleasures are not always ideal for the unadventurous. Thailand and Vietnam are the most popular destinations for backpackers, but the temples of Angkor Wat, located near the city of Siem Reap in Cambodia, are consistently touted as one of the alternative wonders of the world. **Book to Bring:** *The Beach*, by Alex Garland—obvi!

The "Ancient Wonders of the Middle East" Trip. Sure, some areas in the Middle East are not advisable travel destinations (e.g., Baghdad, Kabul, the Gaza Strip), but don't let that deter you from all the great places to visit there. For those interested in ancient history, Jordan is steeped in Biblical lore and Syria boasts the world's oldest continuously occupied city: Damascus. Israel, Lebanon, and Turkey offer rich culture and staggering landscapes—float in the Dead Sea, visit Bethlehem, and explore Istanbul's East-meets-West influences. Many travelers combine a trip to the Middle East with a stopover in Egypt—Cairo and the Great Pyramids of Giza are easily accessible from the Mediterra-

Tips & Tricks: Cheap Places, Expensive Flights

The one "gotcha" with super-cheap travel destinations like Southeast Asia and parts of Eastern Europe is they can cost an arm and a leg to get to in the first place. When planning your itinerary, remember to factor transportation into the budget rather than clinging to the fact that beers will cost five cents. Look into cheap connecting flights or around-the-world tickets (see p. 34) to make the airfare affordable.

nean and can serve as a launching point for a riverboat up the Nile. When heading to the Middle East, be aware that visiting heavily Muslim regions during major holidays like Ramadan can pose some logistical problems. **Book to Bring:** *Exile*, by Richard North Patterson.

The "All-American Roadtrip." Nothing says "I just graduated" like five dudes in a Jeep with the system blasting and the smell of B.O. wafting into the muggy summer air. The cross-country trip is a classic option—hit Vegas, Austin, and New Orleans, or take the high road through Chi-Town, Ann Arbor, and Yellowstone National Park. Cruising up and down the coasts is also an option, but just remember the golden rule of road trips: whoever smelt it dealt it. If you have an early commencement, try to plan a route that allows you to crash all of your other friends' graduation parties. **Book to Bring:** *Fear and Loathing in Las Vegas,* by Hunter S. Thompson (the audiobook).

The "Party 'Til You Die" Trip. It seems counter-intuitive to travel somewhere for the purposes of getting so lit up that you forget where you are, but it takes all sorts to make the world go around. If Mediterranean waters and all-night raves appeal to your animal instincts, the Balearic Islands are home to Ibiza, where mega-clubs like Space, Eden, and Amnesia (sounds like a science fair) have broken the backs of the world's hardiest party-goers. For a similar scene a bit closer to home, Mexico furnishes *muchas* tequila slammers in Cancun, Acapulco, and Tijuana. **Book to Bring:** Reading will make your head spin—bring a copy of *Pure Drum & Bass* and brace yourself.

The "Shredding in the Summer" Trip. Skiing during the summer is one of those mind-blowing experiences that will make you question everything you thought you knew about the world. Argentina and Chile are renowned for their great snow and beautiful scenery, and since it's winter there during our summer, the slopes are open for a post-commencement shredding session. (In Argentina, Cerro Catedral, located outside the city of Bariloche, is a popular destination for skiers, trekkers, and rock climbers.) If you want to stick to the Northern Hemisphere, Whistler in British Columbia is the capital of shorts-and-T-shirt skiing and snowboarding. **Book to Bring:** Just rent as many Warren Miller films as possible.

The "Camping with High School Friends" Trip. Cheap, cheerful, and potentially hilarious, this trip is a spiritual twofer, allowing you to reconnect with nature and the past at the same time. Pitching your tents within walking distance of a water park or mini-golf course is always a power move, but if you have the opportunity to go to a great national park like Acadia or Yosemite, you should definitely leap on it. **Book to Bring:** *SAS Survival Handbook: How to Survive in the Wild, in Any Climate, on Land or at Sea,* by John 'Lofty' Wiseman.

The "Brazilian Hedonism" Tour. Few places on the planet get it cracking quite like Brazil (you know a place is crazy when the boys are born with mustaches). Ipanema Beach in Rio has great surfing, beautiful bodies, and amazing caipirinhas. Plus, you always have an enormous statue of Jesus looking over you—a comforting thought, I'm sure. Salvador is one of the most laidback party towns you're likely to find anywhere—the heavy Afro-Caribbean influence in the Bahia region finds its articulation in the non-stop smorgasbord of food and music. When you're all partied out, venture into the Amazon for some hardy trekking and wildlife-watching. The rapidly growing city of Manaus is the port of entry into the rainforest, and from there you can take guided camping excursions or make daytrips from the comforts of a jungle lodge. **Book to Bring:** *Brazil*, by John Updike.

The "Che Guevara Wannabe" Trip. From the steakhouses of Buenos Aires all the way up to cigar shops in Havana's Old Town (note: Americans need a visa to get into Cuba), there's plenty of territory to cover in a trip based loosely on a dude whose face you saw in someone's dorm room. Grab a motorcycle and a diary, and don't forget to bring an Epi-Pen in case you go into anaphylactic shock. (If you don't know what that means, don't worry about it.) **Book to Bring:** *The Motorcycle Diaries*, by Che Guevara.

The African Vacation. There are all sorts of reasons why people overlook Africa when planning trips. "It's too dangerous." "It costs too much to get there." "Hippos have killed more humans than any other semi-aquatic animal." Though hippos are undoubtedly dangerous beasts, all of these excuses hold about as much water as the Sahara Desert. From the amazing markets of Marrakech to the world-class surf of Cape Town, there's literally an entire continent of amazing places to visit. Many companies offer safaris specially designed for the budget-conscious, and camping in the desert will always be free (if slightly unsafe). Explore the forests of Madagascar or track down lions in Tanzania. Africa is waiting to reward those who think beyond the tourist trail. **Book to Bring:** *Things Fall Apart*, by Chinua Achebe.

The "Sports Lovers" Trip. From major events like the World Cup and the Olympics to more off-beat affairs like the Highland Games and the Ashes cricket test, the summers

Tips & Tricks:
Around the World Ticket

The "Around the World" ticket is the stuff of legend amongst travelers. For better or for worse, there are a lot of myths circulated about ATW fares, but don't worry—you don't have to make it around in 80 days, and you don't have to sit in the cargo compartment. Let's nip those rumors right in the bud. The good news is they do exist, and for about $2,000 you can wend your way around the globe and see some truly amazing places. The bad news is that they come with restrictions galore, so you have to be flexible and red-eye ready. Check out world fares from airline alliances like Star Alliance, OneWorld Explorer, and SkyTeam, but make sure to pay close attention to the conditions, which usually include a mileage limit, a 12-month time limit, a minimum (generally 3) and maximum (5-10) number of stops, and an eventual return to the starting point (so if you end up trying to reenact *Seven Years in Tibet*, you can kiss your return fare goodbye). Most tickets also stipulate that you must travel in one direction, so you can't just get one to visit your ladyfriend in Paris for a year. All that said, the net result is monumentally more budget-friendly than buying a gang of one-way tickets, and you can pimp the system to get your penny-pinching self to some traditionally expensive locales. It pays to be flexible.

are always chock full of international sporting extravaganzas. Depending on the profile of the event, you may need to get tickets well in advance, but sometimes just being around all the madness can be half the fun. Just don't become a sports hooligan—it's not a real job! **Book to Bring**: *Being Gazza: My Journey to Hell and Back*, by Paul Gasgoine.

Travel Resources

There are as many approaches to travel as there are places to see in the world, and where some prefer a live-life-in-the-moment, fly-by-the-seat-of-your-pants approach, others globe-trot with such painstaking precision that you'd think they were searching for Carmen Sandiego. No matter what your steelo is, we suggest at least a *little* bit of forward-planning, if only to ensure you get the best deals, stay safe, and don't find yourself suddenly wishing you had taken some malaria pills after waking up in a sweaty fever with enormous welts all over your face. Before you hit the road, check out these great resources to help you make the most of your travels.

STA Travel. Just because you are out of college doesn't mean you can't be a student in the international sense of the word. Are you young (i.e., under 26)? Are you cheap? Do you think "gap years" are the jam? You are still a student. STA International has offices all over the place (especially near college campuses) and will help you plan your itineraries, book your flights, and snag deals at hostels. They also offer package deals and a host of other useful resources. In order to get discounts worldwide you should cop a $22 International Student Identity Card (ISIC). Consider it a membership fee, as well as a chance to feel young again.

Travel Zoo. Sign up for the newsletter to find out about great package deals that are perfect for a spontaneous trip. The site has a daily deluge of bargains, and it often offers a list of airlines that are having major ticket sales.

Smarter Travel. The name says it all—deals, news, and advice to help you travel with the efficiency of Condoleezza Rice.

Priceline. Do you wonder what all those William Shatner commercials are about? Well, here's your answer: it's a website where you pick a travel route, name your price, and see if any airline can match your bid. Pretty handy, though you may not have much flexibility in choosing your flight times. And don't try bidding $0—it doesn't work!

Airfare Watchdog. This site allows you to search for the cheapest flights to and from every major city in the U.S. and Canada, with results including Southwest and JetBlue. There is also a daily list of the top 50 fares currently on offer.

Eurail. This is only applicable to European travelers under 26, but it is a great resource for those who want to travel inexpensively by train. Check the website for ticket options, all of which offer flexible rail travel through the 18-country Eurail network at a set price.

Air Ninja. A great starting point for any budget-conscious traveler. Simply enter in your starting point and destination to find out which regional and discount airlines fly between those airports. These carriers are generally absent from searches on major travel sites, but they often offer the lowest fares.

Project Visa. Get up-to-date visa and embassy information on all of the countries you are considering visiting.

U.S. State Department. Check for travel advisories to make sure you are not venturing into the midst of a civil war. The

State Department site also offers visa and passport information, embassy details, vaccinations, and tips for safe travel.

Further Resources

Here are a few more resources to help you bring your travel dreams to fruition, and also figure out what to do once you get to your destination. When staying in hostels or crashing on people's couches, always exercise common sense and put safety first. Enjoy!

Cheap Lodgings
Hostels.com
Hotels.com
Hostelworld.com
CouchSurfer.com
GlobalFreeloaders.com

Good Guidebooks for Grads
Lonely Planet
Let's Go
Rough Guides
Road Trip USA
TimeOut city guides

Cheap Flights
Kayak.com
Expedia.com
Orbitz.com
Mobissimo.com
Sidestep.com
Cheapflights.com

Good Travel Websites for Grads
Gridskipper.com
Travel.nytimes.com
Guardian.co.uk/travel
VirtualTourist.com
TripAdvisor.com
TheBathroomDiaries.com

(Note: If you're flying domestically, don't forget to check Southwest Airlines, which doesn't submit its flights to external searches.)

The Post-college Gap Year

Maybe three months of traveling feels way too short. Maybe living at home doesn't appeal to you, but you also aren't too fired up about jumping straight into the rat race. Have you considered taking a year off?

We could devote a whole book to the subject of gap years—who knows, maybe we will!? But let's not get ahead of ourselves. The point we want to make is there is a wide range of viable alternatives to finding a traditional job as soon as you leave school. You don't have to be Prince William to take a year off. Just don't feel bad when your activities are not chronicled by *Hello!* magazine.

After graduation, pressure to find a job and earn your keep doesn't just come from parents. Even if they are not particularly boastful, listening to your friends talk about their jobs and watching them charge extravagant dinners to their corporate cards can make you feel like you're stuck at the kids' table. But the thing about the kids' table is that it's mad fun (I still try to snag a spot there every Thanksgiving), and the thing about your friends' work stories is that they are full of smoke and mirrors. You have the rest of your life to work the proverbial 9-to-5, and a year delay is not going to sentence you to a permanent spot at the back of the pack. Doing what your friends are doing is not a good reason to discount a post-college gap year.

So what are good reasons to take a year off? Obviously, it's not the right choice for everyone. But if you decide to do it, make sure you have a goal and a plan. Bumming around European cities to attend all-night raves on daddy's dime is not a great opportunity for growth and enrichment. Better reasons to take time off include learning a language, seeing new places, or volunteering, especially if you are burnt out from college or unsure of what you want to do. Rushing into things will only fuel the fires of a midlife crisis later in life, so at least give the possibility of a gap year some thought.

Tips & Tricks: How to Play Time Off on Your Résumé

Unless you spent the year trying to beat *Mario Bros.* without getting small, time off is not something you need to hide from employers. The key is to not look like a directionless wanderer who will pick up at the drop of a hat and move onto something new. Employers like loyalty, but they also value a range of experience and a proven ability to be independent. Moreover, many companies report that employees who have taken gap years demonstrate greater maturity and stay on longer than their peers. So, in many ways, time off can make you an even more attractive candidate (especially if you went to Australia and got a nice tan). The important thing is to present your time off in a way that shows it had a purpose and wasn't just a ploy to put off the inevitable.

Holy S*%#, I Just Graduated!

Chapter II: **Apartments & Homes**

Apartments & Homes

Have you ever seen MTV *Cribs*? What about *Lifestyles of the Rich and Famous*? Well, unless you are really good at skateboarding or selling ringtones, your first apartment definitely won't be on one of those shows. However, you will be able to *watch* them all you want, sans the irksome distraction of your mom yelling at you to "turn off that garbage." (You can also create the illusion of being on *Cribs* by owning *Scarface* and lining up all your Gatorades neatly in the fridge.)

Life beyond the dorm and your parents' house can be a bit intimidating if you've never had to take care of yourself before. But it's important to remember that even though some prisons are massive and have very good facilities, they still feel very claustrophobic and small for the simple fact that they are prisons. The golden goggles of freedom, on the other hand, can make the tiniest, coldest, most roach-infested apartment look like Buckingham Palace. Maybe that's a bit of an exaggeration. But like Paul Bunyan's height, it's an exaggeration with a point.

Let's be real about things: if you're like most recent grads, your first place is not necessarily going to be palatial. If it is, well played. But if not, don't fret. The important thing is that by moving to a new city and/or renting your first apartment you are taking a huge step toward independence and personal responsibility. Having your own place will give you the space you need to thrive socially and creatively. Furthermore, it will force you to become more self-reliant as you learn to deal with landlords, pay utility bills on time, buy your own groceries, and maybe even clean up after yourself once in a while.

Needless to say, apartments vary quite dramatically across the country. In New York, the norm is to shoehorn yourself and your belongings into an absurdly small unit within a large building, whereas in L.A. and many other cities it is more common to rent houses or condominiums. In Boston you will develop chronic bronchitis without heating, while in Phoenix heating might be irrelevant. For the sake of simplicity, we will refer mostly to "apartments" here, but the basic guidelines for finding somewhere to live, getting a lease, and settling in can be applied anywhere and to any situation.

In this chapter, we'll provide you with all the know-how you need to transition to life beyond the nest. After discussing the decision to move to a new city, we'll tackle the specifics of searching for an apartment, preparing the necessary documentation, living with roommates, and even buying a place. Ultimately, finding a nice spot can be one of the most bellicose bees in a recent grad's bonnet, but where you sleep each night is so fundamental to your daily happiness that it's worth giving the process the respect and attention it deserves. Fly, pelican, fly!

Choosing a Post-grad City

So, you've made the decision to move out of the nest and make your way in the world. We salute you and sincerely hope that you didn't fall victim to a *Failure to Launch* situation in which your parents secretly plotted to force you out of the house even though you are Matthew McConaughey, the most handsome dude in the world. (Number one on a laundry list of things that didn't make sense about that movie...)

Subject to a few restrictions, you now have the world at your fingertips. Close your eyes, spin the globe, and point. Gary, Indiana! Okay, forget that plan. A more logical approach may be in order.

Let's start with some real talk: the first city that you move to after college isn't necessarily the one you'll end up in for life. So go sow your nomadic oats (and, if you're lucky, maybe even spread your seed like Flavor Flav on Viagra). Always wanted to live in Los Angeles before settling down in Boston? Or how about Beijing before Kansas City (who said you have to settle "Stateside" right after college)? Now's the time to explore and experiment, when your responsibilities are at an all-time low and all you need to worry about, in most cases, is putting a roof over your head, eating food, and possibly repaying student debt (but no kids, mortgage, etc.). In the worst-case scenario, you move in less than a year. We promise, it's not a big deal.

Apartments & Homes

City Selection: A Chicken and Egg Situation

Let's just point out the elephant in the room: picking a city solely because you want to live there is all gravy, but doesn't it ultimately come down to your job? There's no simple answer here. Mostly, it depends upon what you're looking for right out of college: a few years of fun, a *Mario Kart*-esque turbo start to a career, or a mix of both (a chicken and egg sandwich, if you will... a 'Wich Came First?). One thing to keep in mind is that to pursue a specific career, you don't necessarily have to move to the city that's famous as the industry hub (e.g., while you could do investment banking in New York City, you could also do it in San Francisco). Assess your options with an open mind before ruling anything out.

The Chicken: Pick a City for Yourself

If you aren't the type that's rushing to make the "millionaires under 30" list (or you are that type but think you can do it without being in a business hub), you've got a ton of options for your first post-grad city. Is there a place where you've always seen yourself living, or a city that appeals to your gut for no particular reason? Some criteria to consider include the following:

- **Weather:** are you a surfer, a skier, or someone who avoids going outside at all costs?
- **Demographic:** do you want to be surrounded by other recent grads, stroller-pushing newlyweds, or incredibly old people?
- **Cost of living:** can you afford the lifestyle you're looking for in the city of your choosing?
- **Culture:** do you want a city that has non-stop entertainment in the form of art and museum exhibitions, classical music, opera, Jonas Brothers shows, and other concerts?
- **Attitude:** do you like a fast-paced or laid-back vibe?
- **Friends and Family:** do you need to be around your friends and family or do you want to blaze your own trail for a bit?
- **Nightlife/Bar Scene:** do you want to club hop, pound Miller Lites with cougars, or drink Trader Joe's wine at home while tearing through your Netflix queue?

The Egg: Pick a City for a Job

If the "right job" is at the top of your priority list, we salute your self-starting 'tude and offer one piece of advice: seriously consider what job you want before you pick your city. Once you choose the industry you want to break into, your city will be picked out for you (assuming you want to be in the hub):

- **New York City:** finance, fashion, advertising/marketing, and publishing
- **Boston:** consulting and venture capital
- **Miami:** anything having to do with Latin America
- **Atlanta:** big business (e.g., Coca Cola, Home Depot, Delta)
- **Los Angeles:** everything entertainment
- **San Francisco:** technology (from computers to health)
- **Washington, D.C.:** politics
- **Seattle:** big-biz technology and tech-related venture capital
- **Chicago:** aerospace, finance, and consulting

You Don't Need to Move to Where Your Friends Are

There's nothing wrong with moving in with friends post-college (indeed, it can really ease the pain of transitioning), but don't move to a city just because your friends will be living there. Odds are, during the first few years after graduation, a diaspora of sorts will occur: some friends might decide they want to chase their Hollywood dreams and move out to L.A. Others might move abroad for studies or "to find themselves." You don't want to be the one who moves to the city where everyone else lives and then gets left in the lurch. Moreover, "keeping the dream alive" with high school or college buddies can turn out to be sort of depressing and stunt your personal growth. Move to where you really want to move, and in the end, you'll probably end up with some friends, anyway. (Note: this goes for significant others as well. You are not married, so there is no reason to act like you are. If you are married, mazel tov—just don't put your wedding photos on Facebook, please.)

Apartments & Homes

Top 10 Cities for College Grads

- **New York City.** The city that never sleeps is the center of the finance and publishing worlds, and there's never a dearth of carrion for culture vultures to devour.

- **Los Angeles.** The entertainment biz isn't for everyone, but few can complain about beautiful weather, excellent tans, and miles of beaches.

- **Washington, D.C.** Politicians-in-training storm this manageable Mid-Atlantic city—be prepared to raise your voice if you want to be heard.

- **San Francisco.** Culturally diverse and uniquely situated, the jewel of the Bay Area is more than just a techie's dreamland.

- **Chicago.** Combining the most interesting architecture in America with top-notch food and a beautiful location on Lake Michigan, Chi-Town delivers cosmopolitanism with Midwestern warmth.

- **Atlanta.** Big business brings recent grads in droves, and "the A" remains the unofficial capital of American pop music. Just don't forget to bring a car.

- **Boston.** Not too big, not too small—Beantown is just right for a lot of recent grads, as well as hordes of students who make a temporary home in "America's College Town."

Top 10 Cities for College Grads Continued...

- **Seattle.** Technology reigns supreme in Microsoft land, but the extracurricular schedule is full and varied. Great skiing and hiking just outside the city are big draws for those who don't enjoy the concrete jungle.

- **Houston.** Texas feels like another country to some, but the home of NASA and big oil might appeal to recent grads who believe that "bigger is better."

- **Denver.** Join the Mile High (City) Club and gain various membership perks, including greater lung capacity, an active arts scene, and easy access to amazing skiing and hiking.

Deciding Where to Live

Once you've chosen a post-college city to live in, it's time to find a place to set up camp. The "sorting hats" of parentage and college housing offices are no longer responsible for assigning you rooms, so the onus is on you to figure out what you value in a living space, how much you are willing to spend, and where exactly you want to live. To do so, it is necessary to balance the three main criteria for judging an apartment: neighborhood/location, cost, and space.

Neighborhood

In most cities worth living in, there exists a wide range of neighborhoods, each boasting its own inimitable flavor. Some are filled with hipsters who aspire to be starving artists even though their parents own Fortune 500 companies. Some are filled with octogenarians, while others are havens for young families. If you are new to a city, get a sense of the landscape by reading guidebooks, grabbing local magazines and newspapers, and talking to people who have lived there. Walk around neighborhoods during the day and then go back at night so you can see what you can do and whether or not it feels safe—saving money is great, but if you are going to end up getting the shirt stolen off your back twice a month on the way home from work, maybe it's not worth living on "the other side of the tracks."

It's easy to get suckered into thinking that the coolness of a neighborhood trumps the practical concerns associated with living there, but in most cases it doesn't. The place

Apartments & Homes

you like to shop, party, or hang out does not necessarily have to be the place you live, particularly if it costs an arm and a leg. The truth is that you will not think that the specialty bookstore down the block looks so cool as you walk past it in the morning, when it's closed... and then again at night, when it's also closed. Here are some more pressing concerns to consider first.

- **Proximity to work.** Will an hour commute to and from work make you want to impale yourself on a rusty spike? If you drive, what will the morning traffic be like? Would you rather wake up half an hour later every weekday or be closer to your friends on the weekends?
- **Proximity to transportation.** Can you get everywhere you need to go without a car? Note that if there's an express bus, train, or highway to shoot you to work in the morning, it might be easier to live in a different area or town than it would be to live geographically closer but three trains and a 10 minute walk away.
- **Cost.** Basically, can you afford it? (See p. 48.)
- **Safety.** We'll just mention it again so as not to get sued. (Just kidding— we really do care about you!)
- **Convenience.** Grocery stores, banks, and pharmacies should be easily accessible, or else you might get aggravated and/or hungry.
- **Other.** How much do you value being close to friends, restaurants, bars, parks, and anything else that will make your life more convenient and enjoyable?

Top 5 Tips for Moving With and Without a Mover

Whether you're moving out of your college dorm or into your new place (or both!), you are going to have to deal with the arduous task of transporting all of your stuff from point A to point B. Here are some tips for moving solo, or with the help of a professional mover:

Moving without a Mover

1) **Prepare.** Figure out what you'll need (e.g., boxes, tape, truck) and secure it before moving day so you won't have to scramble. If you wait until the last minute like every other kid in College Town, USA, you may be stuck riding the Greyhound. This eventuality, in turn, will give new meaning to the word *depressing*.

Top 5 Tips for Moving With and Without a Mover Continued...

2) **Get help.** Ever tried to load a mattress into a car/truck on your own? Now imagine trying to repeat this process with all of your furniture. Ask friends and family for help. If that backfires, then scour Craigslist for freelance strongmen. You don't need to be a hero.

3) **Pack smart.** Save some cash by getting your packing materials online or from a hardware store. Also, put some thought into what goes in each box and how to avoid wasting space. Storage/packing is an art form that should be treated with due respect.

4) **Wheels.** Check U-Haul, Budget, and Penske to see what kind of ride you will need and compare prices. On pickup day, arrive early to get first dibs. When loading up, remember to distribute weight evenly. If you are renting a trailer, make sure the truck and/or your car has a hitch to attach it to.

5) **Assume it will be annoying.** I don't care what people tell you; moving yourself is a big pain in the butt. If you have the cash, do yourself a favor and spend it to hire movers.

Moving with a Mover

1) **Make a reservation.** This is not your Intro to Philosophy term paper—just because you are paying someone else to do it for you doesn't mean you don't have to give it any thought before the date of pickup. Most moving companies recommend making a reservation two to four weeks ahead of time.

2) **Comparison shop.** In comparing movers, you will naturally want to consider pricing, but you also want to learn a bit about the company that will be sending someone to pack all of your worldly goods into a truck that could double as a getaway vehicle. Make sure your mover has insurance and uses fulltime staffers that will be mindful of their own job security when moving your stuff.

3) **Check the fine print.** Once you are given an initial estimate, it is helpful to rattle off any potential obstacles you envision to ensure the movers don't hit you with any hidden fees. Do they charge an additional fee for large items like an armoire? Will the company transfer your goods mid-move to a different truck (thus increasing chances of breakage)?

Apartments & Homes

Top 5 Tips for Moving With and Without a Mover Continued...

4) **Get directions.** If you are at a point of indecision about where you want to live, hiring a mover in the hopes that they will make the decision for you is probably not the way to go. Printing out specific directions ahead of time will save time and money. It will also force you to pick a place to live and thus prevent the possibility of homelessness.

5) **Pack yourself.** Not only do movers generally charge by the hour, but they also won't care if all of your belongings are supposed to be sorted by "awesomeness factor." Moreover, they will charge more for packing supplies, and use way more boxes than is necessary. Handle this part of the process on your own and then use the pros for what they do best—heavy lifting.

Cost

How much you are willing to pay is pretty much up to you, though we encourage you to think about saving your money rather than blowing it on an unnecessarily extravagant apartment. In economic terms, rent is a sunk cost, meaning it cannot be recovered once you've paid it. It is not an investment that will accrue value over time (unlike buying a place, which you can learn more about on p. 68). On the flip side, the place where you sleep and spend most of your free time has a huge impact on your happiness quotient. Just keep things in perspective when you are hunting. If two apartments are essentially identical, but one comes with a gym in the building and costs $100 more, don't think, "Wow, this apartment building is so much better because it has a gym!" Rather, you should think, "Would I pay $100/month for a gym membership?" Rent is money you never get back, so make sure you put it toward the things that are actually important to you on a day-to-day basis. Also, remember that roommates can significantly cut the cost of living (see p. 62 for more on "Roommate Living").

So how much is reasonable? Property prices vary so drastically from place to place that it is impossible to say, but *The Quarterlifer's Companion* offers the following rule of thumb:

Generally, it is advisable not to spend more than half (this may vary by area) of your monthly income on rent and utilities. Therefore, if you make $35,000 a year and bring home $2,000 a month after taxes, Social Security, and health care, you should not be spending more than $1,000 on rent.

It is important to settle on a range before you start apartment hunting so as to narrow the search and make sure you don't waste time. Also, be very explicit in asking about the average cost of utilities and the services each building provides (generally trash removal, water, and maintenance). To figure out a reasonable price range, consider creating a budget to get a sense of your monthly expenditures (see p. 144).

Space

As the fictional British broadcaster Alan Partridge once pointed out, "People always go on about space. But people forget, you can get lost in space!" Though your getting lost in your first apartment is about as likely as Baghdad winning the next Olympic bid, the fact remains that space is not always all it's cracked up to be, particularly when it comes at a high premium.

We should note that you could probably rent an old ranch in Mississippi for the same price that it costs to live in a cramped Manhattan studio, and in many ways that's an awesome idea. But for now let's assess the realities of city living. When looking at an apartment, think about how much natural light it gets and how important that is to you. If you end

Tips & Tricks: Flex/ Convertible Apartments

Before you start wheeling and dealing on the real estate scene, make sure you are familiar with the industry lingo—not understanding the terminology on a listing can lead to a lot of wasted time and maybe even a grave mistake. One concept that is particularly relevant to recent grads living with roommates is that of a *flex* apartment, also known as a *convertible*. These terms refer to apartments that have the space (generally in a large bedroom or off the living room) to add an extra bedroom by putting up pressurized walls. So a "flex three" or "convertible three" is a two-bedroom apartment with room for a third. It does not mean that it is a three-bedroom that can be *flexed* or *converted* to four, so if you have more than three people look elsewhere. Like a convertible car, these apartments are usually pretty cramped, and unfortunately you can't pop the roof to get more sunlight. However, this type of arrangement can make the rent much more manageable for recent grads on tight budgets.

up renting a convertible, will the added room block out most of the light? Next, assess the floor plan, which is generally much more important than the square footage number quoted on the listing. Do you have to walk through another bedroom to get to the bathroom? Are the hallways awkwardly narrow? Finally, think about your unique lifestyle and needs. If you live with a social group of friends and you plan to spend most of your free time in the apartment together, then maybe it's worth sacrificing large bedrooms for a bigger living room and kitchen. But if you hate people and basically just want to be able to play *World of Warcraft* in peace, hold out for a suitably comfortable bedroom. Finally, if you have worked out a rental scheme in which you and your roommates will pay different amounts, make sure you look for places where the rooms match their respective price tags.

Perks and Special Needs

If you require wheelchair-accessibility or you own a pet, you'd better make sure that any building you look at can accommodate these needs. Beyond the essentials, you need to determine how much you value the various "bells and whistles" of the building.

- **Laundry.** A laundry room (or better yet a washer and dryer in the apartment) should be the first point of investigation. However, bear in mind that laundry rooms cost money, so look around the neighborhood before ruling out a laundry-free building—there may be a Laundromat next door that will wash, iron, and fold your clothes for little more than it would take to use the machines.

- **Kitchen.** A refrigerator, stovetop, and oven are basic, but a dishwasher can be a godsend to a busy and lazy grad. That said, if you never cook at home (let alone eat outside the office), maybe it's irrelevant. Determine your cooking needs and aspirations, then proceed accordingly. You can also roll with paper dishes and plastic silverware to make things easier. Just don't expect Al Gore to show up at your dinner parties.

- **Gym.** Having a gym in your building is pretty fresh, but again, assess your actual schedule and habits. Does your job provide gym membership somewhere better? Would you prefer to work out at home or closer to work? Have you even worked out since '99? Maybe it's not so fresh after all...

- **Doorman.** A doorman apartment is not only safer, but also more convenient when it comes to dealing with packages, guests, and other building-related issues. However, if packages are your main concern, remember that you may also be able to get packages shipped to your office.

- **Patio, balcony, or roof access.** If you like "grilling and chilling" as much as Bobby Flay, a little deck space can be very agreeable. But make sure you adjust the value of this luxury for the effects of global warming. Next thing you know, you'll be flipping burgers in July with gloves on—and I'm not talking about oven mitts!

- **Parking.** Do you need it and are there cheaper alternatives?

Apartments & Homes

Confessions of a Nomad: The Modern-day Odysseus, by Gritz

Nomad, n.

1. *A member of a group of people who have no fixed home and move according to the seasons from place to place in search of food, water, and grazing land.*

2. *A person with no fixed residence who roams about; a wanderer.*

After living with my mom in Washington, D.C., for the first fall after I graduated, I decided to seek fame and fortune at an Internet startup in New York, where I shacked up with my best friend from college and his parents. Everything was going great until I was fired three weeks later, less than 24 hours after I had signed a sub-lease on a place with my buddy. Suddenly, I found myself at the most daunting crossroads of my post-college life: Should I bail out and go back home to D.C. with my tail between my legs, or should I soldier on with no job and zero prospects? Needless to say, my hubris got the better of me, and thus my life as a nomad began.

Over the next eight months, I would live at six more locations, including two couches, one hotel, a solo sublet that everyone I know refused to visit, and a room that leaked dirt from the ceiling—when I woke up in the morning, I often felt like someone had tried to bury me alive. Sometimes, I wished they had finished the job.

Though it's rarely easy, the nomadic lifestyle is a reality for many recent grads that move to a new city before securing employment. But while job-hunting, apartment hunting, and sleeping on a different futon every couple of weeks can be an exhausting endeavor, there are many hidden benefits to the life of a wanderer.

Firstly, a good nomad will have to develop admirable social graces if he plans to make it for very long. Be it an aunt or a friend of a friend from college, your host is doing you a huge favor by providing you with room and maybe some board, so you have to be on extra good behavior. Clean up after yourself, keep your things neatly packed away, leave the house as much as possible, and always bring your own towel (and bedding if possible)—no one wants your juices on their linens. On a similar note, don't bring

Confessions of a Nomad: The Modern-day Odysseus Continued...

a "tenderoni" back from the bar unless you are staying with your best friend. When you're a nomad, the whole idea is to snag a spot in someone else's bed! The need for a roof over your head actually adds a bizarrely Darwinistic subtext to the act of flirting, because getting it cracking means free shelter and another night of survival in the concrete jungle. (Needless to say, I never actually achieved this level of nomadic prowess. Boo-hoo! I guess that is the price one pays for having uneven facial hair and eczema—conditions which are only exacerbated by the nomadic lifestyle.)

Next lesson: a nomad shall become extremely resourceful and knowledgeable about the city where he subsists. On the one hand, you may become familiar with many different neighborhoods, which will come in handy if you ever decide to get your own place. However, you will also need to develop the ability to kill time on the streets, ideally for free. Sometimes you will have to wait for your host to get home, or you'll wake up on a Saturday morning and literally not know where you are going to sleep that night. Lurking around a city is an art form that requires a little outside-of-the-box thinking. Street performers become your TV; Barnes & Noble is not just a bookstore, but also an opportunity to catch up on world affairs and take a deuce. Best Buy is the rec center, where kids play Guitar Hero and lounge in gaming chairs all day. Help yourself out by using some of the money you're saving on rent to join a nice gym—it will serve as an unofficial clubhouse where you can shower, utilize various hygiene products, and hang out if you have nowhere else to go.

Finally, the consummate nomad shall develop an intimate appreciation of life's necessities. If you are going to be nomadic for any extended period of time, you will need to scale down your belongings to a bare minimum. A few changes of clothes, toiletries, a pillow, and a towel are really all you need—wait until you find a place before calling in the Ps2s, humidifiers, and other household luxuries. When it comes to food, channel your Neanderthal lineage and learn to be a hunter-gather. This involves pulling moves like eating all of the free samples at Whole Foods and taking home food from buffets for dinner.

At the end of the day, being nomadic can be an invigorating experience, because you haven't really lived until you've sat on a park bench wondering whether or not you might have to sleep there. Also, if things go well, the experience can reaffirm your faith in humanity. The modern-day nomad is a sympathetic character that people love to help, so foster good etiquette and enjoy the fruits of others' hospitality!

Apartments & Homes

Subletting an Apartment

The term *sublet* refers to an arrangement in which an existing lease is passed on to a third party by the original lessee. In layman's terms, someone who already has an apartment rents it out to you. For the subtenant (most likely you), the benefits of this practice are two-fold. Firstly, subleases provide greater flexibility for short-term stays. A regular lease will usually last at least one year, but you can always find people subletting their apartments for almost any amount of time, from a week to many months. This arrangement is ideal if you are still unsure of where you want to live, or if you do not know how long you will stay in a city. Secondly, you can sometimes get incredible deals on fully furnished apartments through subleasing. If a banker suddenly finds out that he has to go to China for two months, time constraints may force him to sublet his apartment at a fraction of its market value before boarding the plane. If you are on the ball, you could be the intern who lives like an i-banker for two months! Before you dive in head first, here are a few tips for making the sublet game work in your favor.

Know where to look. Because sublets are generally listed by individual tenants rather than management companies, Craigslist is the best place to start your search (check out the "sublets & temporary" section). Also, check Gradspot.com's "Roommate Finder" to find people who are looking to fill space in their apartments, and do a Google search for local sublet sites. Finally, note that subletting is very much a word of mouth business—don't forget to let friends, coworkers, and family know that you are on the hunt. Put the word out through Facebook and MySpace, and stay in touch with alumni networks, as well.

Make sure everything is above board. If a random dude on Craigslist is subletting his room in a four-bedroom apartment, you had better go visit the place to meet all of his roommates and make sure they know what he is doing. Perhaps more importantly, make sure the sublessor has cleared the arrangement with his landlord. Some buildings forbid subleasing, so you don't want to end up getting tossed out through no fault of your own. (Of course, you can always just risk it and hope for the best.)

Have a written agreement. We'll be honest—this may not happen. Whether they are negotiated with friends or strangers, sublets are often fly-by-the-seat-of-your-pants arrangements, and as a result they can be disconcertingly casual. Unless you can trust the person completely or the sublease is extremely short, a legal document is ideal (if you don't have a buddy/colleague/dad who's a lawyer at your disposal, the Internet Legal Research Group offers sublet forms for each state). At the very least, make sure you cover these issues explicitly at the beginning of negotiations to avoid problems down the line:

- **Rent.** Will you pay the rent to the sublessor, or directly to the landlord? If you are still going through the person who sublet the apartment to you, what will happen if they fail to pay the rent to the landlord on time?

- **Security deposit.** Will you be required to cover a portion of the security deposit? What happens if you accidentally punch a hole in the wall while watching a Jane Fonda aerobics workout on VHS? Note that if you pay a security deposit directly to the tenant, they may not be able to pay you back until they get their original security deposit back from the landlord at the end of the lease. Will this delayed repayment work for you?

- **Apartment issues.** If there is a problem, are you expected to deal with it (or, worse still, pay for it)? Will the sublessor be easy to contact if you can't figure out how to fix the Internet connection, or is he going to be in the Ecuadorian rainforest the whole time? Will he give you the green light to make game-time decisions on repairs?

- **Are you allergic to cats (or responsibility)?** Sometimes presumptuous sublessors will expect you to do things like take care of their eight cats or water their plants. For some of us, it ain't that type of party. Before moving in, read the whole listing with an eye for personal red flags like pets, smoking, or religious needs (e.g., Kosher).

- **Think about the future.** If your sublease takes you to the end of the original lease, you may be in a position to take over the lease and stay in the apartment. Play it right and this move could be a good way to "test-drive" an apartment before making a commitment.

Finding an Apartment

Back in the days when the West was still wild and the Oregon Trail had yet to become an incredible videogame, the U.S. government used to sponsor "land runs" in which homesteaders would line up with their wagons, wait for a gun blast, and race to claim a plot of land from the U.S. government. It was pretty insane, but in the end the most motivated and aggressive settlers got the land.

These days, the process has changed drastically with the advent of real-estate brokers, Craigslist, and actual laws. Nonetheless, in cities like New York and San Francisco, the general vibe is not so different from those days of yore. Crazy competition for the best apartments is driven by the fact that 1) many twentysomethings want to live in the same areas and in similar types of apartments, and 2) the majority of recent grads move in and out of apartments at the same time of year (see p. 56).

If you're lucky, you have a couple of weeks set aside solely for apartment hunting. For those who will be working during the search, be prepared to wake up early and spend all of your lunch hours racing around to different apartments. Most people see between 10 and 40 places, so it can be a grueling process—depending on your schedule and budget, you may want to use a broker. In the meantime, you'd better familiarize yourself with the secrets of subletting (p. 53) and being a nomad (p. 51).

But enough small talk—it's time to make moves. Survey the land (on the Internet), load up your wagon (with the proper documentation), and get ready to throw some 'bows in the pursuit of the perfect pad. Oklahoma! Oklahoma! Oklahoma!

Broker Versus "No Fee" Apartments

Tips & Tricks: **How to Be a Super Hunter**

When it comes time to seal the deal, you're going to have to gather a whole bunch of money and documentation for the landlord. Preparing these items in advance—and even bringing filled-in forms and documents with you when you visit apartments—can be the difference between getting an apartment and seeing it slip through your fingers. Indeed, the competition for apartments can be so fierce that anything you can do to improve your candidacy helps. Consider getting a guarantor even if you don't think you'll need one. Ultimately, landlords have no obligation to be fair when it comes to deciding who will get the place (no "first come, first served" policy applies here), so you want to make an effort to look like the richest, most responsible candidate. Go to page 59 to find out exactly what landlords require from prospective tenants.

Apartments & Homes

There are essentially two ways to find an apartment: getting a broker or searching on your own. (There's also a third option called "getting your mom to do it for you," which should be exercised if possible.) Brokers are more prevalent in some cities than others (e.g., Boston), so depending on where you live you may not have much of a choice. In general, however, the decision boils down to a question of time and money. Let's consider the pros and cons of the two approaches.

Option #1: Do It Yourself

If you're determined to save some extra cheese (or if going it solo is the only viable option in your city), be prepared to put up with some serious hassle when looking for

Tips & Tricks: When to Look

When it comes to figuring out what neighborhood you want to live in and what type of apartment you want (e.g., studio, loft, two-bedroom), it's never too early to start getting a sense of the market. The more places you visit and neighborhoods you wander around, the better perspective you'll be able to bring to the hunt. However, it's important to realize that actually sealing the deal on a specific apartment is something that requires good timing and a bit of last-minute jostling. Since most recent graduates move into new apartments in the early fall, August and September are often the most competitive months for apartment hunting. These are also the months with the most openings because those recent grads that came before you also signed one- or two-year leases around the same time of year. Once you reach the stage of the process when you are actually ready to sign a lease, "starting early" does not really help—apartments are flipped very quickly when the last lease ends, so there is usually a two-week rush to compete for a place before someone snags it.

"no fee" apartments. Hopefully you have roommates lined up who can pitch in, because you will inevitably consider moving back home after wading through the detritus of inaccurate, unavailable, or undesirable listings. Still, if you enjoy the thrill of the chase and don't like paying others to do what you can do yourself, then it's certainly feasible (and an entire month's rent cheaper) to find a place on your own. Just follow these tips to avoid a major headache:

- **On the prowl.** Let family, friends, and coworkers know you're in the market for a new place. Ask friends about their search to get a list of good websites and managing agents. Also, if you like someone's building, have him ask the super if there are any apartments up for rent.

- **Go to the source.** This is often the best strategy: if you've narrowed down your search to a neighborhood, visit each building in the surrounding area and ask people going in or out whether there are apartments available, or try to find the number of the managing company (usually found on a plaque in the entranceway) and call directly. Even if they don't have an apartment in the building you're calling about, they might have one nearby.

- **Craigslist.** Start your search here before moving onto the other sites we recommend at Gradspot.com. It doesn't require registration, paid subscription, or a tolerance for pop-up ads. And while crafty brokers have even infiltrated

Apartments & Homes

the "no fee" section, there are still plenty of diamonds in the rough.

- **Ad language.** You will need to become adept at decoding the language used in apartment listings. "Cozy" generally means "incredibly small," "full of character" translates roughly to "falling apart," and so on and so forth. As a rule of thumb, avoid any building featured in an ad with flashing lights, size 98 font, or exclamation mark abuse.

- **Pictures.** Look for any fine print under a photo that says "photo is similar to actual apartment." Note the use of the term "similar," as in "not exactly" or "could be literally anywhere."

- **The phone call.** When calling different listings, try to get as much info as possible (e.g., exact street location, price, and, most importantly, size). Then be ready to run over to see the place at the first available time slot.

Option #2: Real Estate Brokers

The reason for using brokers is that they go through all of the listings for you to separate the wheat from the chaff, and they can show you a lot of apartments at once, thus saving time and avoiding scheduling issues. They may also have access to rentals not listed anywhere else, and they can sometimes get better deals from managing agents than you could negotiate yourself.

> ### Tips & Tricks: Apartment Resources
>
> While some buildings still put up signs reading "Rooms for Rent," finding apartments has gone digital like everything else. Craigslist is the go-to online classified source for the independent hunter in most cities, but there are also tons of great regional and city-specific resources for both brokered and "no fee" apartments. For example, NYBits.com is great for brokered apartments in New York City, while Westside Rentals is a must for hunters in L.A. and San Diego. Check in at Gradspot.com/book for a list of resources catering to the top cities for recent grad.

Apartments & Homes

Broker fees are occasionally "negotiable," but they usually run between a month and 15% of the yearly rent. Some brokers are great: resourceful, empathetic, and not criminal. But many are none of the three. So if you do seek their services, you have to learn how to cut straight to the real talk. And remember: since you shouldn't have to pay anyone until you actually find a place, feel free to get a number of brokers working on your case at the same time (warning: they'll drop you if they find out). Here are some rules of engagement to keep in mind:

- **Fix a price.** First figure out the highest rent your budget will allow. Then shave off a couple hundred dollars to account for the broker fee.

- **Ask around.** Try to find good brokers by asking friends what companies and specific brokers they used.

- **Play the field.** Work with several brokers. Remind each one (in a tactful way) that there are many others who are just a phone call away. That way the broker has to go above and beyond if he wants to get his hands in your pockets.

- **Get a schedule.** The first dirty broker trick is to show places way out of your price range, and then bring you to a dilapidated hut within your actual range. See the con? Ask for an itinerary before seeing any apartments. Then nix anything that doesn't fit your budget. If that doesn't leave anything left to see, tell the broker to get back to work. Or ditch him.

- **Under pressure.** The second dirty broker trick is to pressure you into settling on a place by mentioning the six other people waiting to put in an application. Whether those six people actually exist or are merely figments of the broker's f—ed up imagination is irrelevant. Don't let the broker pressure you into a hasty decision. That being said, if you know you like it, mount up and take it—those six people may be out there after all.

- **Do some recon.** The Better Business Bureau is a good place to check up on the credentials of specific brokerages.

- **Negotiate.** If you (or the broker) have no luck negotiating the rent, try to negotiate the broker fee instead.

- **Beware of contracts.** If a broker wants you to sign anything, read it very carefully, and remember that the window for negotiation closes once you lay down a signature.

Apartments & Homes

Sealing the Deal

If you thought *finding* an apartment was a struggle, you are in for a treat, *mon frere*. Actually sealing the deal is half the battle, and in most cases it involves an infuriating mix of timing, luck, and favoritism. Fortunately, a little preparation and a light sprinkling of gamesmanship can give you the head start you need to nip all those other bammas at the finish line. Prepare the necessary documentation beforehand and bring it with you when you visit apartments to put yourself on the leader board from the word "Go." Next, make sure that any roommates have their things in order, as well. If anyone is out of town, you will need to fax all of the documents and have them sent back immediately. In some states, these documents may need to be notarized (the same goes for guarantor's forms, which are discussed below). Finally, try to buddy up with the super and doorman when you visit the apartment—they are on the front line and will know exactly the right time to strike if something opens up.

What You'll Need

Not every landlord requires exactly the same items, but you will almost always need to provide some combination of the ones listed below. Once the process is done, make sure anything you handed over is returned to you.

- **Copy of photo ID.** Driver's license or passport should suffice, even if the picture resembles someone who still requires a legal guardian to get into Rob Zombie movies.

- **Letter of employment.** Must verify duration of employment, position, and salary.

- **Two most recent pay stubs.** Get 'em from work.

- **Tax return copies.** Some places require just the past year, while others require the past two years. Bring both just to be extra safe.

- **Most recent bank statement.** Get it from the bank.

- **Copy of previous lease.** Make sure the lease has the previous managing agent's info and let's hope there are no skeletons in the closet. If you did have a falling out with your last managing agent, pretend you spent the last few years living with the 'rents.

> ## Tips & Tricks: Read the Lease (and Take Pictures of the Apartment)
>
> Don't be lazy—this is a healthy portion of your salary we're talking about, so make sure you are not committing to anything that will bite you in the booty. For example, did you plan to leave for three months in the summer and sublet your room? Some buildings do not allow subletting, so check the fine print. If you can't decipher the legalese, try to find a lawyer, or let your parents take a look. Then, once you have signed, take pictures (with date and time display) of the apartment when you first move in so that you have evidence of that giant crack on the ceiling that the landlord will likely try to deduct from your security deposit.

- **Letters of recommendation.** In the absence of written notes, names and phone numbers of personal or business references should be enough.

- **Rental application and fee.** The application will be provided by either the landlord or broker. Most often it is filled out on the spot, but occasionally it can be done in advance if there is a particular building or management company to which you are confining your search. The fee (about $50) is used to process the application and run a credit check.

Guarantors

Most management companies require that a tenant's income be above a minimum level, usually about 40-45x the monthly rent (income of roommates can be combined). For a $2,000/month apartment that means you have to make between $80 and $90K. If you don't stack this type of money (you're not alone), you may need a guarantor to co-sign the lease. The guarantor agreement is provided by the landlord or management company and requires some basic personal and financial information. Signing it legally obligates the guarantor (usually a family member or close friend) to pay rent if you default. They must earn a greater percentage of the rent, on average 80-90x the monthly rate, but combining the incomes of two guarantors is often allowed. Even if you can hack it alone, having a guarantor is never a bad idea, since it makes your candidacy that much more attractive.

Get Your Money Right

On top of the application fee, there will be other lump sums of money to pay either upon application or at the lease signing. Unfortunately, you will usually have to pay a bit more than just the first month's rent—that arrangement only works at a halfway house. Have your finances in order or risk seeing the apartment you searched so hard for go to those better prepared hunters who got there after you. Below is a list of what you'll need (note: landlords often require the security deposit and first month's rent to be on separate certified checks or money orders—no personal checks or credit cards).

- **Broker fee.** If you go through a real estate agency, it will most likely charge a fee that is tantamount to highway robbery. (The norm is 10-15% of the yearly rent.)

- **Hold deposit.** Used to reserve an apartment prior to lease signing, this fee is generally just deducted from the security deposit. If the potential tenant has a change of heart, it will be deducted from his or her bank account instead.

- **Security deposit.** Paid at lease signing or move-in, this charge ensures that damage to the apartment is covered. It is usually equal to one to two month's rent and refundable as long as the apartment is left in the same condition as when you moved in.

- **First month's rent.** Essentially another security deposit to lock it down once and for all.

Renter's Insurance

Many recent grads never even consider purchasing renter's insurance because they either A) falsely assume that the landlord's insurance covers the tenant's belongings, or B) don't think they own much that's worth protecting. However, the reality is that owner's insurance (paid by the landlord) only covers structural damages to the building, and if you ended up copping that plasma TV and Tempur-Pedic bed, you might have more to protect than you think. Renter's insurance generally covers stuff like fire, smoke, theft, vandalism, and lightning. And while it protects all of your personal belongings, it also has other unexpected benefits—for example, it provides temporary housing should you need to relocate or wait for repairs to be made, and it covers medical and legal expenses if someone gets hurt in your crib and sues you. With typical plans running about $150-300/year, it's not such a ridiculous thought after all. Allstate, Geico, and State Farm all offer coverage, but as with any insurance policy, be sure to comparison shop like there's no tomorrow (or perhaps like there is a tomorrow in which your apartment is going to catch on fire).

Apartments & Homes

Roommate Living

Ah, roommates—can't live with them, can't live without them.

Actually, you can live without them, but it's more expensive and sometimes sort of lonely. If you were the type of person in college who preferred the privacy of a single room (or, alternatively, were banished to a "psycho single" after searching for Kylie Minogue sex tapes on your roommate's computer), don't overlook the fact that you still lived in a dorm full of students that you could fraternize with on a whim. Living alone in post-college life can be a bit more solitary, and sometimes it's nice to have someone to come home to at the end of the working day (or the day of being unemployed and depressed, as the case may be).

Sometimes, however, it is not nice at all—particularly if you come home to find your roommate smearing chocolate mousse on a call girl while listening to the *Ducktales* theme song. The sword cuts both ways, as they say (the good news: sometimes that sword cuts the rent in half). But if the above image doesn't put you off and you do decide to shack up with a roomie (or eight), consider what you are getting yourself into and how to make it work.

Finding (Compatible) Roommates

In this menagerie, there are three distinct beasts: friends, strangers, and lovers. (Sometimes the first two can morph into the third, but only if you decide to "s—t where you eat"—something I think we can all agree is a bit odd.) If you haven't found anyone to live with yet, visit Gradspot.com and use our "Roommate Finder" tool to find an ideal match. Alternatively, try to link up with other apartment seekers via friends, family, and alumni networks. Finally, Craigslist is always something to fall back on, as its pages are always packed with people renting or subletting individual rooms for recent grads in large apartments or houses. However, it is also a refuge for nutcases, so be aware of the risks involved.

Friends. As long as you don't allow things to get too "college," living with friends can be a nice way to ease the transition into the "real world." However, it's not necessarily going to be all gravy, all the time. Getting kept up by a noisy roommate might have been passable the night before your noon lecture, but waking up at 7 AM every day will make you a bit more conservative in terms of what you deem to be appropriate nighttime behavior. New responsibilities like getting your own food, paying rent, and trying to be moderately clean can draw unspoken tensions to the surface. In England, where apartments are called flats, BFF stands for "Bad F—kin' Flatmate." (That is untrue, because they don't use the phrase BFF. But I have dual citizenship so I have taken the liberty of mixing and matching.)

Strangers. If you are good enough friends with your roommate, you will hopefully be able to work past any problems and still find that there is a modicum of love left in your hearts at the end of the day. Strangers are a different story–if someone you just met eats your Fage yogurt or slightly offsets your sleep patterns, you will have no problem declaring your blind hatred for him and blaming him for all of your post-college problems. (A good scapegoat, but not necessarily a healthy one.) Some people choose to live with strangers as a sort of experiment. For example, they might live in a house full of "artists" in order to get in touch with their creative side or mitigate the soul-sapping effects of their job. (Note: artists are terrible at cleaning up.) In general, however, the decision to subject oneself to strangers is a purely economical one. If you become friends then you've got "cashback" situation on your hands, but the more realistic goal should be to get along moderately well. Stack the odds in your favor by always meeting each and every roommate before making a decision. General compatibility issues include the following:

- **Smoking.** Will your roommate be smoking tobacco, weed, or crack on a regular basis? Probably something to broach before move-in day.
- **Pets.** Don't try to hide your ferret: I can smell it from a mile away!
- **Lifestyle.** Is your prospective roommate more Mike Jones or Bridget Jones? (In other words, will he or she party and yell a lot, or sit around gaining weight and crying?)
- **Work schedule.** Depending on the bathroom situation, the morning shower rush can be a real source of frayed nerves (and split-ends).
- **Significant others.** Do any of the roommates have boyfriends or girlfriends who are always around?
- **Gender.** Are you cool living with someone of the opposite sex?
- **Race and sexual orientation.** Beware of racists and bigots!
- **Religious and/or dietary needs.** Kosher? Deathly allergic to nuts? Be clear about your needs, and make sure you can respectfully comply with theirs.
- **Other.** Cleanliness, weird habits, etc.

Lovers. Shacking up with your boyfriend or girlfriend is definitely an aggressive post-college move. The most important thing to consider is your motivation. The only real reason to move in with a lover is if you both think it is the right time to up the ante. Doing it to save money or because it seems convenient will probably end in tears, so don't take it too casually. For better or for worse, living together will push your relationship to its limits and give you a better sense of whether you're compatible enough to build a long-term future together. Remember all those nights when you said, "Let's not sleep over," because you wanted to play *Tony Hawk's Pro Skater* or watch *Sex in*

Apartments & Homes

the City reruns with a carton of Chunky Monkey? Well, now you *have* to sleep over, so you'd better hope that your mate is understanding of your idiosyncrasies (and the fact that you leave enormous logs in the toilet after eating Indian food).

Laying Down the Ground Rules

No matter whom you end up living with, you have to sort out paying the rent and buying the cleaning supplies. Otherwise, you'll either be evicted or carried out on your couch by an army of rats while the Pied Piper upper-decks your toilet. Here's how to keep it all in check:

(see p. 152).

- **Lease.** The lease question is a tricky one. If you want ultimate control over the apartment you may want to keep the lease in your name, but not having your roommate's name on the lease also means you become the landlord by proxy. You'll be responsible for getting the rent together on time, or covering the whole rent yourself if your roomie decides to do a runner. Heavy is the head that wears the crown.

- **Rent.** Will one person pay more due to certain privileges like a bigger room or parking spot? Rooms can be pro-rated based on square footage, but you may also want to take other things into account like closet space, number of windows, or proximity to the bathroom.

- **Utility bills.** Divide the duties—if one person covers cable, the other should make sure the lights stay on. If you only watch Wu-Tang videos online and your roommate keeps the cable box in her room, she should pay more of the cable bill. Consider signing up for automatic bill pay to reduce hassle and avoid late payments (see p. 152).

- **Groceries.** Decide up front whether food will be separate or shared so that tension doesn't arise when someone lays a finger on your Butterfinger. There are some things the apartment will regularly need, like toilet paper, napkins, and trash bags. Will these items be bought as needed by whomever, or should there be a monthly Costco outing together to stock up Y2K-style?

- **Furniture.** You may have some stuff left over from college, but chances are it's been thoroughly "compromised." Figure out what's usable and then discuss who will bring what. If items need to be bought, decide whether the cost will be split or if one person will foot the bill and maintain sole ownership. The problem with splitting is that eventually you move out and somehow own a quarter of a flat-screen TV and a third of a chez lounge. One potential

Apartments & Homes

solution is to agree upon what big-ticket items everyone wants to have (e.g., couch, TV, dining room table), and then have each person handle an item in full.

- **Visitors.** How late is too late and how long is too long? A roomie whose friends overload the couch and stay for weeks on end will get annoying faster than a Carrot Top special.

- **Chores.** Keep in mind that people have different cleaning habits—some tidy up every day, while some do a big *Trading Spaces*-style overhaul once a month. If your roommate cleans less often than you do, don't try to force him onto your schedule. Instead, try to make a compromise with other chores or get him to pitch in for a maid service.

Top 10 Ways to Go Green in Your First Apartment

These days, it's not so much "go green or go home" as "go green in your home." Making some environmentally friendly tweaks in the crib is not only easy, but it will also cut down on your gas, water, and electricity bill. Everyone wins!

1) **Change your bulbs.** Compact fluorescents last up to 10 times as long as incandescent bulbs and use a quarter of the energy. You do the math!

2) **Look for certified Energy Star products.** An Energy Star TV set can use 30 percent less energy than uncertified ones, and an Energy Star washing machine can save more water than one person drinks in a lifetime.

3) **Control your climate control impulses.** Experts suggest setting the AC to 78°F (an insistence on 72°F will cost you 39 percent more energy). Keep the heat around 68°F during the day and 60°F at night.

4) **Kill the "energy vampires."** Unplug appliances like cell phone chargers when you're not using them—they keep sucking down energy even when nothing's connected.

5) **Buy organic and recycled products.** Organic mattresses, sheets, and towels are increasingly mainstream and affordable. Opt for recycled glassware, clean up with eco-friendly household products, and get a reusable shopping bag for trips to the grocery store.

Apartments & Homes

Top 10 Ways to Go Green in Your First Apartment Continued...

6) **Downsize your fridge.** Most recent grads don't keep much more than beer, milk, and a few condiments in their refrigerator, so why go for a massive energy-guzzler?

7) **Build good habits.** There are so many easy ways to save water and energy that people just overlook. Turn off lights when you leave the room, don't run the water while you're brushing your teeth, and take shorter showers (consider installing a low-flow shower head). After a while, these habits will become second nature.

8) **Use your dishwasher wisely.** Only run your dishwasher when there's a full load and always use the energy-saving setting. Savings earned: 100 pounds of carbon dioxide per year. If you're doing dishes by hand, use cold water.

9) **Buy some plants.** Houseplants not only add a little color to the room, but they also suck down pollutants and purify the air in your apartment. Just remember you'll have to water them once in a while.

10) **Get a home energy audit.** Many utilities providers offer free home energy audits to find where your home is poorly insulated or energy inefficient. You can save up to 30% off your energy bill and 1,000 pounds of carbon dioxide a year, according to the *Inconvenient Truth* peeps.

Dealing with Apartment Issues

Once you move into your apartment, you've still got to sort out a few key details before it becomes worth living in. Setting up your utilities, buying a mattress, and getting the cable hooked up will require a bit of time and money, but a visit to Gradspot.com should cut out a lot of hassle. What we want to discuss right here, however, is what to do if anything goes wrong in your new place. From roach infestations to leaky faucets, apartments (especially cheap ones) are full of problems waiting to rear their heads at inopportune moments. There's a D.I.Y. approach to handling most issues (many of which can be found on the website), but for first-time renters, the most important advice we can stress is to develop good relations with the **superintendent** and the **landlord.** These two people can single-handedly make you a happy camper or a miserable squatter, so it's worth taking a second to understand who they are and what their roles are in the building.

The Super

Your superintendent serves two purposes. First, your super is an apartment
steward/stewardess. When you first move
in, make sure your super informs you
of all emergency numbers and contacts,
shows you the circuit breaker, and walks
you through the ins-and-outs of your
apartment. The super is also your maintenance safety net. He (or she) is not
there to help you replace a light bulb or
kill a cockroach in your tub. Supers are
the last line of defense—call them only
after you tried to fix the problem yourself or when a situation arises that you
clearly can't deal with alone (e.g., there
was a flood and now there's a hole in your
wall). Granted, you can call them for every little issue, but then you'll end up being known as the recent grad who cried
"rat." Your super will probably set some
ground rules with you before you move
in, but unless there's an emergency, you
should only contact him between 9AM
and 9PM. After you've dealt with your
super a few times you'll get a handle on
how helpful he's willing to be.

Tips & Tricks:
Tipping in Your Building

The only thing worse than an
overflowing toilet filled with diarrhea
is an overflowing toilet filled with
diarrhea that won't be fixed for a
week. Tip the super $50–200 around
Christmas time and make sure he
knows his hard work is appreciated
(even if the work really isn't that
hard). If the building has doormen,
be sure to tip them too, since they
are in charge of your packages, dry
cleaning, and take-out. Depending
on how many visitors you have,
how often you receive deliveries,
and how well you are treated, tips
for doormen should range from
$10–$80. If you're in a building with
a ton of people, make sure you know
who's relevant to your life; you don't
need to tip all forty people on staff.
Next thing you know you'll be evicted
for defaulting on the rent!

Apartments & Homes

The Landlord

The landlord is not just a person who takes your money each month and laughs all
the way to the bank (though he is that too). He's also supposed to be responsible for
any problems with the building. Has the super still not fixed that leak in your ceiling
you've complained about five times? Enough is enough: call the landlord directly. Your
lease will include some legalese about the "habitability" of your apartment, and that
basically means that the landlord must resolve anything that makes your home unliv-
able (e.g., lack of clean water/heat/sane neighbors). If he does not rectify a situation,
threaten to stop paying rent or bring in the real authorities: an attorney, the police, or
the Department of Housing and Communities.

Sometimes, you might be in hot water with the landlord. Perhaps you were too busy with your new job and forgot to pay the rent. Usually, landlords will charge you a late fee, but if you've been a good tenant, they tend to waive it. But what if you can't make the rent one month? Instead of just ignoring the problem, you should speak with your landlord and see if you can work something out—most of the time it's not a huge deal. However, if the worst-case scenario occurs and your landlord tries to evict you, be sure to know your state's tenant rights and contact the Department of Housing and Communities. A landlord can't just kick you out without the law behind him.

Buying a Place

You might be thinking that we've officially lost the plot. You're an intern with piles of student debt and zero credit history—how the hell are you going to buy a house or an apartment!?

Admittedly, buying a place is not feasible for everyone in the first few years out of college, but these days it's not as insane an idea as it might seem at first glance. While property markets are out of control in places like New York and Los Angeles, many cities are quite affordable. We understand that you might not want the headache of mortgages, insurance, and other home-owning responsibilities, but 90% of the motivation for buying property is pure economics (the remaining 10% is knowing where your home will be for the next 5-10 years and being able to make any modifications you want to it). Rent, as we discussed before, is a completely sunk cost—it does not appreciate in value and you will never get it back. In many cities that are popular among recent graduates, rents are inordinately high because landlords know that we need housing and are willing to pay a lot for it.

Property that you own, on the other hand, is an investment that can appreciate over time, sometimes quite significantly if you choose wisely. Also, homeowners get a sizeable tax break on their mortgage payments, which is a nice bonus, and can make the total monthly costs of owning a home equal the rent you would otherwise be paying (thus, for many, the real challenge of buying is having enough money for the down payment). Getting a loan as a recent graduate is never easy, but buying a house is still viable. If you do decide to go for it, however, you should look for a place that you actually want to live in and that you think holds good value, rather than treating it solely as an investment (some people even consider it a "consumable" investment). Otherwise, you will drive yourself crazy if you spend all of your time worrying about how every little problem that comes up (in your house or the market as a whole) will affect the value of your "investment." Ultimately, you're buying your home for the next decade.

Apartments & Homes

Of course, there is a huge amount of research and preparation that goes into buying property, but we just wanted to put the thought out there for people who hate seeing $1,000 go down the drain each month. If you expect to be in one place for at least 5-10 years and you're making a healthy salary that you can reasonably expect to maintain, at least consider it. And remember, even if you have to leave before you think it's time to sell, you can always sucker the most recent crop of recent grads into renting it while you bide your time.

Buying Versus Renting

Many recent grads are surprised that the monthly payment on a house or apartment can often be less than they pay in rent. Check out this chart to see how the financing breaks down:

Price of House/Apt	Cash Down @ 10%	Total Monthly Payment[1]	Year-end Tax Savings[2]
$100,000	$10,000	$640	$1,890
$150,000	$15,000	$959	$2,835
$200,000	$20,000	$1,279	$3,780
$250,000	$25,000	$1,599	$4,725
$300,000	$30,000	$1,919	$5,670
$350,000	$35,000	$2,239	$6,615
$400,000	$40,000	$2,558	$7,560
$450,000	$45,000	$2,878	$8,505
$500,000	$50,000	$3,198	$9,450
$750,000	$75,000	$4,797	$14,175
$1,000,000	$100,000	$6,396	$18,900

Apartments & Homes

(1) Total Monthly Payment includes mortgage repayments and apt/house maintenance. However, it does not include the tax benefit of owning a mortgage. We did not include the benefit in this number because we wanted to look at the monthly cost of owning a house/apt, and the tax benefit only accrues at year end when you file your taxes.

(2) Since we don't think you should ignore the tax benefit all together, we wanted to present the annual tax savings you would receive at year end.

Notes

· Assumes a monthly interest rate of 6.0%, a tax rate of 35%, a 30-year mortgage, and that monthly maintenance is proportional to purchase price.

· Some simplifying assumptions were made. For example, we assumed an average maintenance, but it can change depending upon real estate taxes, amenities, and the general level of home upkeep.

Chapter III: The Job-hunt

The Job-hunt

Here we stand at the true crossroads of the post-grad experience. While commencement day serves as a communal ceremony to mark the transition into the "real world," there comes a moment of more personal epiphany when each recent graduate acknowledges his or her independence. Whether it's a day, a week, or a year after leaving campus, the real transition begins when you say to yourself, "Yes, I will look for a job to support myself, and maybe I'll even consider moving out of my childhood bedroom."

The job-hunt is a rite of passage for recent college graduates in the same way the fox hunt is a rite of passage for young, ruddy-cheeked British lads with aristocratic lineage. In many ways, it can be the most trying of all post-college obstacles because it distills so many doubts and challenges into one seemingly all-important process. Once you figure out what type of work you actually want to do (an arduous decision for some), you then have to tackle the thorny issue of actually *getting* a job. And that, in turn, takes more time and effort than you may have realized. According to outplacement firm Challenger, Gray and Christmas, the average job search lasts four months, so don't be discouraged if nothing falls into your lap immediately.

In spite of its many merits, the American educational system does not do a particularly good job of seasoning its young charges for finding employment. The immediacy of work and reward in academia does not always exist in the professional world. At school you take an exam and, a couple of weeks later, get a grade in return. Needless to say, ambiguities do exist, thanks in part to rogue professors who decide that they are going to single-handedly combat grade inflation by handing out horrible grades. But, for the most part, you still know what you need to do to get into a good college, receive academic honors, and so on. Along with the massive salaries they provide, careers in law, consulting, and finance are attractive to many recent grads because the steps for advancement are well-delineated. Most often, they involve either attending more school or applying for jobs in a way that feels very similar to the college application process.

For the rest of us, the job-hunt can feel like an enigma wrapped in a conundrum tucked inside of a difficult to reach cabinet—or whatever that expression is. Inexplicable rejections, unanswered e-mails, and botched interviews can take the wind out of anyone's sails. But unlike activities such as hiking or being really cold for an extended period of time, I can honestly say that the job-hunt builds character. The challenges of networking and presenting yourself as more than a transcript will push you to develop a fuller sense of what your strengths are and what gets you fired up.

Remember that while finding a first job can feel like a permanent decision, it is really just the beginning of a long working life. Take it seriously, but don't lose sight of the fact that you're still building a résumé and skills set.

In this chapter, we'll debunk the mysteries of the job-hunt. This isn't *The Secret*, so you're not going to learn how to take over the world simply by *thinking* that you're the jam. Instead, you will learn things that are actually useful, like where to search for openings, how to construct an effective résumé and cover letter, and how to network your way to interesting people and places. Enjoy yourself—this is where things really start to heat up!

What Should I Do with My Life?

You should figure out what you are passionate about... then find someone who will pay you for it! Or how about calling up your high school career counselor, and asking if he was serious when he said you were cut out for "clerical work." Don't forget about finding some peyote and going on a vision quest in Yosemite National Park. Obvi!

When it comes to deciding what type of career to pursue, there's all sorts of advice that people will give you, ranging from the New Agey ("do what you love, man") to the depressingly practical ("whatever pays the bills, son"). Somewhere between the existentialist and realist approaches you may find something that resonates with you and sets off a light bulb. But our take is that finding "the right job" is more of an active process than a philosophical one.

The first step, as cheesy as it sounds, is simply to expand your frame of reference and realize that there are a lot of jobs out there (see p. 77 to start brainstorming). Campus recruiting and the high profile of certain career tracks (e.g., law school, finance, consulting) can skew toward a limited conception of the job market. Thinking that those are the only options would be a huge mistake—if they aren't up your alley, you just have to dig a little deeper to figure out your alternatives. From there, it's really a matter of taking a calculated risk and trying a job that you think you will enjoy. If you like it, then you've chosen well; if not, then you've at least narrowed down the field and picked up some valuable perspective.

Of course, even after you've acknowledged the range of opportunities available, it can be tough to satisfy that internal yearning to find something that really grabs you. One simple litmus test for figuring out a good starting point is suggested by Lindsey Pollack in her book *Getting from College to Career*: start picking up the paper every morning and see what section you gravitate toward. Do you hone in on the front page or flip straight to the arts section? Are you more interested in the stock prices or the box scores? It seems kind of silly but it makes sense. As a whole, a good newspaper provides a representative swath of what's going on in the world. Whatever you find most interesting is probably where you should focus your efforts.

New Ageism for the Job-hunt

When our writer Gritz graduated from college, he decided to put his fate in the hands of the most powerful mathematical concept in the world: the Venn diagram! The Venn diagram is used throughout the modern world to solve problems large and small, and it was single-handedly responsible for bringing together Jay-Z and R. Kelly on *The Best of Both Worlds*. So why wouldn't it work for a recent grad looking for a job? Let's see how the experiment panned out.

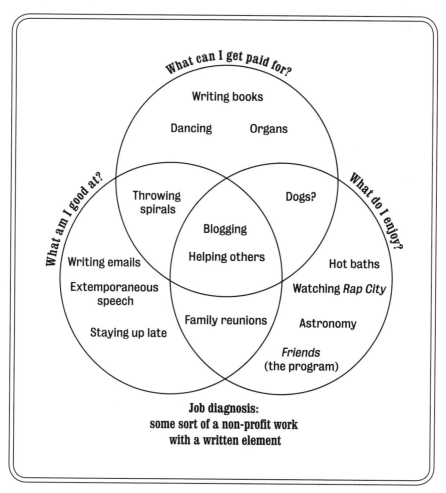

The Job-hunt

Interview: Doing What You Love

After meeting at the University of Pennsylvania, emcee Naledge and producer Double-O formed the rap duo Kidz in the Hall. In 2006, they released their critically acclaimed debut *School Was My Hustle* on Rawkus Records. We talked to Naledge about translating an Ivy League degree into a rap career.

What other careers did you consider when you left college? I was interested in music journalism, public relations, and possibly advertising. Whatever I ended up doing was going to involve the world of media and entertainment.

How did you make the decision to pursue music full-time?
I did what most of us artists call "jumping off the ledge." I just quit my job cold turkey and told myself I was going to either sink or swim. I lived for a year as a starving artist in Los Angeles. Eventually I made enough contacts and got enough people interested in my music that I knew a deal was going to come. I wouldn't have been able to survive if it wasn't for my savings account that my parents left me and money I saved while I worked at a public relations firm.

Did you receive any discouragement from parents, friends, or teachers? My parents supported me 100%. To most of my teachers, hip hop music was a foreign world to them so they would often stress to me that I needed to use my education as a backup plan. Most of my friends thought I was crazy to not go the conventional route and get a corporate job. Most of them didn't think that I could really get a record deal. Oddly, they are the same ones that say they believed in me all along.

Do you have any advice for recent graduates who feel pressure to get a traditional job instead of pursuing their passions? Chasing your true passion is always going to be most rewarding, but it is key to be realistic about your situation. Sometimes you will need to supplement your passion with a "9-to-5."

Are there good and bad reasons for getting involved in a creative industry? The monetary return is not always great, but you will be much more emotionally rich.

The Job Lottery: Take Your Pick

The nice thing about jobs is that you can often utilize your natural talents more fully than you did at school. In academia, there are few classes where being hilarious or having good people skills really help you that much. But out there beyond the ivory tower, there are jobs that match all sorts of talents. Do you have a nice way with children? Do you have an extraordinarily refined palate? Can you stay up extremely late? All of these are marketable skills on the job-hunt. The key is to determine where your talents will be valued and then figure out how to sell them effectively on the job-hunt. By the same token, just because you feel that you don't fit the traditional mold of a particular industry doesn't mean you shouldn't bother trying. Passion and perseverance will most likely take you further than talent anyway—just ask Wilmer Valderrama.

The Wide World of Jobs

Sometimes the pre-graduation job rush can make the working world feel remarkably small. It sort of makes you wonder how many lawyers and bankers the country really needs. That's not to say that those aren't careers worth considering, but remember that the job market has a lot more to offer. Just to get the wheels turning, here's a smattering of potential vocations waiting to be explored. Remember: this is just the tip of the iceberg...

Professional Blogger	Video Game Tester	Head Hunter
Internet Entrepreneur	Travel Writer	Management Consultant
Franchise Owner	College Student Advisor	Construction Manager
Archaeologist	Interior Designer	HR Manager
Graphic Designer	Tutor	Real Estate Agent
Public Relations (PR)	Musician	Farmer
Non-profit Fundraiser	Personal Assistant	Environmental Engineer
Sommelier	Pharmacist	Financial Advisor
Dog Walker	Social Worker	Paralegal
Astronaut	Radiologist	Computer Systems Analyst
Website Programmer	Alaskan Crab Fisherman	Talent Agent
Advertising Salesperson	Ski/Surf Instructor	Art Gallery Manager
Civil Servant	Tour Guide	Actor
Photographer	Teacher/Professor	Truck Driver
Fashion Buyer	A&R Rep	Actuary
Car Reviewer	Flight Attendant	Stock Agent
Chef	Wedding Planner	Airline Pilot

The Job-hunt

Where to Look for Jobs

In his ever-popular book *What Color Is Your Parachute: A Practical Manual for Job-Hunters and Career-Changers*, Richard Bolles discusses the ways in which the Internet has revolutionized the job-hunt. Gone are the days of a soot-covered young lad traversing the back alleys of a dangerous city, looking for the "Help Wanted" sign that will be his only beacon of hope. Romantic as it may sound, I don't think anyone wants to *literally walk around the streets* looking for a job. Think about how insane that would be!

The new paradigm, in the extreme, involves millions of people punching their personal information and preferences into a computer and waiting for the Internet to match them up with the perfect job. As Bolles explains, "The Internet now permits encounter between job-hunter and employer, *at warp speed*."

Of course, he goes on to explain that the system does not actually work so perfectly, and the majority of jobs are still landed through networking rather than applying out of the blue online. That said, the Web is still an invaluable tool for finding opportunities, and it should be the starting point of any well-executed job-hunt.

Full-time Job Information Resources

Whether you've decided to pursue a career or you are just exploring your options, there are many online resources that provide information on specific companies or industries in general. These sites also provide cover letter and résumé writing advice, as well as other full-time job search tips and tools:

- Gradspot.com (listed first due to contractual obligations!)
- Vault.com
- WetFeet.com
- Occupational Outlook Handbook (Google it)
- Salary.com
- Your college's career office site

Above, we've highlighted the sites that, in our opinion, offer the best career information on the Web. However, there are even more options. Some of the other sites include QuintCareers.com, JobWeb, and CollegeGrad.com.

The Job-hunt

Where to Find a Full-time Job

Tips & Tricks: Network

The job-hunt is extremely competitive, and unfortunately, being well-qualified does not always translate to getting offers. Sometimes you need a connection to even be considered in the first place. Before, during, or even after you apply, be sure to stack the cards in your favor by networking. Go to page 99 to learn the networking essentials you'll need to pull off a *coup d'employment.*

Once you get past the brainstorming, the skill assessments, and all the other self-searching exercises, it's time to find some actual positions wherein you might be able to render your services. A job search is a right of passage, and no right of passage would be complete without a ritual. Don't worry, you don't have to shave a Labradoodle and burn its hair in a terra cotta oven—this ritual is all about making the commitment to scan job listings on a regular basis. It can become a bit of an obsession, but that's okay—you don't want to miss out on a sick job just because you didn't have your head in the game.

While most people browse Monster.com and CareerBuilder.com (and we suggest you do as well), everyone scours Craigslist. Why? We can only assume it's because the twelve-hour-a-day job you're about to get will only start to look good after you've browsed the odd-jobs section of Craigslist and seen what life could have been: toenail-clipping collector, poop shoveler, or full-time Furry.

After a quick scan of those behemoths, it's time to get down to the nitty gritty. Each industry has its go-to destination for job postings, and you should always check the "Careers" section of a company websites. In addition, you're a soon-to-be or recent grad, and as such, you should take advantage of one very unique resource: your alma mater.

Alma Mater Job Resources. Recent college grads have three unique and effective resources at their fingertips, and most grads get their jobs through one of these avenues:

- **College Office of Career Services.** Not only will the office hook you up with other alums on similar career paths, but it will also furnish you with openings from companies that are specifically targeting your school.

- **Alumni networks.** For some reason Hoyas like helping other Hoyas, Tarheels follow Tarheels, and so on and so forth. Contacting fellow alumni can put you on the receiving end of some odd reminiscences (you might not want to know what those class of '66 dudes got up to), but it is a must for anybody on the job-hunt.

The Job-hunt

Tips & Tricks: Don't Spend Money to Get a Job

Regardless of which career resources you end up using, check with your school's career office prior to shelling out cash for any subscription fees that might pop up. More often than not, career offices will offer free subscriptions to their students and alumni. That said, be prepared to shell out a few dollars here and there for résumé photocopies at Kinkos, stamps for mailing applications, etc.

- **Professors.** Usually, the people with the coolest jobs are the ones who were set up by professors that took an interest in their future. Think about professors with whom you've developed special rapports and talk to them. They might have some great ideas.

Investment Banking & Consulting Resources. The best time to apply for an entry-level finance or consulting position is in late summer to early fall, a year before you'd start working. Since most major banks and consulting firms have structured programs for their entry-level employees, they hire the majority of their recent grads during this time. Your first step should be applying through your career office. However, if you've been otherwise directed, or a specific firm that you're interested in doesn't recruit on your campus, you can apply to any of the major banks and consulting firms directly through their website. Investment banks Citigroup, Goldman Sachs, and Morgan Stanley accept online applications, as do consulting firms Boston Consulting Group, Bain & Company, McKinsey, Monitor, and Mercer. Note that this list only scratches the surface. You should also check out a financial head-hunter organization (e.g., glocap.com) that can find you placements at a variety of companies.

New Media & Marketing/Advertising Resources. Comp Sci majors aren't the only people applying for jobs in New Media, which are listed on Paid Content and MediaBistro. Start-ups are always on the lookout for marketing directors, researchers, and content producers. The trade-off of working with a start-up is the lack of stability associated with a new company, but with this risk comes flexibility and high growth potential. In light of the shifting forms of consumption from traditional media to innovative online formats, marketing/advertising is also an incredibly interesting field to get into right now. There is a lot of overlap between New Media and marketing/advertising, and joining one of the major marketing/advertising companies (e.g., Grey, Ogilvy, BBDO, Digitas, SBI.Razorfish) might be a nice first step. Check with your career services office for advertising firms that recruit at your school, and also browse the career sections on the websites of any advertising company that might pique your interest.

Publishing & Journalism Resources. If it's a career in publishing or journalism you seek, check out Mediabistro, Ed2010, journalism school listings, IWantMedia, and even *Variety*. After surveying those resources, it often helps to go straight to the source in this industry. Track down your favorite websites and publications online, then check to see if they have a "Careers" section. Don't be dismayed if you only see internship programs—while we know you see yourself as a staff writer or editor-in-chief, sometimes internships are the only way to develop the contacts and clips you'll need to get there.

> ## Tips & Tricks: Odd Jobs
>
> Whether you want to supplement a salary or just make a little cash, there are tons of ways to make a quick buck, both online and on the streets. Check out our list of money-making schemes on page 25.

(For more on interning, see p. 82.) As a final word of advice, find out who publishes the magazine or newspaper where you want to work. For example, the Condé Nast media empire includes *Vogue*, *GQ*, *Wired*, and *The New Yorker*. Maybe you know someone at a publication that falls under the same umbrella as the one you want to work at, or maybe you can get a gig at *Teen Vogue* but not *Vanity Fair*—at least you'll gain access to the Condé Nast HR department. Just that connection alone will give you a leg up on the competition when the next *Vanity Fair* position opens up.

Paralegal & Lab Resources. The best way to get these jobs is through connections, since getting in the door is the most important part. Contacting fellow alums or friends' parents is the best way to find those doors in which to insert your foot. For paralegal positions, check out ParalegalJobs.com, Employment Spot, or the paralegal jobs forum at Indeed.com. For lab jobs, check out eLabRat.com, lab positions at Indeed.com, or postings at university medical schools.

Non-Profit Resources. Not feeling the corporate route? There are plenty of resources for finding non-profit jobs. If you know what you're interested in doing, first head to the organization's website. Non-profits such as the Red Cross, the Salvation Army, the World Wildlife Fund, UNICEF, the Peace Corps, and Global Education Partnership all offer positions through their websites. If you don't know what you want to do, check out Idealist.org and World Volunteer Web, the Monster.coms of the non-profit world.

"Other." If you don't see the industry you hope to enter here, don't despair. In fact, the best way to find a job remains your alma mater's career office, because if a company lists a position there you know it has a vested interest in your school (and, by extension, you). Unfortunately, even your career office will not have every job you want. If it doesn't, head over to your dream employer's website and apply directly. If you just know the industry that interests you but not the companies that might have openings, check out one of the job information resources we listed on page 78 to find lists of the top employers by industry.

The Job-hunt

Interview: You're Never Too Old to Intern

The late Notorious B.I.G. once said, "The key to staying on top of things is to treat everything like it's your first project. Like it's your first day and you're the intern." Wise words, Biggie. But how can you emulate the perspective of an intern if you've never been one? We called upon our good friend Theodore Bressman of the *Intern Memo* to break down the internship game for us:

Why would I want to be an intern after I've graduated from college? Aren't internships just for students? No! Being an intern after you graduate is just the first of many difficult professional lessons you're gonna learn in your first couple years out of school. Many people graduate college all idealistic and jacked up about changing the world because they just spent four years studying luminaries like Winston Churchill or Jacques Cousteau. But unless you're Intern Will and you actually wrote your thesis on Churchill, you never really spent much time studying that awkward time when he was filling the proverbial coffee orders of Parliament members. Being an intern may seem lowly for a college graduate, but keeping a good spirit is all you can really do until you prove yourself and they take you on full-time. The truth is that an internship is a great way to naturally ease into a full-time job, so look at it that way.

Do you have any rules of thumb for being a great intern? I've never believed in rules of thumb... psych, I live by them exclusively!

I think the main credo to live by as an intern is similar to the credo you should live by as a human: "Be earnest, but relax!" Nothing entrusted to an intern is of life or death importance, so if your boss assigns you something, don't bother him every five minutes with minutiae. If he wastes his time working on your task, he might as well have done it himself.

But that doesn't mean you should just cross your fingers and hope you're doing a halfway decent job. Every task you're assigned is a chance to prove yourself to your employer and show him that you're willing and capable of doing anything you're asked to do. So don't get too stressed, but don't get too comfortable, either. I think that's a credo we can all get behind.

You're Never Too Old to Intern Continued...

How can you ensure that you're making the most of an internship? Make sure to have a laugh, but make sure it's a strategic laugh. Your ultimate goals should be to learn, foster positive relationships with your supervisors, and get an offer for a full-time job. You don't want to be some wound-up momma's boy, but you also don't want to be some slick Johnny Come Lately who's too cool for the gig.

How do I turn an internship into a full-time gig? Prove that you're reliable, not insane, and willing to do anything asked of you. A lot of interns waste their time complaining that the work is beneath them. Not to be blunt, but those jokers are fools! Think about it this way: would you rather be making photocopies or sitting at home combing online job databases wishing you weren't unemployed?

Where are the best places to look for internships? On-campus recruiting, your college career office, friends, and targeted job searches... and, of course, InternMemo.com. Getting an internship, though slightly more non-committal than a job, is still really tough, so keep a positive spirit. One specific thing you can do to help yourself out is to follow up any application with a phone call. This is one of those things that is so easy to do, but for some reason not that many people do it. Do it. It can make all the difference.

Going to Grad School

While we discussed the decision to either get a job or take a year off in Chapter 1, there is another option that's popular among recent grads: going back to school. Whether you decide that a business degree is the best way to advance your career or you just have a yearning to be back in academia, there are graduate degrees to match almost any intellectual or professional goal. There are also good and bad reasons for getting them. Good reasons: you need a graduate degree to get the job of your dreams, you want to be an academic, or you have the opportunity to study abroad. Bad reason: you want to avoid the real world and "keep the dream alive." While you are allowed to remain in semi-aimless mode as an undergraduate, a worthwhile Masters or Ph.D. requires a certain degree of focus and purpose.

Before you get too excited about getting back on campus, remember that like colleges, grad schools generally require an annoying application process. If you're going to apply while working, make sure you give yourself time to write the essays, fill out the apps, and study for the appropriate standardized tests. Law schools require the LSAT, med schools look at MCATs, and business schools will want to see some GMAT scores. The general test for most degrees outside of those fields is the GRE, though most schools will accept a GMAT result as well. Along with testing, there's also the question of how you're going to pay for the whole thing. Look into fellowships, scholarships, and grants, or find out if your employer will subsidize your further education.

To learn more about grad school and to find programs that fit your goals, check out further articles at Gradspot.com.

Compiling Your Life on Paper

Once you've put a little bit of thought into what industries you might want to explore, it's time to get your job-hunting ducks in order. For most positions you will need to present a résumé and a cover letter. If you are applying for a creative position or media job, you may be required to submit some samples of your prior work (called "clips" in journalism). Only certain jobs will require references.

A sloppy résumé or typo-riddled cover letter will leave you grounded before you even get a chance to takeoff. Put some time into nailing these items down—they will not only be crucial in helping you snag interviews, but they will also give you confidence as the search progresses and things start happening quickly. When someone calls and says, "Meet me for coffee in half an hour. Bring your résumé," you don't want to be scrambling like an idiot. Preparedness is the cousin of "getting a job." And they are cousins that actually like each other.

Ultimately, keep in mind the purpose of these documents when preparing them—a résumé basically lists your background and skills, while a cover letter ensures that you have "intangible qualities" like a personality and an enthusiastic approach to work. It's often said that an employer should be able to glance at your résumé for 20 seconds and have a strong impression about whether or not you're a good fit for the job. I prefer to run a little thought experiment: if you dropped your résumé and cover letter in the street and a con artist picked them up, he should be able to perfectly mimic your behavior in a professional environment. Ironically, he would then just be working like a normal person, which sort of ruins the whole *modus operandi* of a con man. But that's probably the least of your worries right now. Let's start with the basics.

Résumé

Résumé. Curriculum vitae. Autobiography.

Surprisingly, these words are not synonymous. In this section, we'll discuss the differences and give you some tips on how to craft the perfect appearance on paper.

When people say that various products, ideas, and athletes "look good on paper," they are invoking the concept of a résumé. When writing your own, the idea is to elicit this response off the bat. During the interview, you can prove that you look good in the flesh as well.

To download a résumé template, visit Gradspot.com/book, then read through the guidelines provided below as you fill it in.

Contact Info. Make sure your name is displayed prominently at the top of the page and all of your contact information is up-to-date. You want to make yourself accessible in the long-run, so don't give the landline number in the apartment that you might move out of next month.

Tips & Tricks: Customize Yourself for Each Job

Different industries, and sometimes even different jobs within the same industry, expect different things from new hires. Consider reworking your résumé and writing a variation of your cover letter for every position. When putting together an application, always check the original job post and the career section of the company's website to pick up buzzwords and figure out what the employer is looking for. Then, tailor your skills and experiences to show that you are the ideal candidate for the *specific* position. Indeed, this approach should have a trickle down through the entire job-seeking process—from the résumé and cover letter right through to the interview. To help customize your pitch, we've polled professionals across many industries to see what traits they look for in prospective hires. For a full list of skills to stress by industry, visit Gradspot.com/book.

The Job-hunt

Even if you don't get a job immediately, a company may keep your résumé on file for a later opening—don't sabotage yourself by disappearing off the face of the Earth. In most cases, it's ideal to use a cell phone number. At home, you never know who might pick up. It could be your senile grandmother who says that you have moved to the family's native Deutschland. Furthermore, give a professional e-mail address. Make sure it is permanent (e.g., Gmail) and will not expire when you leave school or another job.

Be Clear, Concise, and Honest. Don't get bogged down in jargon because you think it will make your duties sound more official. While it's acceptable to candy-coat tasks like coffee-making and photocopying with phrases like "performed administrative duties," there is no reason to pack your résumé with white lies. Use action verbs (e.g.,

Tips & Tricks: Change Your Voice-mail Recording

It's huge turn-off for a potential employer to call your cell phone and be redirected to a scene from *Scarface*. Be brief and professional. Go with something along the lines of, "Hi, you've reached Frederick Werner. I'm unable to answer the phone right now but if you leave your name and number I will get back to you as soon as possible." You'll sound like a dingus to your friends, but it's a small price to pay.

administered, built, reviewed) and articulate each task in one or two phrases. If anything comes up in an interview, you should be able to expound upon it without having to say, "I guess by 'managed the books' I meant that I opened the mail, and my boss often received a lot of books..." Similarly, don't be dishonest about your skills and background. Even if you pull the wool over an employer's eyes by saying you are proficient with Quark and Excel, they are not going to be too pleased when you arrive on the first day and suddenly need a tutorial. That said, you should certainly emphasize these skills where applicable, and in general make an effort to be as precise as possible in your résumé descriptions.

In today's age of Monster.coms and massive HR departments, you need to make your résumé highly searchable online by packing it with keywords.

Objectives. State your objectives in one to two tight sentences. Make them as specific and compelling as possible—if you are applying to a range of places, tweak this section for each version of the résumé that you send out. "Stacking cheddar," "baaalllliiinnnn'," and "getting out the house" are not great reasons for wanting a job. Understand your audience and let them know exactly what you hope to get out of the experience. Also, if you are applying in an industry where you have no experience, tell a story (the extreme Cliffs Note's version) of why you want to go from finance to non-profit work, for example.

The Power of One. Keep it to one page. Most employers of recent grads are dealing with a high volume of résumés, so HR managers don't have time to wade through multi-page documents. But more importantly, the résumé is the first test to see if you can present information clearly and concisely. If it takes you more than a page to outline yourself, then you are effectively outlining your professional aspirations in chalk. Ya digg?

Prioritize. There are no set rules for chronology or layout on a résumé. However, you want to prioritize the most relevant information so that it appears near the top of the page. Generally it makes sense to start with your educational background (if you need to save space, consider nixing your high school—it is obvious that you went to one, and it's unlikely the employer will know the school). Then move on to your relevant work experience (including internships). Under each entry, the bullet points describing your duties and achievements should be prioritized as well. Leave activities and interests for the bottom.

Design. Unless graphic design is essential to the job you're applying for, having a slick looking résumé is not going to help you, and it certainly won't gloss over a lack of relevant experience or skills. Avoiding a lot of white space on the page will help you fit more information, but in general don't get hung up on aesthetics.

Tips & Tricks: What Did I Do for the Last Year?

If you get to the end of an internship or leave a job and are having trouble articulating what exactly you did there, check the job posting for the position you are leaving and see what the description is. Hypothetically, it should cover what you did (or were supposed to do).

What If I Have Never Done Anything?

Recent grads are often sorely lacking in the "Work Experience" category. If this is the case for you, emphasize your skills in other ways. Maybe you led a team on a semester-long project or organized a charity race in your town. Don't think that you can't mention something from school or activities you have done in the past. The bottom line is that you are trying to sell yourself as trustworthy and capable—if a job or internship can't speak for you, that doesn't mean your relevant talents shouldn't be noted.

To Include My GPA, or Not to Include My GPA. In the realm of résumé quandaries, this is one of the trickier situations to navigate. Everyone wants a rule of thumb, and the one that gets invoked most often is that you should include your GPA if it's over 3.0, or only include your GPA within your major if it's significantly better than the overall number. But every thumb is different, just like a snowflake. Generally, technical jobs (think engineering, Google, etc.) will definitely be interested in your GPA, and if you don't include it they will ask in the interview. In this case, leaving a GPA off your résumé will read like an admission of guilt, so you'll have to decide whether it's really bad enough to try to keep under raps. If it is particularly low and there is a good reason (e.g., you worked a job while going to school or held multiple leadership positions), be sure to address this in the cover letter and/or interview. Finally, specify the scale used—different schools have different ways of expressing GPAs, and 3.5 out of 4.0 is quite different from 3.5 out of 15.0.

Proofread. Proofread. Proofread. The administrative staffing service Office Team reports that 47% of executives said they would throw out a candidate's résumé for just one typo. This statistic might strike you as absurd. Should a typo really be that big a deal? But you've got to think of it from the perspective of the employer: HR departments have to wade through a huge amount of résumés, so separating out the typo offenders is a quick sorting device to make their job easier. Furthermore, a typo on a one page document does not really scream "detail-oriented" or "professional," which are

The Job-hunt

two qualities that you should be shouting about. Basically, don't give a potential employer an excuse to not consider you.

Read This, It'll Knock Your Socks Off. Once you feel confident in your résumé, run it by as many people as possible. The extra eyes will help weed out the typos and also provide you with feedback about how well you're selling yourself. It's ideal to get some feedback from someone working in the industry you're interested in, because he or she will have a sense of what specific employers will want to see.

Curriculum Vitae

You wouldn't be alone in thinking that this is just a fancy way of saying résumé. It's a pretty fun phrase to toss around, no doubt. But the reality is that CVs and résumés are quite different documents. Whereas a résumé is a sort of "highlight" reel of educational background and relevant experience/skills, a CV is the uncut version—the uncircumcised junk of résumés, you could say. And like uncircumcised junk, CVs are more popular in places like Greece than they are in America. They detail your entire educational background and list every single job—dating back to your high school camp counseling days—in chronological order with a description of job duties. They are presented in paragraph form. And they include "vital statistics" like date of birth, nationality, and even height and weight.

When to use a CV: International jobs; academic, education, scientific or research positions; and in applications for fellowships or grants.

Autobiography

This is something else entirely. For examples see *The Autobiography of Benjamin Franklin, It's Not About the Bike: My Journey Back to Life*, and *Confessions of a Video Vixen*.

Sample Résumé

JANE DOE

1234 Pine Avenue, Apt. 1 • Beverly Hills, CA 90210
(646) 402 5557 • jdoe@gmail.com

OBJECTIVE [Optional]

Detail-oriented Computer Science graduate seeks position as member of a software engineering team in a fast-paced, challenging work environment [Highlight relevant skills or strengths]

EDUCATION

University of California, Los Angeles (2004 – 2007)
Bachelor of Science in Computer Science, with Minor in Electrical Engineering
GPA in Major / GPA: 3.79 / 3.54 [Show GPA in Major if higher than overall GPA]

Relevant Coursework and Projects
- Coursework heavily focused on practical aspects of Computer Science, including *C++ for Programmers*, *JAVA for Programmers*, and *Machine Structures* [Technical skills]
- Head of the Berkeley Machine Learning Project Group, leading a team eight undergraduates in the design and development of an original machine learning algorithm [Leadership, Intelligence, Passion]

Redondo Beach High School (1999 – 2004)
Valedictorian, June 2004

WORK EXPERIENCE

[Focus time spent on relevant jobs and qualities]
Google Inc., Mountain View, CA   2007 - Present
Intern
[Describe the company and position, especially if it is not well known]
- Selected as one of 100 summer interns in the highly competitive Search Media Group at the world's leading Internet search company
[Projects & Accomplishments – Focus on relevant responsibilities]
- and developed source code for a variety of projects focused on search-based product offerings
[Relevant programming experience]
- Designed large scale distributed file systems and other infrastructures to reliably and efficiently manage and process hundreds of terabytes of information [Technical skills]
- Part of a team of six software developers responsible for optimizing performance of database of over 10 billion cached websites [Teamwork]
- Achieved proficiency in COBAL without any prior experience and successfully tested and debugged over 60,000 lines of legacy software code [Fast learner, attention to detail]

[Do not spend too much time on less relevant work experience]
Reborn Computers, Los Angeles, CA   2006 – 2007
Computer Repair Technician
- Repaired all brands of desktop and laptop computers, and performed diagnostic services on computers and peripherals [Technical skills]

SKILLS

- Sun certified Java developer and fully proficient in a wide variety of other programming languages including Unix, Linux, C, and C++ [Technical skills]
- Fluent in English and Spanish, proficient in French [Be careful not to exaggerate]

INTERESTS AND OTHER

- President of the UCLA Computer Science Student Association (CSSA) [Leadership, responsibility]
- Vice-captain of Barrack House softball team [Teamwork]
- Avid scuba diver with Advanced PADI Openwater certification [Include something interesting!]

The Job-hunt

Cover Letter

Cover letters involve a curious mixture of personality and homogeneity, confidence and humility. In many cases, writing a cover letter is harder than actually performing the job you are applying for. Though the cover letter should logically be an introduction that says, "Hi, here are some things to know about me before you look at my résumé," the reality is that it's probably going to be the reverse. Most employers just don't have the time to read a bunch of cover letters. Thus, the cover letter is the icing on a well-baked résumé.

With that realization in mind, the main objective of a good cover letter should be to explain why you should get the job. It should tell a story of where you've been and where you are hoping to go, so it's important to spin your experiences specifically toward the job in question. This is particularly important if you appear to be shifting gears (e.g., you're a chemistry major interested in PR or you're dropping out of med school to do finance). A cover letter is a test of your personality and your written communication skills, but mostly it's a personal sales pitch. Stay focused—anecdotes and tangents, no matter how hilarious, should be kept to a bare minimum.

Thankfully, there is a basic formula for a strong cover letter. Follow these guidelines to ensure that you make a good first impression on paper.

Length: One page, including any headers, footers, or whatever other design flourishes you include. (No negotiations here.)

Heading: Whenever possible, you want to address your cover letter to an actual human being. Headings like "To Whom It May Concern" and "Dear Hiring Manager" should be used only as last resorts. If you aren't given a name off the bat, do a little research. Applying to a magazine? Check the masthead for the editor's name. If it's a large office, try calling HR, telling them what job you're applying for (you don't have to say who you are), and asking for a specific name within the department. The personal touch will show that you are resourceful and that you care enough to figure out whom you are dealing with.

Paragraph One: What are you applying for and why? The cover letter is, in essence, an introduction to a stranger. So what do you do when you meet a stranger? You find some common ground. You announce your purpose for addressing him or her. You figure out if you "know the same people." This doesn't mean that you find out your potential boss went to Stanford and say, "OMG do you know my friend Brittany?" It means covering a few basics:

1) What position are you writing about?
2) How did you find out about the job?
3) Do you have a networking connection? (If so, mention this as early as possible.)
4) Why, in a sentence or two, are you interested in the job? (This is like the thesis statement of your cover letter that will be illuminated in the subsequent paragraphs.)

Second Paragraph: What have you accomplished in your life that is relevant to this job? You'd like people to "read between the lines" of your résumé and realize you are a wonderful person with great perspective. But if they didn't even realize that Dumbledore was gay, you've got to keep your expectations realistic. Here's where you expound upon your experience and spell out the subtext for them.

> ### Tips & Tricks: Naming Files
>
> When naming your résumé and cover letter files, make sure they are distinctive. Recruiters get hundreds of documents titled "resume09.doc" or "myresume.pdf"—make it easier for them to find your information later by saying who you are in the filename (e.g., "Joe_Public_Resume.pdf"). You will be more searchable and your name will be more memorable. The same applies to cover letters.

For example, you can talk about a specific project that you handled well but weren't able to fully convey in a simple bullet point on your résumé. Or you can talk about the type of feedback you got from your boss and coworkers. Remember to be specific: only highlight things that are relevant to the position you're applying for. Don't be humble, either. That doesn't mean that you should be arrogant or act like you're above the job, but rather that you can dispense with phrases like "I think" and "I believe." You don't "think" you're a good fit—you *are* a good fit.

Third Paragraph: How do you match up, why do you want the job, and why should you get it? If you were playing *NBA Jam: Tournament Edition*, this is where the announcer should be yelling, "That's the nail in the coffin!" Tie up your experiences and interests to convince the reader that you are the man or woman for the job. Show the employer that you are enthusiastic and passionate. Don't say, "If I don't get this job, I will literally kill myself!" But give a strong indication of why the job interests you and what you hope to get out of it.

Closing Statement: Mind your Ps and Qs. When closing out a cover letter, remember a few key things:

- Reiterate your contact information.
- Thank the reader for taking the time to consider your application.
- Sign your name if you are not sending electronically.

The Job-hunt

Sample Cover Letter

JOHN DOE

8888 W. 16th St., Apt 5B   john.doe@gradspot.com   (646) 402 5557
Philadelphia, PA, 19147

Mr. Derek Anderson
Head of Undergraduate Recruiting
Diamond Group
720 Lexington Avenue, 12th Floor
New York, NY 10022

Dear Mr. Anderson,

I am writing to you to apply for an Assistant Strategist position with the Diamond Group. After speaking with Daniel Kelly and conducting my own research, I know that Diamond would be a perfect match for my talents and aspirations. I recently graduated from the University of Michigan, where I maintained an overall GPA of 3.85/4.00 with a major in Marketing and a minor in English Literature and Language. Through a diverse range of professional experiences, including internships at *The Milwaukee Journal Sentinel* and Lehman Brothers, I have consistently been intrigued by the way in which companies both predict and shape the desires of consumers as they build their brand. By joining the Strategic Planning team, I hope to pursue this interest and further develop my knowledge of the industry as a whole while producing for your company.

While working on the arts desk at the *Sentinel*, my coverage of commissioned music in Nike's viral marketing campaigns garnered the interest of the business editor, who asked me to write a piece about the role of authenticity in the company's branding strategy. I continued to follow this trend on my blog, eventually leading to a successful pitch to Slate.com last year. Meanwhile, my internship last summer at Lehman Brothers offered me an intense immersion in the basic mechanics of M&A corporate advisory, as well the investment banking industry in general. I acquired a great deal of business acumen from being part of such a hard-working environment, and I greatly enjoyed researching the potential for market growth in a variety of industries. However, while I received encouragement from my supervisors to pursue a fulltime position with the company, I did not find that the job played to my creative strengths.

At Diamond, I hope that I can pursue my passion for corporate branding and marketing strategy within the context of a more focused and creatively challenging environment. My background in print and online media provides me with a lens through which to analyze a brand and assess its marketability, while my investment banking experience has helped me develop a high level of professionalism, attention to detail, and analytical skills to review businesses. I especially hope to apply these skills to aid Diamond's shifting focus toward digital advertising. I am extremely excited by the prospect of translating my skills into a market strategy role, and I look forward to speaking with you about the possibility of joining your company. If you have any further questions you can reach me by email (john_doe@gradspot.com) or via phone at (646) 402 5557.

Thank you for your time and consideration.

Sincerely,
John Doe

Salary Requirements

Many jobs will ask you to include salary requirements with your application. While it might sound awesome to say you require, "Cheddar, gouda, and other denominations of cheese," this is actually sort of a no-win situation. On the one hand, the company may be using the salary requirement as a screening process—if you are too high, you might not be considered. On the other hand, it might be trying to save money by finding people who will work for cheap. Unless you're Criss Angel, you don't want to dig your own grave, because you may not be able to get out of it. There is no cure-all to this irksome malady, but here are a few suggested remedies:

Do your research. Look into the industry in which you're applying for a job and find comparable positions. Visit Salary.com to gauge ballpark figures, talk to people you know in similar positions, or cold-call a competitor and try to find out what they offer. The compensation should be pretty standard across the board. If you think you can get away with it you might consider writing something like, "I expect a competitive salary," but you're avoiding the question, which is not what you want to do in the face of a potential employer.

Give a range. You really don't need to say, "I expect to receive $34,553.78 per annum." Figure out the industry standard and say something like, "A salary in the low- to mid-thirties." Covering the basics without being evasive shows that you are a diplomatic wizard.

Stall. Say you would prefer to discuss compensation in an interview, but you don't imagine it will be a problem. Some people claim this is a good move, but it seems pretty suspect.

Don't forget benefits. Make sure you know what benefits are offered, such as healthcare and 401(k) plans. Often, it is easier to negotiate for wider benefits than a higher salary. Assess your own needs to figure out if a $35K salary with full benefits is better than $40K with none (hint: it probably is).

E-mailing Résumés and Cover Letters

An HR professional once said, "The three most important factors in screening an application are delivery, delivery, and delivery." But that's absurd: we all know that it's not delivery. It's DiGiorno!

In this day and age, it's rare to physically mail in an application. Often there will be an online application where you simply plug in your info and upload your résumé and cover letter. However, sometimes you will be asked to e-mail your materials. While this system is supposed to make things easier and more efficient, it also adds new trauma-

The Job-hunt

inducing variables to the equation. What do I put in the subject line? What do I put in the body? Don't get too antsy, though. It's basically a matter of common sense and following directions.

Sometimes HR will tell you to put a job code or phrase in the subject line so that they can easily sort applications. If so, follow directions, attach your résumé, cover letter, and any other relevant materials, and then write a quick note in the body saying that you have done so. In general, you will not be penalized for sending documents as Word files, but sending them as PDFs is preferable because this format generally looks the same across all operating systems. The format you choose is not a huge issue, but just remember that if a company receives a lot of applications and they can't open your résumé, they probably won't ask you to resend it—you're out of the running.

If there are no instructions for the subject line, include your name and the title of the position. A catchy or offbeat subject line (e.g., "Will Work For Food") is rarely appropriate, though it's up to you to judge the attitude of the organization. As a final point, don't be afraid to paste your cover letter directly into the body of the e-mail as well as attaching it. This is the one document you really want someone to read, so serve it up on a platter.

Sample Application E-mail

From: Samuel Bentley <sbentley@gradspot.com>
To: Mrs. Daniels <Mrs.Daniels@fakeweb.com>
Subject: WX957 – Production Assistant
Attachment: Sam_Bentley_resume.pdf, Sam_Bentley_coverletter.pdf, Sam_Bentley_clips.pdf

Dear Mrs. Daniels,

I am writing to submit my application for the role of Production Assistant, which I learned about through your listing on Media Bistro. Attached you will find my résumé and cover letter, as well as a PDF of my writing clips. For your convenience, I have also pasted the text of my cover letter below.

If there is any other information I can provide, please do not hesitate to contact me by e-mail (sam.bentley@gradspot.com), or by phone at 646 402 5557.

Thank you for your consideration,
Samuel Bentley

Cleaning Up Your Online Identity

Corporate America has a stick up its booty; we won't refute that. But even so, companies are not so naïve as to think that none of their potential employees has ever had a few Buds too many or lit a fart on fire in a crowded space—it is corporate *America*, after all. Everyone knows you went to college and probably got caught on camera acting a fool. The point of cleaning up your online identity is simply to ensure you are putting your best foot forward when presenting yourself to the people who need to be able to trust you. Don't give them excuses for thinking you're a rogue element—using a profile picture of you rocking a kegstand in your underwear is probably unnecessary during the application process. You don't have to censor all personality out of your online game. Just use some common sense and avoid shooting yourself in the foot for no reason at all.

Okay, enough of that sermon—let's get down to business. For most recent grads, protecting your rep online is mostly about rethinking your Facebook profile, which basically boils down to two words: privacy settings. (A similar process can be iterated across other networks like MySpace, Bebo, etc.) Facebook actually gives users a high level of control over their profiles, but most people never think twice about what they are posting or who can see it. Basically, there are five "access levels" on Facebook: friends, networks, strangers, limited profile, and "blocked." There are also three basic types of content that could get you in trouble: your personal profile, photos/videos, and wall posts. The trick is to decide who you want to see what and then adjust your privacy settings accordingly. (Privacy settings can always be accessed on the top right side of the page.)

Needless to say, it's really up to you to decide how private you need (or want) to be. If you are working for the government or a very conservative bank, you may have greater concerns than others about employers or coworkers viewing your profile and pictures. Moreover, some people don't feel comfortable being easily stalkable, while others derive great pleasure from online exhibitionism. For anyone concerned about their Facebook identity, here are the most important ways in which you can change your privacy settings, as well as our suggestions for avoiding a misstep:

Profile. If you are only concerned about specific people viewing your profile—a hip, thirtysomething boss who insists on being Facebook friends with everyone in the office, or a young child that you tutor—you might want to employ the **limited profile** feature. You can choose exactly what parts of your profile will show up and then choose exactly who you want to see this version. Of course, you can also go all out and **block** people. Beyond that, you have the ability to choose who can see each distinct profile

Tips & Tricks: Cleaning Up Your Google Search

Affecting Google rankings is no easy task. Whole books are devoted to improving search engine results, and major Internet companies spend millions of dollars each year on search engine optimization (SEO). Before you even think about going into battle with the rankings, make sure it's worth your time. Google all variations of your name and nicknames and see if you find anything you're not happy about. If there is nothing unsavory, or if your name is common enough to render you anonymous for search purposes, then you are in the clear. Otherwise, the best you can usually do is to contact webmasters and ask them to take down anything that you'd prefer not to have on the 'net. This approach may be useful when your friends tag your name and the phrase "superman that ho" on pictures they posted at Urban Dictionary. But if the *The Waterloo Courier* ran a story about the time you were arrested for streaking through the mall, there's not too much you can do about it.

feature, as well as your general contact information. The simple solution is to make your profile available only to your friends—this makes it easy to monitor who sees it since you must accept or decline all friend requests. It is also probably best to let only your friends see your photos, videos, groups, and wall.

Search. Unlike the old days, when you had to construct insanely complex advanced searches to find the person you made out with the night before, it is now extremely easy to search Facebook. Since people can only see the most basic info about you when they search (i.e., name and picture), it is not really necessary to limit their ability to do so. What should be considered is whether you want to create a **public search listing**, which will be submitted to search engines like Google. On the one hand, this makes it easier than ever for employers (and anyone else) to track you down. However, if you are concerned about the quality of your Google search, the Facebook public search listing should rank high enough to appear on the first page of search results.

News Feed and Mini Feed. How many ways do you want to allow people to stalk you? That's basically what you should ask yourself when considering what settings to choose. Posting a note is usually a consciously public gesture and you probably want to alert your network that you've written something. But do you really want everyone seeing that you ended a relationship or commented on a specific discussion board? If not, adjust your settings to determine what actions will be publicized and which will be kept for vigilant visitors to figure out for themselves.

Poke, Message, and Friend Request. When you perform any of these functions, parts of your profile (which you can select) become available to the recipient. If you poke or friend someone, you are probably not too concerned about them seeing your profile. However, the place to be careful is with messages—for example, you may message a networking contact because you can't track down his e-mail address. It's worth it to think about what parts of your profile he or she will be able to see. You should probably provide just enough information to show that you are not a completely random stranger, and that you have some connection through a high school, college, or mutual friend.

Oh, and one last thing: just to make sure you read this chapter thoroughly, we'll be systematically Facebooking each and every one of you. Watch your back!!

References

Hiring is always about trust. Unfortunately, the prevailing code on the streets is "don't trust anyone," so you'll often need to bring in some backup to vouch for your good name. The good news is you usually won't be asked for references until you're being seriously considered for a job. The bad news is you have to ask yourself a tough question—who thinks you are the bee's knees other than your mother? Hopefully one of these people:

- A former boss
- A professor or a dean
- A coworker
- A coach
- A family friend in the industry
- Someone who already works at the company you're applying to (money in the bank)

Here are some tips for providing references during your job search.

The Job-hunt

Choosing Your References

The most important thing to note about references is that a personal relationship speaks louder than a fancy name. If you had a great rapport with your thesis advisor and never spoke with the dean, go with the thesis advisor—he or she will know a lot more about your strengths and will have a genuine interest in promoting them. Maybe you want to get into trading and your second cousin's great uncle is T. Boone Pickens—utilize this connection for networking, but don't ask for a meaningless reference. You don't want HR calling up someone who barely knows you. This makes you seem like you've got something to hide or can't find anyone to say something good about you.

Building a Reference Network

A good rule of thumb is to ask for a written reference from a supervisor or coworker whenever you leave an internship or a job (and ask as early as possible so you are not putting them on a ridiculous deadline to help you out). This way you'll have a nice little stash of kind words to deploy at will. But playing into the whole theme of mistrust, most employers won't be interested in written recommendations because they can be easily forged. Instead, you will provide contact information so they can get a reference on the phone and ask hard-hitting questions like, "What is Teddy's greatest strength. And, as a follow up, what is his deepest, darkest secret?" In this case, always get permission by asking a potential reference if he or she would mind being listed.

Maintaining a Reference Network

While you can't give out your home phone number and have your little brother pretend to be the CEO of General Mills, you can definitely take steps to ensure your references aren't burning your bridges like some sort of anti-transportation terrorists. The first way to achieve a little editorial control is to choose your references wisely (see above). Once you've done that, keep them in the loop about the status of your job search. If a company recently asked you for references, contact your people to tell them they should expect a call. While you're at it, describe the position so they'll know how to pitch you. Never forget that they are doing you a huge favor. Thank them often and stay in touch.

How to Present Your References

Don't put your references in your résumé, and unless the original application instructs you to do so, don't send them out with your other materials. Generally, references come into play once you are being seriously considered for a job. Upon request, provide a Word document with the name, title, company, and contact information (work phone and e-mail) for each of your references (usually three to four). No major formatting is required, but make sure the file name is easily identifiable, and remember to list your name and contact information on the page. In addition to the attachment, it is appropriate to paste this information into the body of an e-mail.

Networking

No matter how great a candidate you are for a job, you may never get an interview without the help of someone on the inside who can make sure your application finds its way to the right eyes. And you might not even know about a job in the first place until you meet the right person who thinks you can do it. This is where networking comes into play.

Consider the following situation: you're applying for a job and are up against one other candidate. The two of you have the same credentials, and you both come off well in social situations. But now for the X-factor: the other candidate is best friends with the interviewer's daughter. Peace out! Another of life's bitter herbs, but that's just the reality of the job market. Rather than crying about nepotism and pursuing some sort of proto-Marxist vendetta á la Ryan from *The O.C.*, get out there and do something about it. The nice thing about successful networking is that it doesn't matter who you know when you start.

The other nice thing is that it's actually not at all about kissing ass and taking names (in your PDA). Good networking essentially involves being friendly, polite, proactive, and reasonably adept at expressing your interests to people. You do not have to be a slimy, shallow a-hole. At the end of the day, the more you network, the less "net work" you will end up doing in life. Doors will begin opening for you. Exciting opportunities will materialize out of thin air. And you'll have a lot of meals and coffees with semi-interesting people. Basically, it's like going to the Mall of America, something I think we all agree is pretty fun.

Networking Doesn't Start With Your Dream Employer. If you were talking to the employer of your dreams then you wouldn't need to be networking in the first place. Networking starts by talking to anyone. The key is to understand that just because you aren't talking directly to the CEO of the company you hope to work for doesn't mean that another person can't help you get to that point. Ironically, the CEO is probably not the one who would ultimately be making the decision to hire you, so shoot for the people who would be your immediate superiors or coworkers. **Don't underestimate the influence of people one to three years out of college, as they are often asked to review résumés submitted by applicants from their alma mater.** In fact, when it comes to networking, don't rule out anyone—that means your family, friends, professors, receptionists, and random kids you meet at parties. The more people who you talk to, the better chance you'll have of connecting with the right people (because eventually somebody knows somebody who knows somebody who knows your future boss).

The Job-hunt

Don't Expect to Get a Job Right Away When Networking. While networking is the art of getting the job before the interview, that doesn't mean you're going to get the job immediately. In fact, the first step should just be asking questions about the industry you're seeking to enter, the company you're hoping to be employed by, and any advice in general. Ultimately, this is a soft-sell and you'll learn something. If you impress someone, they'll remember the conversation even if you haven't asked them for a job—maybe they'll connect you with someone else or even employ you later themselves.

Networking Isn't Ass-Kissing; It's About Finding Commonalities. Many people pursue the following tactic of networking: locate anus of powerful human. Implant nose in said anus. Repeat. But no one likes a brown-nosing sycophant, so try to be a bit more genuine. Don't launch into a conversation with people you're networking with by asking them who they know or if they can help you land a job. Also, don't just agree with everything they say or talk about how great the company they work for is. Instead, be completely candid. Ask them about their job and their interests. Share your genuine passion for the industry with them. Try to find some common ground—if need be, feel free to talk about something completely non-work related (e.g., current events). If you establish a rapport first, then the conversation will eventually turn toward what you want to do (or you can politely nudge it in that direction). And when that happens, you're effectively networking.

Don't Forget Networking Etiquette. You'll never get yourself in trouble by being too polite (to start). Call people Mr., Ms., Mrs., etc. Always meet/speak with people at their convenience. If you're getting drinks, don't be ashamed to offer to pay for your drink (although nine out of ten times they'll pick up the tab). Get a vibe from your interactions as they go on and loosen up accordingly. For example, if they tell you to call them by their first name, it's most likely not a "test," so go ahead and do it. Finally, always write a thank you letter (see p. 112).

Informational Interviews = Good Networking. Informational interviews are the perfect way to get your foot in the door because they're easier to score than job interviews. An informational interview is an opportunity to talk with someone in an industry or at a company you find interesting. It's not an interview for a job, but rather a way to become more informed about your dream job. This approach will provide you with two advantages: it will enable you to be more knowledgeable when the real interview rolls around, and it may actually turn into an interview. Remember that anytime you're talking with an employee of a company you one day hope to work for, you're being interviewed (even if they don't say so). For a sample informational interview request see page 102.

Where to Meet for a Networking Meeting. Let's start with where not to meet: over dinner. Or "drinks," for that matter. That's just weird (unless they offer). Instead, ask if they would be willing to talk over a cup of coffee, or during a quick breakfast or lunch. Other options include meeting at someone's office, or finally, talking on the phone. Of course, an in-person conversation always has more impact, but you should be meeting when and where it is convenient for the other party.

How to Prepare for a Networking Meeting. We can't stress enough that you should prepare for any networking meeting. This means reading up on the person you're meeting with (thank you, Wiki-Google), the company they work for, related recent news, and the industry as a whole. This will help with conversation topics and your preparation will reflect your enthusiasm. That said, don't go wild with displaying your knowledge of someone's personal history—you don't want to transform from "job candidate" to "restraining order candidate."

What to Bring to a Networking Meeting. Always bring some type of notebook and a pen. If you can do so discreetly, bring a résumé in the event the person you're meeting with asks for it. If you are networking over the phone, you can compensate for the lack of face time by being extra organized. Spread out your notes in front of you or keep a Word document open—the person you're speaking with will never know and it can make you look extremely knowledgeable. This also works when leaving voice-mails for people you want to hook up with.

Always Send a Thank You Note After Every Networking Meeting. So, you've spent an hour talking with someone about a job, and that person has been kind enough to share his career insights with you. He did you a favor. Acknowledge it by sending a thank you letter (or e-mail, as the case may be these days). Depending upon your relationship with the person you just spoke with, the letter can be formal or just a sentence. Referencing something you discussed during your conversation goes a long way. You can even ask a follow-up question.

Professional Karma. Networking never ends. Even after you've gotten the job, you should be sure to not only inform the people who helped you, but also to stay in touch with them (as well as anyone else who you networked with along the way). Who knows when you'll need your next job? Or better yet, when you can help someone else. Because when it comes down to it, networking is a pay-it-forward game. Sometimes the student doth become the teacher, and someone you help may also be able to reciprocate down the line.

The Job-hunt

Sample Informational Interview Request

The first sentence of your request should not only introduce who you are, but also explain your connection to the individual you are reaching out to. Maybe he or she is a friend of a friend (as per the below example). Or maybe you found the person in your alumni network. Or maybe this is just a cold call and you pulled the name from a newspaper article.

From: Michael Humphrey <mike@gradspot.com>
To: Mrs. McGregor <McGregor@fortune500.com>
Subject: Interview Request

Dear Mrs. McGregor,

I recently graduated from the University of Miami, and after my good friend, David Johnson, learned that I was interested in a career in marketing, he suggested I contact you to request a brief informational interview.

While at the University of Miami, I majored in marketing. In addition, I had an internship last summer at Razor Corp, where I assisted media buyers on several high-profile interactive marketing campaigns. I now plan to apply both my education and my work experience to a career in marketing. At your convenience, I was hoping to learn what types of positions you suggest for a recent college graduate, and also to hear your thoughts on the future of the industry as a whole.

Thank you very much for your time. If you are available to speak with me, we can talk over the phone, or I can meet you at a location of your choosing. I can be reached at 646 402 5557 or by e-mail at mike@gradspot.com.

Appreciatively,
Michael Humphrey

The Job-hunt

Phone Call Script: "Hi, my name is Michael Humphrey. I was fascinated by the recent article about you in *The New York Times*, so I thought I would get in touch because I'm very interested in pursuing a career in marketing. At your convenience, I was hoping you might be willing to spend a few minutes talking on the phone or in person to provide me with some advice based on your experience. Would it be possible to set up an informational interview? Thank you very for your consideration. You can reach me at 646 402 5557 or via e-mail at mike@gradspot.com."

Top Places to Network

- Family
- Friends and fellow students (don't forget about their parents)
- College alumni networks
- College professors or deans (depending upon your relationships)
- Career services office
- Facebook, LinkedIn, Doostang and other online communities (see below)
- Charities
- Teams
- Organizations
- Trade conventions (many are free)

Professional Networking Sites: The Anti-social Solution

While it's wise to protect yourself from prying employers online (see p. 95), the Internet is also a great place to self-promote, get your name out there, and network your way toward great jobs (and even dates, if you're into that sort of thing). Online career networking is growing rapidly as the first legitimately web-savvy generation of workers begins to make its mark on the professional world. Needless to say, it will only get more relevant with time, unlike other Internet phenomena like Soulja Boy's "Crank Dat."

The big three in the arena of career-oriented social networks are LinkedIn, Doostang, and Ryze. As an increasingly multi-purpose platform, Facebook has its place in the hierarchy, as well. If you decide to take the online career networking route (and we suggest you at least give it a shot), ditch whatever habits you've developed on other social networking sites and keep your profile purely professional. As a rule of thumb, treat it exactly as you would a résumé: list all of your accomplishments, but don't lie or exaggerate. Keep in mind that you're not just friending people to share party pics or appear popular anymore; you're attempting to connect with specific recruiters and future employers. They will catch you in a lie quicker than a jealous ex-girlfriend. (Well, maybe not...) Either way, there are plenty of tips and tricks to getting the most out of online career networks.

The Job-hunt

LinkedIn

LinkedIn.com was the first online career network to gain widespread popularity, and today it boasts a user base of 17 million "professionals." Basically, it's like one massive cocktail party, minus the cocktails and the human interaction. (If you want to set the mood, however, just fire up a gin and tonic and play some music softly at your computer.) All online career networks have the basic features you'd expect (create a profile, make friends, etc.), so we're going to assume that you can figure out the basics. What we want to dig into are the ways to make your profile stand out and get exactly what you want from the site:

- **Bond. James Bond... @Gmail.com.** When filling out the first name and last name fields on your profile, consider filling in your entire name in the first name field and your e-mail address in the last name field. Thus, whenever you appear in search results, your e-mail addy will be on full display. Why is this good? Networking is about putting yourself out there; by including your e-mail address as part of your name, you're making it extremely easy for people to reach out and connect to you.

- **Consider making your profile public.** This means anyone can view it, and Google will even display it as a search result when people Google your name (see p. 96). To do so, go to your account section and edit your "full profile." But before you plaster your name all over the 'net, make sure that you've fine-tuned every part of your profile.

- **Utilize the Advanced Search feature.** Instead of just browsing for people by industry, search for specific companies or positions, as well. You can even use Boolean searching, the illest search technique of them all. (You might recall from 5th grade library sessions that these searches use AND or OR to tailor your result—for example, you might search "IT Department AND Apple.") When searching for a phrase, make sure you enter it within quotation marks (e.g., "IT Department," not IT Department).

- **List every job you've ever had.** Even the bad ones, unless they involved doing something illegal. By including all of the companies you've worked with, you make it easier for old coworkers to find you. The bigger your network, the better.

- **Ask questions.** LinkedIn enables you to send a message to your entire network in the form of a question. So, once you've built up your LinkedIn buddies, ask a question like, "Is anyone connected with a friend who is working at Google?" to start the ball rolling on your job search. You may be surprised to find several responses from friends who know someone who knows someone else who works at Google. Even if you only have a second-degree connection, it's better than blindly submitting a résumé.

- **Dig deep for connections.** Found someone who works at the company of your dreams but don't want to cold call? Check his or her LinkedIn profile to see if you have any connections. LinkedIn shows connections that have up to six degrees of separation—you could probably even find a way to holler at Kevin Bacon! In a bind, you can have your friend ask her friend to put you in touch with a friend's friend. Again, it may not sound ideal, but it's better than sending a random e-mail to a potential employer before you have laid any groundwork

- **Don't stop short of the finish line.** Remember that networking isn't just about getting an interview—it's about getting a job. If you managed to land the interview, take things one step further and see if you can network to your interviewer. And even if you can't, check out his or her LinkedIn profile to see if you have any commonalities (e.g., you're from the same town or previously worked for the same employer). This way you can enter any interview strapped with ammunition.

- **Don't be shy about asking people for LinkedIn recommendations.** LinkedIn enables former bosses and coworkers to add letters of recommendation to your profile, similar to traditional references. There's nothing better than an objective source lauding your talents. And don't forget about karma—you may need to return the favor one day, so be careful about whom you ask to recommend you and whom you're recommending.

- **Don't accept everyone and every offer you get at face value.** More and more, recruiting companies are popping up on LinkedIn. When you think

> ## Tips & Tricks: The Point of Online Networking
>
> While online career networking can feel more casual and less intimidating than striking up conversations over cocktail wieners, remember that it is a means to an end, not an end in itself. The key is to turn your online contacts into offline phone calls, meetings over coffee, and interviews. Nothing can replace face-to-face contact, but online networking can broaden the scope of your search and help you connect with people even if you're from the middle of nowhere, attended a tiny school, and have no friends.

The Job-hunt

you're networking your way to a job at Nike, you might just end up networking your way to contact with a recruiter.

- **Stay informed.** There are blogs that follow career networking as well as entire books written on LinkedIn. Don't fall behind the curve on the newest networking techniques.

Sample LinkedIn Profile

Doostang & Ryze

Doostang and Ryze are also very popular with the online career networking community, but they are much smaller than LinkedIn. Of course, that doesn't necessarily mean they're worse; often the employer you are trying to track down may be found only through a smaller site. Doostang is similar to LinkedIn, except it's a little more

The Job-hunt

exclusive in that you need to be invited by a current member to join the community. Once inside the fold, you'll be privy to job postings from today's hottest companies. In addition, if you convince twenty people to join, you'll be given access to the premium area which has "premium-member-only job postings." Back of the 'net? Not exactly. On the one hand, this reeks of a pyramid scheme developed to drive user accounts. But on the other hand, we might just be cynics—one argument is that by proving that you can get twenty people to sign up, you show that you are a leader and are more qualified than the next person for a job. Pyramid scheme or not, it does give you access to more job postings, and no one can complain about that.

Ryze enables anyone to join and creates communities around topics that are less specifically geared toward careers (e.g., interests and location). There is a premium option and a growing user base. It also utilizes edgy spelling, which may or may not be worth mentioning.

At the end of the day, it doesn't hurt to take a peek around the various networks to see which ones seem to cater most effectively to your interests. Once you start doing your thing, however, you can apply the same concepts that we've laid out above to any online career network.

Facebook as a Career Networking Tool

Don't forget Facebook (as if you would, you Facebook FREAK). Although not focused exclusively on career networking, Facebook has over 70 million users, many of whom list their employer. Expand your network and scan it to find people in the industries that interest you—or, better yet, people who work for the companies you want to target. Facebook is also useful for letting people know what you're after. For example, you can post notes or use your status to alert your friends to the type of job you want; with any luck, they'll holler at you when they come across something they think might be of interest. Just don't sound too desperate—networking, even online, is a lot like dating. "Why are you still single" and "why don't you have a job yet?" are questions that go hand in hand—in fact, sometimes one response can answer the other!

Applying and Interviewing

Once you've e-mailed, mailed, or uploaded your application to the appropriate place, the waiting game begins. One of the most frustrating parts about applying for jobs is that sometimes (quite often, in fact) you never hear back. Even though you spent six hours perfecting the cover letter and sent an extremely gracious follow-up e-mail a month later, you might get straight-up blanked. Companies receive too many applications to muster the humanity it would require to respond to all of them. For this reason, it's advisable to cast a wide net—you may catch some unwanted things like diseased crustaceans and discarded diapers, but you'll also increase the odds of finding something you want.

The best advice we can give, particularly for newcomers to the job market, is to accept every interview you're offered. Even if you are 99% sure you will not want the job, interviewing is an acquired skill, and any chance to practice will pay off down the line. Each time, you'll learn about your nervous ticks, expose yourself to new questions, and perfect your handshake until it hovers playfully between dead fish and vice grip. The whole process of interviewing can be extremely nerve-wracking for some people, but it's also the part of the game where you can really stand out from the hordes of other applicants with comparable credentials. We hope our tips below will help you shine with the intensity of a thousand suns.

Prep Work

Prepare for an interview as you would prepare for a test. That doesn't mean drink a sixer of Red Bull and stay up all night playing online cribbage. It means anticipate what's coming and make sure you are ready to knock it out of the proverbial ballpark. Research the company, the industry, and the interviewer beforehand. Start with the company website: pay close attention to major divisions of the organization, highlighted products or services, press releases, vocabulary, and who's who. Search Vault.com for company profiles, employee surveys, diversity statistics, and more. Find out if they've been in the news lately using Lexis Nexis (probably available through your college library) or by searching the archives of major papers like *The New York Times*, *The Wall Street Journal*, or *The Washington Post*. Finally, don't forget to do some Googling, and consider checking out online career networks like LinkedIn and Doostang to find the interviewer and see if you have anything in common. (For more on online career networking, see p. 103.)

After you've done your background checks, mock up a list of potential questions that might pop up, including both general personal questions and those specific to the firm.

Ask other people who may have interviewed with the same company or similar companies for advice on the interview. Also, refer back to the job description to remind yourself of exactly what skills they are looking for so that you can stress them throughout the interview. Finally, know your résumé and cover letter inside out—sometimes, your résumé is the only thing that the interviewer will know about you, so be prepared to defend its honor to the death.

Day of the Interview

If you played sports in college or high school, you know how nerve-wracking it can be to anticipate an event where you have to be 100% on the ball. Game day readiness is all about routine and preparation; quell anxiety by avoiding last-minute problems. Print out your résumé and any other materials the night before and put them in a nice folder. Make sure your outfit is pressed and looking sharp. If you don't know the dress code of the organization, call HR and inquire about appropriate attire (you don't have to give your name—you can say you're coming in for a meeting). Looking presentable will give you greater confidence and also create a better first impression. Eat food that won't upset your stomach, pop an Icebreaker, and don't drink too much caffeine if it will make you jittery. Finally, make sure you know how to get to the interview, and plan to arrive early. A late showing is a one-way ticket to Not Getting a Jobsville. If you *are* running late because of an Amtrak strike or legitimate emergency (catching the end of *Pirates 3* doesn't count), call ahead to let them know what is going on and when to expect you.

In the War Room

When the moment of truth arrives, be prepared to cock back a fully loaded clip of wit, charm, and illuminating yet humble tales about why you are awesome. Here are some things to remember:

Check your body language. Along with being well-dressed and well-groomed, body language can make a big difference in how you are perceived by your interviewer. Sit up straight, avoid nervous fidgeting, and make eye contact (though not to an awkward extent). If you are not a very expressive person, try your best to smile and display enthusiasm—someone who does not know you may mistake your natural demeanor for boredom or apathy.

Tips & Tricks: Phone Interviews

Phone interviews are often a critical first hurdle in landing an in-person interview. In rare cases, they can be the only interview you'll get. Since you can't read the various social cues of a face-to-face conversation, you have to rely solely on what you say and how you say it— use enthusiasm and intonation to sell yourself, and avoid gum chewing, smoking, or eating. Be prepared for the call, find a quiet place where you feel comfortable chatting, and find a landline to avoid a cell-related snafu. Finally, take advantage of the best part of phone interviewing—no one can see you, so you can lay out all of your notes in front of you and nail all your talking points.

Go in with a game plan. You know what skills they want, and you know what experiences and achievements you can offer as evidence that you are the best fit. Figure out how you are going to pitch yourself for the job at hand, and know what talking points you definitely want to hit. Even though the interviewer is asking the questions, you can still "topsy-turvy" the situation and put yourself in the driver's seat. If they ask if you can follow directions well, don't just say "yes." Use it to segue into the story of that time you followed directions mad well!

Speak slowly and clearly. Unless you are interviewing to read off the side-effects at the end of a Lipitor commercial, speaking a mile a minute will make you sound insane, incomprehensible, or nervous—either way, not a good look. Before fielding each query, steady yourself with a deep breath, which will have the added benefit of making your answers seem less rehearsed.

Don't panic. If a question throws you off guard, don't stare at your feet for five minutes or go into an epileptic fit of "uhs" and "likes." Getting truly stumped is more likely in finance or consulting interviews where you have to address case studies or logical dilemmas, but you never know when you might just draw a blank under pressure. The trick is to be prepared for this eventuality. Utilize stalling techniques like repeating the question out loud or asking for a clarification. If you are offered a drink at the beginning, accept even if you're not thirsty—a well-timed sip can be a lifesaver when you're flummoxed. When all else fails, thinking out loud is always better than silence, no matter how much you think you are bombing.

"What is your biggest weakness?" You will almost always be asked this question, because everyone in the world mistakenly thinks it's revealing, when in fact it is not at all. Everyone pursues the same tactic (as you should, too): take an apparent weakness and then flip it to seem more like a strength. "I'm a perfectionist" is getting a bit tired, so think of your own variation on the theme.

Don't be negative. Badmouthing ex-bosses or past experiences makes you sound high-maintenance and pessimistic. Rather than talking about what you hated, find a way to describe what you learned and what your new goals are.

Ask questions. 99% of interviews end with an invitation to ask questions about the job and the company. The ball is nominally in your court, but you are still being tested. The questions you ask should demonstrate your enthusiasm and knowledge of the company and industry. Utilize the research methods discussed above to go in with a solid list of questions, and don't make the mistake of assuming that they will think you know everything if you don't ask anything. Refrain from asking about salary, benefits, vacation time, etc. You can handle that with HR, or after you actually get an offer.

> ## Tips & Tricks: Clean Up Your Online Profile
>
> Just as you will research the company, industry, and interviewer prior to the interview, odds are they will also look into your background. First place they'll start: the Web. So, be sure to clean up your online profile before pursuing the interview process. Check out page 95 for a full breakdown of keeping your online identity appropriate for the job-hunt.

Request a response. To give yourself peace of mind, don't hesitate to ask when you can expect to hear back. Ideally, you can save yourself the sleepless nights of wondering why you haven't received a response.

Ask for business cards. Request a business card from each person you meet during your visit to the office, otherwise you'll be kicking yourself when it comes times to send an e-mail and you can't remember anyone's name.

Follow-ups

A follow-up thank you letter is not simply polite; it is also a chance to reiterate qualifications, reemphasize a desire for the position, or bring something up that didn't get mentioned in person. Write a brief note to each individual who took part in the interview within 24–48 hours. If there is any doubt over correct names, spelling, or titles, call the office to double-check. After that, wait until the timeframe that you were given for a response has elapsed before calling or e-mailing again. An overly eager beaver is no one's favorite type o' beaver.

The Job-hunt

Sample Thank You Note

Dear Mr. Alexander,

Thank you for taking the time not only to interview me, but also to share your insights into and experiences at Smithfields with me. It was exciting to hear you discuss how the meritocratic culture truly pervades every facet of the firm. I also enjoyed learning about the lean project teams that enable new hires to assume lots of responsibility very quickly. After meeting with a number of employees on Monday, I feel certain that I would like to become part of the Smithfields community. Thank you again for your time and I hope to be hearing from Smithfields soon.

Sincerely,
Blair Stevenson

Blair Stevenson

Making a Decision

Congratulations! After months of begging and pleading at the feet of employers, the offers are rolling in. Now you've got some swagger! If you get two or more offers, all we can say is to take into account all of the issues we've brought up throughout the last two chapters: geography, salary, benefits, office vibe, and so on. Go with your gut, and if you got job offers in different industries, don't feel that by choosing one you have to stick to that career path. If you got a job offer in another industry once, you can do it again.

So there you have it, the Gradspot guide to landing your first job. Before we move on, there's just one more set of demons to lay to rest...

Settling: Is This the Best Time to Sacrifice Your Dreams?

We won't go so far as to say that starting your first job will cause another existential crisis, but let's be honest: it could. Taking a job that you don't feel is perfect for you can be a tough pill to swallow. Like the pilgrims of yore, today's "settlers" will go through bouts of intense regret about why they gave up a mediocre life of unemployment and mild persecution for "the New World." But if you are stressed out about settling, we suggest that you settle down. Just look at America—400 years down the line and it's not half bad.

We're joking, of course—America is so f—ed up! But settling is all about perspective. On the one hand, there's a dark storm cloud in the post-grad forecast: 99 times out of 100, your first job is not going to be your dream job. But there's a silver lining, as well: the majority of recent grads hold three or four jobs in their first five years out of college, so it really doesn't have to be your dream job. Still, feeling like you've sold yourself short can definitely keep you up at night. There are no simple answers, but it's important to develop a more holistic view of your entry into the work force.

Why Do You Feel Like You're Settling?

There are a lot of factors that go into the decision to settle—your economic situation (usually how long mom and dad will pay your way), the difficulty of entry into a given industry, and the likelihood of other opportunities arising. Not even the great mathematician Leonhard Euler could reconcile those variables, so you probably can't either. Try to pinpoint exactly why you feel like you're settling—by necessity (you need to pay the bills or take a job in Wichita to be near your sick grandmother), by ambition (you have big dreams and will not be satisfied until you run your own company), or because it's the easy option (laziness).

Make a Commitment

Once you've made a decision, it's important to commit to it rather than constantly wondering what could have been. As the old saying goes, "Finding a job is a job in itself." It's sort of like how finding a boyfriend or girlfriend is as annoying as having one. At some point, you have to stop playing the field and commit (for a bit). You can look for other

The Job-hunt

jobs/partners while you're at it, but your hands are going to be tied because if you get caught, it's pretty awkward. And you don't have as much time as you used to. And your work/sex life will suffer.

Okay, this analogy is pretty much aces so far except for one important fact: getting out of a relationship sooner rather than later will make things easier, but when you start a job, a certain level of commitment is expected (it varies, but generally a year is considered the minimum). Here's the thing, though: just as being in a relationship makes you more attractive to other people (the old "I want what he/she has" phenomenon), holding a job will boost your status in the eyes of other employers. Moreover, if you perform well, they'll be more likely to speak highly of you to others rather than badmouthing you 'round the block and on the Interweb.

Should I Take a Pay Cut?

This is a whole different type of settling—forgive us for not feeling bad for you. Presumably, you can either slave from "8 til late" every day doing something you don't love or make a significantly smaller salary doing what you really want to do. We'd like to say go with your heart every time, but we realize that things like student debt and rent are real concerns. Sometimes you just have to get on your grind. But if you are fortunate enough to have a little bit of financial cushioning, think twice before buying into the allure of a six-figure salary. Even though parents and grandparents love to recount their days of "paying dues" in terrible first jobs, it's a slippery slope toward a breakdown when the only thing getting you out of bed in the morning is the paper chase.

See page 137 for more information on deciding when to move on from you first job.

The Job-hunt

Chapter IV: Working Life

Working Life

Congratulations on your new job! You are now a contributing member of society. Working from 9-to-5, using an Internet computer, and enjoying access to an unlimited supply of free coffee... these are just a few of the things our grandparents fought for, so don't take them for granted. It's time to get it started, buddies. The totem poll is ready to be ascended; glass ceilings are ready to be shattered.

When you get that call or e-mail telling you that you've got a job or internship, relief will wash over you in an awesome wave. Maybe you'll have a drink or go to Six Flags to celebrate. But as the big "first day" draws nigh, a creeping sense of dread can begin to sully even the most buoyant of dispositions. What if I am bad at the job? What if it is miserable? Is this really what I want to be doing? Are they going to find out that I don't technically know how to use Excel?

Pump the breaks, homie. Give yourself time to bask in the triumph of employment and enjoy the excitement of starting something new. Save the stress for when you actually have some work to do, and don't get too worried about whether you chose the "right" job. The thing about the "right" job is that it's a myth, sort of like El Dorado or the claim that Burger King puts pickles in its burgers so they can achieve the legal definition of "food." Employment and enjoyment may be spelled very similarly, but they're often quite far removed from one another. Working in a fun office with interesting people can be much better than doing "what you want" in a miserable environment. And for the majority of us, knowing exactly what we want to do is a long way off anyway. So even if you don't end up loving this first job (though we hope you do), it might open up a new door that you never knew existed, sort of like one of those potions in *Mario Bros. 2.* If nothing else, at least you'll know one more thing you don't want to do—sometimes finding a great job just comes down to a process of elimination.

But let's not get ahead of ourselves—this chapter is all about surviving your first day, settling into the workplace, and navigating the treacherous waters of office politics. According to *Young Money*, recent grads hold their first position for an average of 1.6 years, so there's plenty of time to figure things out. Whether this job ends up as the launching pad for your career or the butt of a joke, the important thing is you're putting yourself out there, picking up new skills, and learning just how little some people can accomplish in an eight-hour workday.

Working Life

First Jobs of Famous People

Few careers begin at the top, and many of the people we now idolize started their working lives with some pretty suspect first jobs.

Bill Gates: congressional page

Bill Murray: sold chestnuts outside of a grocery store

Tommy Hilfiger: sold his jeans from the trunk of his car when no stores would carry them

Jerry Seinfeld: sold light bulbs over the phone

Madonna: worked behind the counter at a Dunkin' Donuts

Stephen King: janitor (inspired to write *Carrie* while cleaning a girls' locker room)

Madeleine Albright: sold bras at a department store

Walt Disney: ambulance driver

Coolio: fireman

Jeff Koons (artist): door-to-door salesman

Danny DeVito: hairdresser

Ellen Degeneres: shucked oysters, painted houses, sold vacuum cleaners

Rod Stewart: gravedigger

Sylvester Stallone: lion cage cleaner, porn actor

Surviving Your First Day

Starting work can potentially be one of the most awkward things you've ever done in your life. Waiting to be told where to sit, how to log into your e-mail, and who (if anyone) is going to go to lunch with you can make you feel like a helpless infant waiting to suck at the teat of responsibility. It can also be an incredibly nerve-wracking experience—an unofficial survey conducted by me shows first-day nerves register even higher on peoples' fear factor than losing their virginity! The thing to remember is that adults in the workforce can be as awkward, lazy, or self-absorbed as the people you knew in college, and unfortunately not everyone is going to jump out of his seat to make the new person feel comfortable. You have to slowly work your way into the fold—don't force it. Be polite, enthusiastic, and friendly, and whenever you're given an opening, let people know what you're interested in and where you'd like to be involved. Here are a few tips for lubricating your entry into the office.

Don't Be Late

The cardinal rule of your first day is to be on time. If possible, take the trip from wherever you're staying to the office beforehand to gauge how long it will take. Then add an hour to that. If you're there early you can grab a coffee or something. Maybe you'll have time for a few. But it's worth it, because being late will set a horrible precedent.

The Name Game

Most likely, you'll meet a bunch of people on your first day, from mailroom employees up to your boss. No one will fault you for taking a few weeks to get acclimated and acquainted with the office, but quickly learning people's names can help you make a great first impression. After you've been shown around, try making a quick chart of who people are and where they sit. If you do forget, don't be afraid to ask again—"I'm so sorry, I've been meeting so many people and managed to forget your name. Could you remind me?" Eventually, you will not be able to use this line anymore, at which point you'll find yourself in the extremely awkward situation of mumbling the name of someone you've seen every single weekday for six months. I did this a lot at school because you could get away with just saying "Hey man" or "What up, dude" to literally anyone. I basically knew about 10 people's names in college. But in a working environment that doesn't really fly.

Working Life

Tips & Tricks: Reassess Your Cell Phone Plan

College is all about off-hours—you study when most people are sleeping and F around when most people are working. As a result, you often eat up cell phone minutes during the day by making calls between classes, parlaying with mama bear, arranging the night's festivities, and ordering strippers. But then employment comes along and changes the game. Non-work calls become fewer and fewer during the day, and you probably won't get out of work until after 7pm. Sounds depressing, but there's some good news: your peak cell phone usage just plummeted, so now you can decrease your monthly minutes and save some cash. After you get into a post-graduation rhythm, be sure to check your monthly cell phone usage, gauge how many minutes you really need, and adjust accordingly.

State Your Purpose

Sometimes you will meet your boss or supervisor for the first time the day you arrive for the job. Don't go barging in with the wild ideas you came up with on the ride over, but do be forthcoming with your goals and expectations. Let your boss know what aspects of the company interest you most and where you'd like to get involved. If the response is, "Actually, you will just be buying me frappucinos and doing my son's homework," then go with the flow. Nonetheless, it will be useful to give your boss a sense of your aspirations, even if he appears to ignore them. For more mundane run-of-the-mill issues like hours, vacations, and reimbursements, it may be more prudent to check in with HR. However, feel free to bring these topics up with your direct superior (not necessarily the boss of all bosses) if there is confusion, and make sure you take an approach that does not bear hints of an "I want to work as little as possible and go on vacation next week" attitude.

Get Your Bearings

At larger companies, offices can be like labyrinths, with more barriers to entry than Cuba. If no one shows you, be sure to ask around to locate the following essentials: bathroom, fridge/coffee machine/kitchen, mailroom, office supply cabinet, and the fire exit. You may also need to get an ID card made, so try to look presentable (though the photo will be terrible anyway). It is advisable to get on the good side of the security guards, who are like the Minotaurs of your office. If they decide that they don't like you and you forget your ID, they will pretend they've never seen you and make you contact your supervisor to get in, thus causing embarrassment and annoyance all around.

Write It All Down

During the first weeks and months on the job, you will be recipient of a non-stop deluge of information, ranging from the menial (e.g., how to sign in guests, where to find post-it notes) to the monumentally important (e.g., how to get paid, who is your manager). Even if your superiors don't expect you to take it all in the first time around, you will come out looking on the ball and ready if you do. For this reason, it's important to take copious notes about the who, what, why, when, and how of the office as you go along. You might feel silly writing down something as simple as "BCC Geraldine on all client e-mails," but you will feel even sillier if you mess it up. As a general rule, always bring a pen, pad, and potentially a calculator to all meetings—even if you just draw pictures of beagles humping grenade launchers, at least it will look like you are trying.

Tips & Tricks: Considering the Company Cell Phone Plan

If your company is willing to pay for your cell phone plan, why not let it? Low-balling it, that's $600 per year of extra cash in your pocket. It would be a no-brainer, but of course all corporate generosity comes with baggage—in this case, full disclosure of your minute usage and call logs. The company is compensating you for all the business calls you are hypothetically making, which, believe it or not, does not include calling your boyfriend in London. Some people take the company plan and then get an additional phone with a scaled-down plan for their personal use. However, many companies probably don't really care what you do with the phone, so talk to coworkers to find out how lenient things are before running in fear.

Be Prepared to Fill Out Forms

Over the course of your first few days you will probably be presented with a number of forms to fill out, many of which will require your Social Security number (worth memorizing if you haven't already).

W–4 form. This form will allow your employer to determine the correct amount of withholding tax to deduct from your wages. Don't want them taking any of your money? Unfortunately, it doesn't work like that. If your employer did not withhold these taxes from you, then you would have to pay them all in one enormous lump sum at the end of the year anyway—better to just play it by the books and avoid extra hassle. When filling out the form, you will have to note any deductions that you will be eligible for that year. But since most of us are unmarried with no kids or house, it's pretty straightforward.

Working Life

If you think you may be eligible for any deductions, check out the "IRS Withholding Calculator" online before your first day of work. (For more on taxes, see p. 162.)

Benefits. Landed a job with a 401(k) plan and healthcare coverage? Back of the net! Choosing a doctor or deciding how much of your monthly paycheck you want to put into savings can be confusing (particularly if you've never done it before), so don't feel you have to pick on the spot. Take these forms home so you can do some research and seek advice from parents and friends. Also, never be shy about taking advantage of benefits just because you don't think you'll be with the company for very long—you are working hard and you deserve them! (For more on retirement funds and healthcare benefits, see Chapter 5.)

Direct deposit. Assuming you have a bank account, sign up for direct deposit so your paychecks will be dumped straight into your account and you won't have to worry about losing checks or waiting for them to arrive in the mail. To do this you will need to bring a voided check to the office. (To learn how to void a check, see p. 152.)

Non-compete and non-disclosure agreements. If you are working at a startup or proprietary information company, you may be asked to sign legal documents stating that you won't share confidential information or offer your services to other companies that are deemed competitors. Often, you either sign or don't take the job and that's the end of the story. However, sometimes there is some wiggle room, and at any rate it is advisable to at least take some time to review the documents (and ideally show them to a lawyer) so you know you are not shooting yourself in the foot. The last thing you want is to finally get a job at the website of your dreams, only to realize that you

---

Tips & Tricks: Reimbursements

While no one complains about a free dinner at work, it's important to realize that the proverbial "free lunch" is still elusive. Sure, you can get a filet on "the Man" every now and then. But if he's paying, that only means that it's late at night and you're at the office eating dinner when you could be home or out with friends. Nonetheless, don't look a gift-horse in the mouth. Get anything and everything reimbursed: cell phones (see p. 121), transportation, food, and whatever else the company is willing to cover. Most likely, you'll have to spend cash up front, and then your boss will reimburse you. But there's even a silver lining to this cloud. If you pay for everything on a credit card, you're banking the points without spending any money of your own. Jackpot! Usually, to get reimbursed, you'll just have to hand your receipts to someone in the back office. One caveat: the reimbursement might not come immediately, so make sure you will have the money in your account to pay your credit card bill when it's due.

have agreed to not work in media for at least two years after leaving your current gig.

Don't Hit On Your Coworkers

That's not what we meant by "lubricating your entry into the office." Settle down.

On Work and Boredom

Being bored at work and being bored doing homework have one vital difference: you get paid to be bored at work. For some, the promise of a paycheck can make aimless hours at the computer feel like highway robbery. Needless to say, that's always a nice feeling. But others feel frustrated, wondering why they need a college degree to play Snood all day. If you want more responsibility, you may need to ask for it. This aspect of office life is foreign to recent grads who are used to knowing exactly what they need to do at all times. At work, some people might not even know you exist, or they may feel that it would be easier to just do the work themselves than teach you how to do it. Ask bosses and coworkers if they have any side projects that you could help out with, or pitch your own ideas when given the opportunity. Don't expect everything to come to you—go out and get it, and eventually you'll earn people's trust and they will feel comfortable giving you more responsibility. And then you will be extremely busy, and you'll probably complain about that, too!

According to *The Quarterlifer's Companion*, well over half of recent grads in the workforce complain about severe boredom on the job. In fact, the number is far higher than those who complain that they are stressed out by their workload. Since fresh-out-of-college employees lack experience, many supervisors are careful about putting too much on their plates. However, sometimes whole offices are just sluggish and inefficient. If

Tips & Tricks: Never Stop Looking for Opportunities

When you finally land a job, there's something to be said for giving it your full attention and not being distracted by the "what if" demons. Better jobs than yours certainly exist, especially when you are young and inexperienced, but doing well now will help you get to those eventually. That said, working hard shouldn't put up the blinders on career opportunities. If nothing more, take an hour each month to scroll through some job sites, check up on openings at your dream companies, have coffee with an old boss, or read up on your industry to see what's new and exciting. Networking doesn't just have to be done a few weeks before you apply for a job—building contacts will always come in handy when you decide to make your next move.

Working Life

Internet caches could talk, they would weave a tale of monumental inefficiency across the Webisphere—according to an AOL and Salary.com survey, the average American worker wastes 2.09 hours per eight-hour workday, mostly by hanging ten on the 'net, socializing with coworkers, and attending useless meetings.

Office Romance

While many people employ a "don't deuce where you eat" philosophy with regards to getting it cracking in the workplace, the taboo of the office romance is fading to some extent. Yes, there was a time when office romance was considered anathema to a successful career. "Business and pleasure don't mix," said the conventional wisdom. "Sex in the office is harassment, even if it's consensual." Just watch *Jungle Fever* and you'll know what I'm talking about (though I think that Spike Lee may have been making a point about something else...). But that was the '90s and this is 2008—these days, a growing number of HR departments are actually supporting (if not encouraging) office relationships as a way of fostering good morale. (Note: Some companies and bosses still think office romance is categorically unacceptable, so always tread carefully.)

Young people are working longer hours, and as the work-life balance shifts further toward the "work is life" end of the spectrum, the office has become the new bar. Obviously, that's not really a compelling justification for romance—dating in the workplace is more of a practical response to heavy work loads than any sort of romantic coup. Still, there's no reason why love can't blossom in the office. Before you dive in head first, just ask yourself a few questions: Can I trust my emotions in the workplace? How will an "affair de cubicle" affect everyone else in the office? Will breaking up make it unbearable to work in this job any longer? Here are the different scenarios you might run into:

- **Dating an equal.** If you are dating another new hire, it's mostly up to the two of you to decide if competing for the same promotions, raises, and projects will breed ill will. Otherwise, this type of relationship can work reasonably well as long as you don't annoy everyone else with your antics.

- **Dating a superior.** Juicing your boss is almost always a bad idea. Even if you successfully pull off an unethical plan to get ahead through sexual favors, the rumor mill is quick to spot an unjust promotion. And you probably won't feel good about it in the long run, either. If you really "like" your boss, check your feelings to make sure they are genuine. Then check his or her hand for a wedding ring. Then quit the job and get it cracking.

- **Dating an inferior.** Most of us don't have to worry about this because we are the inferiors. But again, the issue that arises here has to do with maintaining professional integrity. Preferential treatment based on romantic feelings will not go over well with the rest of the office, and if you can't be objective (not many can) then it might be worth reporting your status to HR to make sure there is no conflict of interest. That said, the interns are always fair game, regardless of age. (Just kidding.)

- **Dating a client.** If your job involves going to a lot of dinners or entertaining clients outside of the office, you never know what might pop off once the *vino* starts flowing. Know your own limits (never drink more than the client) and remember that your job is not to jump people's bones (at least we hope not). If your boss finds out, your actions will not be looked upon favorably. If he or she is the one cajoling you to flirt for business, then you need to get out of there immediately.

Regardless of the specifics, avoid P.D.A. at all costs. Petting, kissing, and even subtle hand-holding will alienate both of you (or all three of you!?) and make work uncomfortable for others.

Office Politics

Office politics are one of the mythical aspects of working life that most people cannot truly appreciate until they have experienced their effects first hand. They are the basis of great debacles like Monica Lewinsky sucking Bill Clinton's cory, as well as great works of art like *The* (British) *Office*. Indeed, as long as you stay out of hot water, office politics are one of the best parts of a job, if only because a classic workplace faux pas can be more hilarious than Nick Cannon. Just think about it—unless you are one of those overly braggadocios types, you probably don't go around telling people about what a dope spreadsheet you made at work last week (because you have correctly assumed that no one cares). But when that dude who works on your floor accidentally sends out a company-wide e-mail about his explosive diarrhea, you will regale anyone who will listen.

Despite their mystique, office politics can be easily navigated with a bit of common sense, confidence, and composure. At the end of the day, most disasters boil down to ambiguous power structures, judgment lapses, and the general awkwardness of human beings. Here's a quick field guide to social and professional interactions in the workplace.

Working Life

Gossip folks. If office romances are a "play it by ear" situation, office gossip is firmly in "don't play it at all" territory. Listening to the resident gossip-mongers dish the dirt is all very well and good, and you should feel free to take that information home and laugh about it in private. But once you start soliciting or dispensing gossip yourself, Pandora's box will creak open and unleash a minefield of potential hazards to your good standing in the office. As with life in general, your safest bet is to employ a "don't trust anyone" strategy. Even if others are making fun of your boss or sending around incendiary e-mails, resist the urge to join in with a zinger of your own. Some people talk recklessly, while others consciously backstab—either way, whatever you say will mysteriously find its way back to you.

Bringing baggage to the office. Everybody has problems. But if you don't hear grown folks complaining about divorces and mortgages, why do you think it's appropriate to whine about your boyfriend or messy roommate? Water-cooler chatter is one thing, and if you make a friend at work who is willing to listen to your moaning then all the better. Just don't let non-work related issues affect your productivity or attitude. "Professionalism" means ignoring your emotions and acting like work is literally more important than your own life. (Also, unless people know you are going on vacation, don't bring literal baggage to the office, either. It will be a dead giveaway when you call in sick the next day.)

Socializing with coworkers. The sociability of an office varies quite significantly from place to place (and, quite often, from industry to industry). Some investment banks have a fratty "work hard, play hard" approach that is fueled by popping bottles and sometimes ingesting class-A drugs. Other offices have training programs or "class" systems that attempt to foster strong bonds between coworkers through retreats, volunteer outings, and parties. And, once in a while, people befriend coworkers at normal offices because they actually like them or are just very bored. The thing to remember is this: just because you work with someone does not mean you have to be best friends. Nor does it mean you have to invite him or her to your birthday party. Pay attention to the social dynamics of your office, but realize that you are free to set your own standards and boundaries. Once you've proven to be a good worker, only a huge chach will begrudge you for having your own life outside of the office.

Pushing back on your superiors. The first time you feel you are disrespected or mistreated in the workplace can be a shock to the system and make you want to run to your mom crying. But, depending on the severity, it might be advisable to let it slide before you've gauged your boss's style and expectations. If it becomes habitual and makes you feel uncomfortable, then it is time to talk to HR or speak with a superior. Additionally, it can feel like you are admitting weakness if you say your workload is too heavy. But again, there comes a time when your boss' expectations need to be in line with your own. At the end of the day, most people would rather have you speak up and say that you are overwhelmed than end up with an unfinished or shoddy product when the due date arrives. Over time, you'll get a sense of who will value and reward your hard work and who is just looking to pawn off all the dirty work on you. But when you're a newcomer, the best course of action is to stiffen that upper lip and work hard enough to earn a good reputation. A good rep, in turn, will allow you to push back down the line without being looked upon suspiciously.

Office parties. The company Christmas party is a tried and true tradition in most offices around the country, but it is just one beast in an odd menagerie of social events at work. Whether it's a holiday shindig, Friday happy hour, or a farewell

> ## Tips & Tricks: Find a Mentor
>
> Though some companies have orientation programs, buddy systems, and other initiatives to help new employees settle in, many recent grads feel completely lost at their first jobs. A mentor doesn't have to work in the same office as you—indeed, it's often better to have a third party who you can address freely without stepping into the mire of office politics. That said, sometimes it's useful to have a mentor within the office as well, since every company has its idiosyncrasies, and you may need someone who understands the specifics of your situation. (Remember, you can always have two.) Overall, a good mentor should be able to offer guidance in the industry that interests you. No matter how smart you are, there are some places where a voice of experience can be invaluable.

party for a retiring fossil, the same rule applies: don't get wasted. It seems like it would go without saying, but you'd be surprised at how many bright, hard-working recent graduates embarrass themselves by going hard on the mixed drinks or failing to gauge their limits. Once you've passed the "are you an alcoholic?" litmus test, office party etiquette pretty much boils down to basic standards of sociability. Avoid the obvious taboos in conversation—sex, religion, politics, and off-color jokes. However, don't feel that you have to only talk about job stuff. Office parties are a great opportunity to interact outside of the structure of "work," which is often not very conducive to getting to know people. Being sociable at a work party can put you on the radar of someone you don't know very well or help you impress your boss, both of which can pay dividends back in the office.

Taking responsibility and getting credit. At school, you hand in a paper and you get a grade. Sometimes you do group projects and end up doing all the work while your pot-head partner reaps the benefits, but at least you still end up with the results on your report card. At work, there is a lot more ambiguity not only in terms of the feedback you receive, but also in who takes credit for what. Sometimes a boss might simply make a false assumption about who has completed the work that he or she is receiving, while at other times your superiors will just take credit for your labor in order to make themselves look better. Either way, you've got a tricky situation on your hands. Demanding credit for everything you do might not be realistic or even necessary. However, if you are being systematically overlooked, you may want to address the issue head-on. If you go this route, do so calmly and don't storm in with guns blazing. Ask a mentor or a senior person you have a good relationship with for advice. On the other side of the coin, don't be the perpetrator of poor professional etiquette—give credit where credit's due, and take responsibility when your work is queried instead of passing the buck.

Business Speak 101

Sometimes walking into an office can be like touching down in a foreign country: the local uniform is borderline fascist, and people speak a dialect that you've probably never heard before. But while the garments are unnecessarily uncomfortable and expensive, the language has fewer words than Esperanto and is pretty easy to pick up. Here's a crash course:

Chicken and egg situation
- Corporate meaning: There is an unclear causality at work.
- What it really means: There is probably some sort of logic to the data that you are presenting to me, but it would require too much thought to figure it out. I will just artfully dodge the entire issue with a meaningless cliché!

Grab the bull by the horns
- Corporate meaning: Take control of the situation.
- What it really means: No one grabs the bull by the horns, not even a bullfighter. It's just dangerous. The better move is to wave a colorful sheet around to annoy it then jab spears into its spinal column.

Golden goose
- Corporate meaning: A cash cow, but in avian form; an idea that will produce high returns
- What it really means: Now that things are going well, I no longer worry about whether eggs come before birds, or vice versa. When the egg is golden, don't ask questions.

Business Speak 101 Continued...

Compare apples to apples
- Corporate meaning: When doing analysis, only compare like things.
- What it really means: Apparently, it would sound too negative to say "don't compare apples and oranges" like a normal person would. That said, I'd love to meet the person who can objectively compare a Granny Smith to a Red Delicious.

Don't reinvent the wheel
- Corporate meaning: Let's not try to fix something that isn't broken or come up with new solutions to problems that have already been solved.
- What it really means: If you are not in the automotive industry, why are you even thinking about wheels? But seriously, fear of taking on the wheel has slowed up GDP growth by at least 10% per year. Maybe there is a better solution.

It is what it is
- Corporate meaning: We're all underwhelmed by the situation at hand, but I have no intention of fixing the problem.
- What it really means: Literally the most meaningless phrase in the world.

Deliverable
- Corporate meaning: A tangible piece of work that can be handed in and reviewed.
- What it really means: I don't trust that you are actually doing any work so I will force you to waste time by turning it into a sort of grown-up homework assignment.

Baked In
- Corporate meaning: One solution is enveloped within another (e.g., a spell checker is "baked into" Microsoft Word).
- What it really means: This idea is much like castor sugar in a Sara Lee cake—it is an ingredient. And I don't know anything about baking or measuring different quantities.

Drink the Kool-Aid
- Corporate meaning: You have to buy into the corporate culture and believe in the company.
- What it really means: Working is miserable, so you must trick yourself into thinking that it is awesome, mostly by pretending that Ultimate Frisbee outings and happy hours are better than not doing those things. This phrase originated from a mass suicide orchestrated by Jim Jones—the zealot, not the rapper. Baaallllliiiiinnnn'!

Working Life

Office Etiquette

The office is a minefield of potential faux pas waiting to happen. Let us be your Angelina Jolie as we walk through the Cambodian jungle of office etiquette to pinpoint potentially explosive situations. No Capri pants please—in spite of the ostensible dangers, this "jungle" is actually very well air-conditioned.

Office Dress

Unless you were a certain type of person (i.e., a terrible one), you probably didn't roll around campus on the business casual tip. More than likely, you rolled in the college uniform of sandals, hoody, and mesh shorts. It's time to step up your wardrobe. Certain types of industries will breed a greater emphasis on appearance than others, but looking good will rarely hurt you. And if it does, you can probably sue.

Getting some fresh work-appropriate gear can actually be pretty enjoyable when you realize the dapperness potential you've been hiding under raggedy threads. But at the same time, it's also sort of depressing to realize that the main intent is to blend into the new surroundings by wearing "corporate camouflage." So, while uncouth flamboyance is not recommended, try to do something to keep a little bit of your personality in your work clothes. If not wearing underwear is what it takes for you to feel like you at the end of the day, then that's what needs to happen.

Guys. Essentials to a burgeoning gentleman's wardrobe include dress khakis, gray wool slacks, long-sleeve button-down shirts, and dark shoes. A good black belt will go a long way, as will a couple of versatile blazers and ties. Black wingtips will fly straight in a formal environment, but if your office is a little more casual, then boat shoes will keep you afloat perfectly well. As for shirts, note the difference between nice dress shirts and "clubbing" shirts. The difference is sort of difficult to describe, but if it's black or has extremely colorful stripes, that should give you pause. And if anyone ever asks if you're from Jersey and you aren't, throw away what you were wearing immediately. A good way to save money and hassle is to buy non-iron shirts.

Where to Go: J. Crew, Banana Republic, Brooks Brothers, J. Press, Thomas Pink.

Girls. Dress for the ladies is a whole other Pandora's box. As Hillary Clinton can tell you, showing some skin can draw completely unnecessary attention, and you never want your clothing choices to be the first thing someone notices about you. The key is to strive for stylish rather than sexy—you don't want to stand out too much, but that doesn't mean you have to throw your own sense of fashion out the window.

When you hit the shops, think about choosing fabrics that you can wash at home to save on dry cleaning costs (wool and cashmere are comfy and may be necessary in winter, but they will definitely run up the bill). Furthermore, consider going a size bigger for work than you did in college—work clothes are meant to be relaxed, and they don't need to show "every curve," as they say.

Specifically, you will probably want one or more of the following: slacks and a skirt that stops somewhere reasonably close to the knee (could be above or below, but no mini skirts); sweaters, blouses, and collared shirts; and flats or moderate heels. The shoe department is an appropriate place to exercise a little creativity. Stylish shoes with subdued clothing can make a great fashion statement, and they probably won't garner too many disapproving looks. Accessories are another place to have fun, since it's easy to add a little flavor without drawing undue attention. As for gettin' your hair and nails did, the best advice we can give is to keep it conservative: go with muted tones for nail polish (no hot pink or blood reds) and keep your hair controlled and out of your face (consider wearing it up if it's below shoulder length).

Where to Go: Zara, H&M, Theory, Banana Republic, J. Crew.

Casual Fridays. Casual Fridays are just an excuse for grown-ass men to wear Crocs. Do as you wish, but remember that "Casual Friday" is not a government-sanctioned event, so not everyone else you do business with will understand why you are wearing cargo pants and some Tevas. If you have business with clients outside your office, plan accordingly.

Note: If you're uncertain about the dress code, call HR and inquire about appropriate attire. Get enough clothes for the first week, but wait untill you've seen what other people wear before going on a shopping spree.

Internet, E-mail, and Phone

For most people, one thing that remains constant between unemployment and employment is that they spend most of their time online and on the phone. But while it used to be just Big Brother and "Net Nanny" on your case, you've now got to contend with company HR departments and nosy bosses. You're still surfing the 'net, but there are sharks in the water. Here are some tips for remaining above board.

Internet

We would like to suggest that if you can't go to HoodTalk.org on your work computer, you should probably think about quitting. But we're willing to concede that things aren't always that simple. Depending on what your job is, you may be able to explain frequent sessions on YouTube or Perez Hilton, but sometimes your company will block certain sites. In general, let common sense be your guiding light. Porn, even when used for "pre-gaming" before a bathroom break, is out of the question. On the flipside, if you have unfettered access to the Web, but know your friend is heavily monitored, think before sending out links and be sure to add a lame but useful "NSFW" caveat ("Not Safe For Work").

E-mail

First things first: if the company you work for doesn't block personal e-mail sites (like Yahoo!, Gmail, etc.), then there's probably no reason to give your work e-mail to your friends and family. Mixing business and pleasure in your inbox could be risky, and it can also garner you some mad weird spam that is at once professional and tawdry. Worst of all, things that you don't even send can get you in trouble, so be wary of letting your friends recap your weekend behavior over company e-mail.

Once you've figured out that conundrum, you've also got to deal with the e-mail etiquette expected in an office. Here are some tips for switching up your e-mail game to remain work-appropriate and professional:

- **Formalize your language and tone.** Once you get to know your boss and coworkers, you can gauge how they correspond over e-mail and begin to adapt a bit. But part of professionalism is cleaning up the language and grammar of your e-mails.

- **Proofread, proofread, proofread.** Read over everything before you send it and check the spelling of names against the address you're e-mailing.

- **Don't inundate people with CCs.** If someone doesn't know why he or she is receiving a copy of an e-mail, you have erred.

- **Beware of the reply-all.** One of the biggest pitfalls in the entire office environment is the "reply-all" button. Everyone from government officials to CEOs to interns can fall victim to an inadvertent "reply-all," or a reply that was supposed to be a forward. Usually, replying all is just annoying for other people, especially if you are replying to the entire office. But when you reply to an e-mail that your boss wrote and you say, "WTF, does he really expect us to do that?" then you're flirting with job termination. Best to make a recipient list and check it thrice before sending an e-mail.

- **Forward thinking.** Beware of forwarding confidential documents, even if it's to your dad or best friend to ask for help in deciphering them. A company could easily fire you for this, and someone on the other end could also get in trouble (especially if the FCC catches on).

- **Don't jump the gun.** Make sure you have read through all the replies to an e-mail before adding your own commentary. No one likes to hear the same thing five times (unless it's "How You Remind Me" by Nickelback).

- **Step up your subject lines.** Titling every e-mail "yo" will no longer cut it, not only because it is too informal, but also because most people receive an absurd amount of work e-mail and need to be able to search their inboxes easily. Something along the lines of "January Expense Reports" is better.

- **Don't be a stick in the mud.** Socializing isn't what it's used to be, and people have become accustomed to interacting almost exclusively via the computer even though they work 50 feet away from one another. This is not an excuse to be a recluse (on the contrary, it's important to have real contact with people). You can, however, use e-mail to your advantage in the office. Send a link to a coworker if you think he or she will find it interesting. E-mail someone in another department if you'd like to grab a coffee and learn about what other things the company does. Or join in the joking if you think it's appropriate—avoid racial or sexual jokes and other blatantly offensive things, but don't feel you have to be completely humorless.

Tips & Tricks: Clean Up Your Online Identity

Once you're employed (and even when you're job-hunting), it's sometimes wise to think about the image you're projecting online from a slightly more cautious vantage point. While everyone loves to scroll through hilarious pictures and "About Me" sections, there's just no way you'll be able to justify getting fired for something you posted online. Avoid blogging about confidential information or badmouthing your company/coworkers on the 'net, and be sure to check out our tips for adjusting your Facebook privacy settings on page 95.

Working Life

Tips & Tricks: Log All Work-related Chats

Since you are now chatting about work rather than cheating on your boyfriend or girlfriend, you shouldn't feel scared to enable "logging" in your AIM account (or whatever IM program you're using). People will send you phone numbers, figures, URLs, and other important information. By logging each chat, you save yourself the embarrassment of asking someone to repeat themselves if you forget what they wrote or accidentally close the window.

Phone

Being professional on the horn is something for which many recent grads are woefully under-prepared. Still, as the resident newbs, many are forced to act as stand-in secretaries. Some positions have a specific protocol you need to learn, and if you work on a desk at a talent agency (think Lloyd in *Entourage*), you may even have a script that you have to follow to the tee. Get familiar with the standards expected in your office and learn to take down the necessary details. Few things are as embarrassing as calling back a client and asking them to remind you of their name and vital stats.

When it comes to personal phone use in the office environment, a certain degree of common sense and decorum is required. Ever wonder what it's like to have a wiretap? To find out, you can either sell drugs on a massive scale, or you can work for a big company. As messed up as it sounds, someone might be listening in, so it's probably best not to talk about last night's deviance (unless you were doing your sister's statistics homework). Even if the mysterious "HR" is not piped in, beware of coworkers lurking in nearby cubicles pretending to be listening to music—you know they surreptitiously mute it whenever you get a call! If you need to deal with a personal matter feel free to do it quietly and politely, but if you are going to complain to your mom about your roommates or plan an "Asian Massage Parlor"-themed party with your friend, find the time to step outside and use your cell phone. Or wait until after work.

Instant Messenger

One of the most upsetting realizations about many offices is that IM is the prevailing mode of intra-office communication. On the one hand, it's sort of odd to IM with someone sitting literally a few feet away from you. But on the other hand, it is very odd to IM with someone 30 years your senior. While you may have grown up using IM to gossip and flirt with sexual predators online, your older coworkers were likely introduced to it solely as a business tool. Don't get caught in the trap of treating IM as a green light for being unprofessional. Here's how *not* to do it:

> **SeXyNeWb:** wazzzzzzupppppp, muthafuckaaaa!!!!
>
> **LeRoyJenkins:** Hello, could I ask who this is?
>
> **SeXyNeWb:** im the new asst. can I ask u sumthin? i am so lost! LOL
>
> **LeRoyJenkins:** Oh, hi Karen. I didn't know that this was your screen name. What can I help you with?
>
> **SeXyNeWb:** i don't know where the stapler is. i would ask jon but he's sorta weird, right? LMAO! he smells like full-court basketball.
>
> **LeRoyJenkins:** You can check in the supply closet in the hallway. There should be a few in there, but if not you'll have to order a restock. I believe your orientation packet has a map that points it out.
>
> **SeXyNeWb:** yah i think i lost that! i am a little hungover ;)
>
> **SeXyNeWb:** my boyfriend and I got in a big fight and I got a little frisky with the pinot... hehe
>
> **SeXyNeWb:** brb... sum weirdo from my middle school is IMing me... wt fuuuu
>
> **SeXyNeWb:** u there???? I still can't find anything!
>
> LeRoyJenkins is idle (4:35pm)
>
> **SeXyNeWb:** lataz
>
> SeXyNeWb is away (OMG this is CRAZY guuurls!!! www.twogirlsonecup.com)

What Went Wrong? Ah, so many things. This conversation has more mistakes than Sinbad's Wikipedia page. Let's assess the damage.

- **Change your screen name.** Whatever you thought was hilarious in fourth grade is probably wildly embarrassing or inappropriate now.

- **Announce yourself.** Don't just jump straight into a question or a demand—write something like, "Hey, sorry to bother you. Got a second?" If you've never IM'ed a person before, say who you are. Figure out what screen names you will need in order to correspond with everyone in your department.

- **Avoid IM lingo.** If your coworkers are dropping "LOLs" and "brbs" all over the place, feel free to join in. But don't assume that everyone knows all the acronyms.

- **Be as clear as possible.** Take hormones and booze out of the equation and IM is still a hot zone for mixed messages—get to the point and say what you mean. Similarly, if you've got something lengthy to say, it's better to send someone an e-mail, pick up the phone, or go talk to someone in person.

- **Do some buddy list housekeeping.** If you're rocking a screen name from way back in the day, you might want to change it or consider deleting some of the 400 buddies you've accrued since middle school. You don't want your past sneaking up on you in the workplace, so take precautions.

- **Show your status.** SeXyNeWb wasn't the only one making mistakes (though we can't blame LeRoy for taking a breather from that convo). If you are away from your computer, let people know. Word of warning: "I am here but am playing a computer game that takes up my whole screen" will not be looked upon favorably.

Interview: Do I Have Imposter Syndrome?

When you are at the bottom of the age and inexperience pile, adjusting to the workplace can be particularly tough, and it's not uncommon for recent grads to harbor fears that they are not really as bright as their résumés suggest (and their coworkers assume). To get to the bottom of these feelings of inadequacy, we called Dr. Valerie Young, who studies a phenomenon that she calls "Imposter Syndrome."

What is Imposter Syndrome? Imposter Syndrome is an often unconscious feeling deep down inside, the idea that [you are] not really as bright and capable and competent as everybody seems to think. People who typically experience Imposter Syndrome have achieved some measure of success, whether it's getting into college or graduate school, getting good grades, and so on, but they just have a hard time internalizing that success. They kind of explain it away.

What would be the telltale signs that one is really suffering from Imposter Syndrome, as opposed to just general anxiety about life? I have heard people say, "I figure, if I can get a Ph.D. in Astrophysics from Cal Tech, anybody can." Constantly being sort of dismissive

Working Life

Imposter Syndrome Continued...

of your compliments—that would definitely be one sign. If there is a certainty that every time you do succeed you feel like, "Phew, got through that one, but the next time I'm not going to be so lucky," then that's something you need to pay attention to.

What do you suggest people do on a practical level to address it? I think the first step is to break the silence and realize that there is a name for these feelings. The problem is that people think that they are the only one that feels this way and that's where the fear and the shame of stigma kicks in. Also, I think a lot of it is keeping entitlement in perspective. I think of entitlement as saying to yourself, "Aren't I entitled to make a mistake? And aren't I entitled to not know all the answers?" Finally, redefine competence as not knowing how to do everything yourself, but rather knowing how to identify the resources that you need to achieve the goal.

Is it possible to express to your superiors that you are feeling like a fraud and that it affects your job execution and/or enjoyment? You know, I don't think I would bring up to your boss that you feel like a fraud. Give yourself permission to feel really off base for the first six months or nine months, but recognize that this is how people feel when they start a new job because you are learning new systems, new acronyms, and a whole institutional history that other people know about and you don't. So, you go into this new job and you don't know what's going on and it's not like if you were any smarter you would know what was going on. It's not an intelligence thing, it's looking at it differently and saying, "Well, why would I know what's going on?"

Beyond Your First Job

Depending on when you've come across this book, life beyond your first job might seem way too far off in the future to even begin contemplating. But since the Bureau of Labor Statistics reports that the average American works 10 jobs between the ages of 18 and 40, it's likely that sooner or later, you'll get to the point where you will think about moving on to new pastures. Whether you are considering switching jobs within the same field or trying something completely new, it can feel daunting (and sometimes a bit awkward) to get out of an existing gig that pays the bills. However, it's important to remember that it's the perfect time in your life to take calculated risks. Unlike juicing "unsheathed" or sledding alone, some risks have potential benefits.

Working Life

Tips & Tricks: Job-hunting While You Have a Job

If you can't afford to quit your current job until you've found a new one, job-hunting can be a bit of a struggle (especially if you don't want your current employer to know you are looking elsewhere). In order to play it extra smooth, schedule interviews during your lunch break or take strategic vacation days to accommodate any traveling or interviewing that you might have to do. You can also utilize phantom doctor's appointments (be ready to explain what the hell's wrong with you) or squeeze in early morning breakfast meetings before work.

On his blog (blog.pmarca.com), Netscape co-founder Marc Andreessen offers the following *Fight Club*-esque philosophy on careers:

The first rule of career planning: Do not plan your career.

He argues that instead of trying to map out a 40-year plan, recent grads should spend time developing skills and pursuing opportunities. You are almost certainly not going to spend your entire career with the company you work for right out of college, so don't let it be the reason that you pass on a riskier (but potentially better) opportunity. Furthermore, without kids or a mortgage, you have a lot of freedom to take an "income risk" (a pay cut) and/or "geography risk" (moving to a new city). Being flexible will introduce you to new things and build a foundation of experience and knowledge in diverse arenas. While being the best at one thing is necessary in set-skill jobs like being an NBA power-forward, Andreessen notes that having a diverse range of talents is a very attractive trait in most industries. As *Dilbert*-creator Scott Adams points out, if you can't be the best at one thing, "become very good (top 25%) in two or more."

Of course, hopping around the job market (and country) at random might not be a great idea. But it's never too late (especially not after one job!) to reconsider what you want and figure out an alternative. Only depressed middle-aged people are allowed to refer to work as an interminable prison camp that has been systematically overlooked by human rights watchdogs—you have way too many escape routes to feel like you're battling against destiny already.

As for the interviews themselves, prepare yourself thoroughly for one inevitable question: "Why do you want to leave your current job?" The real reason might be that you despise your boss and feel degraded when he makes you expense his trips to the strip club. But being positive will leave a much better impression—say that you feel you've outgrown your current position, or that you are looking for a new challenge. However, don't forget to talk up all the stuff you've learned at the job you want to leave. You are evolving from a smart but untested college grad into a smart and semi-experience twentysomething. And believe us, employers know the difference.

Good reasons to leave your job:

- It is affecting your health.
- You are chronically tired or depressed.
- You are being harassed.
- You are 100% sure you are in the wrong industry.
- You want to move to a new city.
- You don't think you would like doing what your boss or boss' boss do.

Bad reasons to leave your job:

- You just don't like working in general.
- You are in an office relationship that has turned sour.
- There is not a Starbucks close enough for your liking.
- You have done something illegal.
- The pay is higher at another job but the work is less interesting.
- Other offices have better vending machines.

Working Life

Chapter V: Money, Healthcare, Etc.

Money, Healthcare, Etc.

For the vast majority of recent graduates, life is not all about the Benjamins—it's all about the Washingtons, Lincolns, and Hamiltons. Starting salaries don't go all that far in the world of student loan payments, health insurance, food, and rent. We've got bills, bills, bills like the first coming of Destiny's Child, but unlike those three lovely songbirds, we don't lay the golden eggs of quality pop music. If we're lucky, our parents will help us out a bit. But the longer we stay dependent, the worse off we'll be in the long run. From our money to our health, it's time to take responsibility for the basic infrastructure of our own lives as we make the transition into the world of self-reliance. Believe it or not, insurance and taxes don't pay for themselves.

First and foremost, let's talk dollars and see if we can make some sense. It is sometimes comforting to believe that all the mistakes we make now—like binge drinking, burrito-only diets, and unprotected intercourse—won't affect us when we're older. But one thing we can't ignore is fiscal irresponsibility. Between credit scores and compound interest, the American financial institution is designed to reward long-term saving and responsibility. So while a booze-soaked week in Acapulco hopefully won't be held against you when you're 65, your money and the people you owe it to are the proverbial elephants in the room. They are big, powerful, and have very good memories.

But let's not blow things out of proportion. If you haven't started saving or building a credit history yet, there's no need to freak out and start robbing banks. While handling your finances requires patience and a bit of forward planning, the best place to start is by developing the perspective that your behavior today could make future investments (e.g., mortgages and auto financing) easier and less costly. Even further down the line, it could also lay the road for a comfortable retirement. According to a KPMG survey of college students, 47% of respondents said they would like to retire between 51 and 60. If you are one of those people who wants to be laid out on the beach before you're a sexagenarian, responsible saving is one of the best ways to make that happen.

Furthermore, if you want to even reach retirement, you're going to have to take care of yourself and make sure you don't end up in the ER with a broken femur and no insurance. Getting kicked off your parents' insurance policy does not mean that you should just "roll the dice." Hopefully, your job will provide you with full healthcare benefits, but even then you may have to deal with the hassle of finding doctors and dentists who will take your insurance. Don't ignore these issues, because the risk of ignoring healthcare is really not worth the reward.

In this chapter, we hope to give you the foundation you need to make informed decisions about issues relating to your personal "infrastructure"—in other words, the things that allow you to stay healthy and function comfortably on a daily basis. We'll help you budget your expenditures, pay off your debts, insure your good health, and generally smooth the path toward self-reliance. You could also read

"Self-Reliance" by Ralph Waldo Emerson, but bear in mind that he once harbored known tax-evader Henry David Thoreau on his property. And you've got to ask yourself some serious questions about a man who lets another man live in a cabin in his backyard.

Budgeting

Even though it sounds like something that no one under the age of 60 would actually do, creating a budget is an essential first step in sorting out your personal finances. Until you know how much money is flowing in and out of the coffers each month, it's difficult to make informed decisions about saving, investing, and tackling student debt. Thankfully, budgeting doesn't have to involve keeping every receipt or writing a journal entry every time you buy a smoothie (though getting this granular can work for some). It's more about being honest with yourself and having a sense of where your money goes. If you are just starting to earn a steady salary and handle your own bills, it takes a bit of time to understand how much everything costs each month. One thing is for sure, though—you'll be surprised at how much of your paycheck is missing after taxes, rent, food, and other expenditures have been tallied up.

To start a simple budgeting routine, set aside five minutes to plan out each month's spending: How much is rent going to be? How much is your monthly student debt repayment? How much do you spend each weekend on eating out, going out, etc.? (Multiply by four.) How many nights will you order in and how much does that really cost? How much do you spend on groceries? On transportation? Cable? Haircuts? Movies? Cell phone bills? Electricity? Ebay auctions? You get the idea. Add it all up. Is it less than your monthly salary? If so, you're in the clear (though bear in mind that maxing out each month is not ideal). If not, adjust accordingly. Do you really need to get coffee each morning from Starbucks when you get it for free at work? And what about lunch—could you save $20 a week by bringing your own food a couple of days? At the end of each month, see how you fare—were you above or below what you expected to spend? Over the course of several months, you'll start to see trends and become more adept at monitoring your own habits.

Top 10 Things Grads Waste Their Money On

1) Drinking/Partying. If you want to keep living "the dream" (perhaps something to reconsider), you'd better wean yourself off Grey Goose and become a walking Wikipedia of happy hours.

2) Coffee. Some very bright people have done the math on coffee shop culture, and it is not beautiful like the equations Russell Crowe scrawls on windows. Assuming you average $3 on coffee per day (which is not so drastic considering the prices they charge these days), you could save nearly $700/year and direct that money into a savings account with a 6% yield. After doing this for 10 years you'll have $10,000!

3) "Shared" furniture. A lot of people decide to split all apartment costs with their roommate(s), including furnishings. But what happens when one person owns a fifth of a television and half a dining room table? How do you calculate depreciation when buying out everyone else's share? Deciding beforehand who is responsible for different essential furnishings and then buying them independently allows each person to have ownership over something that they can later sell or take to a new apartment.

4) Dates. Instead of being shortsighted yet simple (i.e., men make the rules), gender roles these days are just confusingly vague when it comes to going out on dates. Do you "go Dutch," whatever the hell that means? Or does the person who issued the invitation pay? These are tough questions, but one thing is clear: dating is a huge waste of money and it's advisable to curb the cash-over-quality approach to courtship. If you're doing it right, making out is free of charge.

5) Enormous TVs. Yes, a huge plasma flatty will make *Willow* look AMAZING, but is it really necessary in an apartment that costs about half as much per month? It's your money, but if you save it you will almost certainly be able to afford something top of the line by the time your surroundings warrant that sort of television experience.

6) Cell phone perks. If you have a job, daytime chatting is much reduced. Also, if you have a BlackBerry, are you really texting as much as you used to? Track your usage for a couple of months and consider scaling back your plan.

Top 10 Things Grads Waste Their Money On Continued...

7) Late payments on credit cards and bills. Unless you have a very shady landlord, there are no massive Samoan men to break your kneecaps when you are late on rent. You will, however, incur penalties and damage your credit. Consider signing up for automated bill pay to avoid late payments on all your bills (see p. 152).

8) Extraneous subscriptions and memberships. Gyms, University clubs, Netflix memberships... it all adds up. Think about how often you use these services and how much they're worth to you. Does your employer offer reduced price gym memberships? Do you really watch enough Showtime to justify the cost?

9) Eating out. Give a grad a fish, and he eats for a day. Teach a grad to cook a fish, and he saves sick amounts of money. Even making your own lunch or bringing leftovers to work a few days a week can make a huge difference.

10) Energy expenditures. Leaving the lights on all day, pumping the heat to sauna levels, and leaving plugs in the wall for no reason are not only bad for your energy bill, but also the environment. Do everyone a favor and budget your electricity and gas usage.

Student Debt

We hate to admit it, but there's a good reason pundits like to call us "Generation Debt." Half of the class of 2007 left school with over $20,000 in student loans to pay off, and many feared they owed so much that they'd be halfway through their working lives by the time they broke even. But this isn't the time to herald the apocalypse—it's just time to get your act together.

Since you probably took out a different loan each year, and possibly from different providers, check the National Student Loan Data System online to see where you stand. Since the NSLDS is not always accurate, you will then need to contact each of your lenders to confirm what you found (you really don't want to get it wrong). Once you've done this, you'll recognize that you've fallen into one of two categories: 1) you can afford to pay off your debt as is, and possibly even prepay some, or 2) the payments are too taxing on your budget and you need some relief.

If you've fallen into the first category, then things are looking up—you can prepay your debt (and thus avoid losing money on interest), or you can just repay it on the original schedule provided by your lender. If you've fallen into the second category, there are still options. You can try to consolidate your debt, thereby decreasing your monthly payments and spreading your repayment schedule over many years. Or, if worse comes to worst, you can attempt to get your loans "forgiven." Regardless of where you stand, it's worth considering the pros and cons of all options.

Prepaying Student Debt

Drumming up the money to prepay all of your debt (or even a portion of it) today may seem daunting, but it's the best way to minimize the net cost of repayment and move on with your life. Why? Because you bypass all of the interest that accrues when you pay over time. Let's recap a little Economics 101: the original amount of money you received from the lenders is called a **principal**. When they ask for a monthly debt repayment, it includes not only a portion of the principal, but also a little "extra" on top of that called **interest**. The interest is derived by applying the interest rate to your outstanding principal. So the more debt you have and the longer you keep it, the more you'll pay overall.

The Perks of Student Debt

In many ways repaying student debt is like going to a good massage parlor—quite expensive, but there are perks. The first perk is the **grace period**. After you graduate, you can stall your debt repayment for up to six months (check with your lender before doing so). However, it's important to note that if any of your debt is unsubsidized, the unpaid interest during the grace period will capitalize (i.e., be added to your principal) unless you pay it yourself. The second "cherry on top" is the fact that a portion of your student debt interest is tax deductible (see p. 165 for more).

What Exactly Is Student Debt Consolidation?

In its simplest form, student debt consolidation on Federal (e.g., Stafford, PLUS) and private loans enables you do to any or all of the following: 1) combine all of your loans into one loan, with one interest rate, and with one monthly payment; 2) decrease the amount of your monthly payment by asking you to pay over a longer period of time (up to 30 years); and 3) lock in your interest rates. It may help you hit your monthly budget, but there's also a downside—the reason that the consolidator is willing to allow you to pay less each month is because it can make more money off of your loan in the long-run. In fact, over a 30-year period, you may pay up to three times as much as if you had repaid your debt on the original schedule.

How to Pick a Student Debt Consolidator

Choosing a consolidator requires a fair amount of due diligence, but it's worth taking the time to do it right—after all, your relationship with the lender may last over 30 years. As of the date of this volume, many of the lenders who consolidated government loans have left the market (e.g., Sallie Mae, NelNet) due to the credit crisis. Thus, if you have Federal loans, you will most likely have to consolidate through the government. The website loanconsolidation.ed.gov is a good place to start, but you'll eventually want to call one of the helpful attendants at the government's hotline (1-800-557-7392) to explore your options. These are basically three-fold: 1) a **standard repayment loan** that does not extend your repayment schedule past 10 years but does fix your interest rate and combines your loans into one; 2) an **extended or graduated loan** that draws out the life of the loan—you can either make a consistent payment each month or pay less now than you will in the future (when you're hopefully making more money); or 3) an **income contingent loan** where repayment is tied to—you guessed it—your income.

In terms of finding consolidators for your private loans, the first step should always be to call your lender (i.e., the organization that originally lent you the cash). You'd be surprised, but many of them may offer to consolidate your debt rather then have someone else do it, or at the very least pass you along to a partner. However, whenever using a private (i.e., non-government) debt consolidator, look out for red flags like companies that resell your debt, non-fixed interest rates, and penalties for prepaying your loans. No matter whom you consolidate with, you should expect some type of discount (0.25%) if you pay your monthly bill with automatic bill pay (see p. 152), and possibly another discount of up to 1% if you make good on all your payments for the first 36 months.

Can I Really Get My Debt Forgiven?

If you *really* can't pay, then yes, forgiveness is possible. But understand that it's forgiveness in the way that your girlfriend "forgives" you for knocking boots with her best friend—in other words, there are plenty of strings attached. Your debt will be paid (at least in part) by a third party if you provide services to their organization for several years. This includes full-time volunteering with organizations like Americorp or the Peace Corps, enlisting for military service, teaching, or offering to help groups such as Equal Justice Works and National Health Service Corps. If you were planning to pursue one of these routes anyway, you might as well accept the added perk of erasing your debt. And if not, at least your karma quotient will be sky high (and your kneecaps will remain intact).

The Bottom Line on Debt

Debt is no joke, and if you don't confront it now it can easily spiral out of control. In dire circumstances (e.g., you're broke and refuse to go to Papua New Guinea with the Peace Corps), you can always come clean with your lender and see if you can work out an alternative arrangement. Remember: bankruptcy and selling organs are not fun options, so if you ever do get desperate, please talk to an accountant or lawyer before doing anything drastic. Also, be sure to visit Gradspot.com for more information on student debt, as well as updates on interest rate changes and lending practices. Good luck!

Bank Accounts

Being suspicious of "banking" is a time-honored tradition that dates back to the days of ancient Greece, when gold was horded in temples by lecherous, inbred priests (at least according to the movie *300*). Sometime later, Adam Smith used his "invisible hand" to invent capitalism, or, as it's now known, "eBay," and banks resembling the ones we know today were born.

Things are pretty well regulated these days, but it is still good to bring a healthy amount of wariness to the process of choosing the right bank. Know that 40% of banks' revenue comes from the fees they charge on consumer accounts. Like going to the movies, the "feature presentation" (i.e., an account) lures you in and then they turn the screws with overpriced concessions like Swedish Fish and Milk Duds (these are the banking equivalent of extraneous charges for things you only sort of want). Unnecessary fees that seem negligible will rack up over time—no matter how many free candies they shower you with, they are out to get you. With a little bit of research, however, you should be able to avoid most extra charges.

Choosing a Type of Account

The most basic account offered by most banks is a checking account, which is preferable to keeping money under your mattress because you can write checks (might be necessary for rent), use ATMs, get a debit card (see p. 158), and not get robbed as easily. You receive little to no interest on your money, but you also pay minimal fees. If your needs are relatively straightforward (i.e., security and convenience), then your best

Money, Health, Etc.

Tips & Tricks: Online Banking

One of the benefits of going with a major bank is the convenience it can provide in online banking and phone support. Online banking offers more freedom (you are no longer a slave to "banking" hours), avoids extraneous fees, and helps reduce the paper trail that is a bullseye for identity theft. (I thought I was immune to identity theft until someone tried to steal my thunder and I realized my identity would be the next logical target.) On top of all that, it's good for the environment. If your employer offers "Direct Deposit" you should sign up for that as well—it's easier for everyone and avoids "human errors" like leaving paychecks at the bar.

bet is to just shop around with different banks and figure out which account has the lowest fees (see below). However, if you decide that you want to earn some interest on your money while it's sitting around, then you will need to think about savings options. The downside of savings accounts is that there are generally more fees involved, and they are more likely to carry a minimum balance that you will be penalized for dipping below. (To learn more about saving and investing options, go to p. 158.)

Choosing a Bank

After the forest has been chosen, it's time to explore the trees in this arboretum of banks. Bank of America is a redwood, Citibank is an oak, and HSBC is a beautiful fern. They may look big and powerful, but 'neath the branches lurk predators. Before choosing a tree on which money may or may not grow, consider the fine print: fees that you didn't bother to read about when you saw the cool Super Bowl commercial will be your downfall. Here are some common traps to look out for when settling on a bank:

- **Minimum balance.** Many accounts will carry a built-in fee for dipping below a set balance, which obviously hurts young people who live paycheck to paycheck and are prone to hover right around that balance.

- **ATM fees.** Some banks have a maximum number of times a customer can use an ATM in a month without being charged. Also, going to another bank's ATM may incur charges from both that bank and your own. Convenience is a big part of choosing a bank, so don't team up with a bank that has no ATMs anywhere near where you live or work. That said, consider using your trips to the ATM as a way to budget—take out all the cash you expect to use for a given week and try to avoid going again.

- **Checking balance.** Some banks charge customers to check their balance over the phone, but online it's always free.

- **Bounced checks.** Be wary of "bounced-check protection" policies that many banks enroll customers in automatically. The bank then covers your "non-sufficient funds" checks up to a certain limit, but you still end up paying the standard NSF fee until you settle the score. Generally, it is better to enroll in the standard overdraft protection plan; the fee is smaller and the bank will just cover overdraft expenses by drawing on your savings, credit card, or line of credit.

How to Write a Personal Check

Never written a personal check? Don't be embarrassed. Just check out this tutorial showing you what to put in each section:

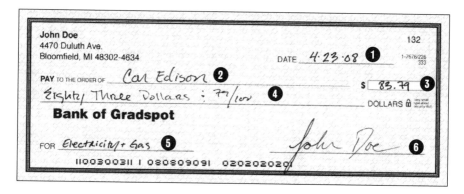

1) The current date.

2) The full name of the individual or organization you are paying. Don't use nicknames or names you just made up.

3) The dollar amount—be very clear with your decimal points and commas.

4) The dollar amount written in long form—cents are written as a fraction in the form of "X/100."

5) Write what the check is for—this part is optional, but it can be helpful for your own record-keeping.

6) Your signature.

Tip: When filling out amounts, avoid blank spaces (someone might sneak in some extra zeros). If you don't fill up the line, you can draw a line through the remaining space.

How to Void a Check

Sometimes you will have to provide a voided check to do things like receive your paycheck from work via direct deposit. To void a check, simply write "VOID" in large print across the face of the check.

Automatic Bill Pay

Automatic bill pay is a simple way to outsource responsibility and maintain good credit. There are two forms of ABP (not to be confused with the semi-delicious coffee chain Au Bon Pain). The more widely used one involves an arrangement between you and a company (e.g., your cell phone service provider) in which you provide them with your credit card or bank account number and they automatically charge you when a bill becomes due. The other, less widely known version of ABP is where you ask your bank to automatically send a check on your behalf to a vendor on a recurring schedule. Setting up automatic bill pay just requires going to your online banking account or calling the bank directly.

Automatic Bill Pay / Credit Cards

Many people are hesitant to use automatic bill pay because they're worried about paying for something without seeing the bill. Conspiracy theorists have their value in certain areas, but we think there are some charges that just aren't worth the hassle and risk of a missed payment. For example, every month you know you're going to pay rent, so why not arrange for your bank to have a check sent the last week of every month? In addition, you know your cable bill should be consistent each month. Other places to consider using automatic bill pay are electricity bills (though you should stay on top of the charges to budget your usage) and any other monthly subscriptions. However, the one place we don't suggest you use it is with your credit cards because who knows when someone will steal your identity and order half of the Hanna Andersson catalog. Just set a reminder each month to pay these, or see if you can create an online account through your credit card provider to receive e-updates when payments are due.

If you do set up automatic bill pay, keep in mind that you can stop it before the pay date. So for example, if you had your rent in the queue and your landlord kicks you out of your apartment, you can stop the check from being sent (although stopping the check is now probably the least of your worries). In addition, companies usually provide a buffer between the dates when you receive your bill and when it is automatically paid, so you can stop it if need be. Think of automatic bill pay as a safety net: you should always review all bills before paying them (automatic bill pay or not), but in the rare event that you forget to pay, automatic bill pay will be there to handle your business and save your credit rating.

Credit Cards

Can't get a job and your parents are kicking you out of the house? There's a simple solution: apply for a bunch of credit cards, max them out on gear and non-perishables, and then fake your own death. Problem solved!

We're joking, of course. Tupac was an exception... credit card fraud is not a foolproof plan. That said, it's a joke with a point: credit cards breed extreme behavior, so beware. Spending that which does not immediately exist is inherently risky, and if impulsivity is the name of your game, it might be good to check yourself before you wreck yourself. **Credit cards should never be used as a way to get long-term loans—at the end of the day, the interest rates that credit cards charge are not competitive.** It's basically like borrowing money from the Mob. And while mobsters are very good in films, you wouldn't want to meet them in real life. If you don't think you will be able to make good on the payments, play it safe and opt for a debit card instead (see p. 158).

Tips & Tricks: Getting Your Credit Report

Even if you feel certain there are no skeletons lurking in your credit closet, you might as well check to make sure there's no funny business going on and to see what organizations have requested to see your information. The three major credit bureaus—Experian, TransUnion, and Equifax—will provide a free copy of your credit report. Forgot about that Target card you got senior year to stock up for Halloween, didn't you?

So, what's so good about credit cards? Glad you asked. There are a multitude of important benefits to having credit cards, assuming that you will always pay them off on time (which we implore you to do). First and foremost, credit cards build your credit rating, which in turn allows you to do things like get mortgages and finance cars later in life. Another benefit of credit cards is the perks they can accrue, such as air miles, free hotel stays, and cash back bonuses. Finally, packing plastic means that when you pay for things, you can just throw down your card and say, "Charge it to the game," which is always a laugh.

Why Don't Credit Card Companies Like Recent Grads?

It's not really a personal thing, it's just business. In college, companies threw credit card offers at us willy-nilly, even tossing in wack T-shirts and mildly inappropriate bottle openers for good measure. But really, they were judging us by our parents, as is the old American tradition. They knew that daddy—with his solid income and established credit history—would be there to bail us out if need be. After graduation, we are judged more specifically on our own merits. Since the two main factors that credit card companies consider are income and credit history, we now look more like charity cases than big ballers. For forward-thinkers, the power move is clear: snag a credit card right before you graduate. It won't expire for at least two years, and if you make good on all your payments, you shouldn't have a problem renewing it as a grad.

Choosing a Card: What to Look For

The main things to consider when choosing a credit card are rewards, cash back, and annual fees. Unless you receive excellent rewards, you shouldn't have to pay a high price for the privilege of using your plastic. Fees might be recouped by the rewards that you accrue, but you often need to do a lot of spending to really make those rewards worthwhile. Furthermore, make sure to find a low interest rate—7% is about the best you'll get. The reason for seeking a low interest rate is just in case you ever have a late payment, but ideally you never will. Instead of getting bogged down in the fine print, just assume the banks never want you to be late and you will be in better shape for it.

Many cards will lure you in with 0% intrest and no annual fee for the first year, but check the fine print and expect things to change for the worse in year two. Use CardRatings.com to compare over 500 cards that are conveniently organized into categories like "Low Ongoing Rate," "Cards for No/Poor Credit," "Cash Back Rewards," and "Gas Rebate Cards." For the needs of most recent grads, the most practical type of card is one that offers cash back on purchases such as groceries, gas, and utilities. Effectively, it's like a magic card that makes all of your essential purchases a little bit cheaper. However, if you travel a lot, it may be worth looking into cards that offer airline miles, or other perks such as free stays at hotels—the American Express Starwoods card receives excellent reviews across the board. As noted above, however, these might not be worth the fees that they carry if you spend relatively little—even $10,000 a year isn't going to get you very far.

Applying for Credit Cards Is Not Like Applying for School

These days, applying to over 20 colleges is considered standard, and Yale doesn't care that you also applied to Michigan and Pomona. However, applying for lots of credit cards in a short span of time makes you look desperate and can adversely affect your credit score. (Here's how messed up the system is: each company you apply to will check your credit history, and the very act of checking hurts your score.) So where should you focus your efforts? For recent grads with no credit history and low income, banks should be the first port of call. If you've been a loyal customer of Bank of America, Citibank, or any other financial institution over the years, they're likely to reward you with some plastic. One fiscal mirage that derails many a thrifty spender is the store credit card. These are easy to get—maybe too easy. Myvesta, a nonprofit consumer-education organization, reports that each time you open a store credit card, 20 points are taken off of your credit score. If you legitimately buy half the J. Crew collection every season, then by all means get a J. Crew credit card. But in general, remember the old saying, "If it seems too good to be true, it probably is."

Deciphering Credit Card Ads

Lawyers can barely decipher the fine print on credit card ads, and even a math major would be hard-pressed to figure out how his bill is calculated. At the end of the day, interest rates should be somewhat irrelevant since you'd ideally pay your balance in full every time. That said, here are a few key things to look out for when assessing a credit card offer.

BALLER BANK

"Charge It To The Game" Credit Card

BALLER BANK
CHARGE IT TO THE GAME

1234 123456 12345

YOUR NAME HERE

CARD OVERVIEW

- Earn up to 5% cash back **1**
- 0.00% APR*
- No minimum payment for 6 months**
- 0.00% balance transfers*** **2**
- No annual fee**** **3**
- $0 fraud liability for any unauthorized use if your card is lost or stolen
- 20 day grace period **4**
- Credit limit up to $20,000

Apply Now!

   * 0.00% APR valid for up to 12 months; Prime Rate + 9.99% APR thereafter. **5** **6** **7** **8**

   ** No minimum payment for 6 months; 3.5% of outstanding balance thereafter. **9**

   *** 0.00% interest rate until the last day of the billing period ending during June 2009; then the standard APR for purchases

   **** Annual fee after first year is $95.

See additional terms and conditions on credit card application.

1) **Rewards:** Air miles? Cash back? Hotel rooms? Are there any stipulations for redeeming the points? Do they offer something you would actually spend your money on otherwise?

2) **Balance Transfer Fees:** Transferring debt between cards may seem like a useful move at times, but look out for the interest charged on these transactions.

3) **Annual Fee:** This fee is paid each year simply for the convenience of having the card. Unless you are receiving exceptional benefits, annual fees should be avoided. Beware of cards that tease with no annual fee for the first year only.

4) **Grace Period:** Kind lenders should offer a grace period, which is the period of time before the lender starts charging you interest on new purchases. You will want a reasonable grace period (e.g., 20-25 days) if you don't always pay your bill in full each month.

5) **APR:** This is the beginning interest rate that you pay on your outstanding balance. Usually, it is a "teaser rate" (e.g., "0% APR!") that will shoot up after the first year, or even sooner depending on your credit score.

6) **Prime rate:** A benchmark used by banks to determine the interest rate. Generally somewhere between 6-10%.

7) **Fixed rate:** This is ostensibly good, because the lender is claiming they won't change the interest rate (e.g., "fixed for life!"). The problem is, they can still just go ahead and change it whenever they want.

8) **Variable rate:** An interest rate that is tied to a standard index. This may sound good if interest rates are going down, but it's not like you can predict the movement of rates for the whole time you're going to hold the card.

9) **Minimum Payment:** Ignore this misleading figure. If you only have to pay 5% of the balance each month, remember that the remainder is just racking up interest that you'll have to pay down the line.

Proper Credit Card Maintenance

First and foremost, **make your payments on time, every time.** Credit cards provide financial flexibility and convenience, as well as some nice perks, but part of the reason for having them at an early age is to build credit and develop responsible habits. Don't cancel any old cards, regardless of whether or not you use them anymore—building a long-term history with a card improves your credit rating, even if you are just maintaining a balance of $0. Never max out a card or charge something that's over 50% of the limit. Creditors see this type of spending as a red flag. That said, credit cards are best used for big ticket purchases that you can easily keep track of, as well as online purchases because of the extra level of security that they provide. The negligible rewards you will earn on small purchases like lattes and gum are not worth the risk of losing track of your spending and then not being able to pay the bill in full at the end of the month. Set up an online account for each credit card to receive alerts and avoid late payments. Finally, make sure you are rewarded for your responsible behavior—request a credit line increase after six months.

Debit Cards

Debit cards won't solidify your "baller status" quite like credit cards, but that doesn't mean they should be thrown out the window (especially if you haven't shredded them into little pieces first). Debit cards are great for people who don't have the financial stability to get a credit card, or who don't trust their ability to spend responsibly and make the payments on time. A debit card is linked directly to your bank account and basically just gives you the flexibility to carry a card instead of cash money. However, there are a few caveats associated with debit cards. Firstly, some merchants don't report debit card transactions immediately (especially if your PIN is not used in the purchase), so stay on top of your balance to avoid an accidental overdraft. Furthermore, certain types of purchases (e.g., meals, gas, car rentals) can result in a "hold" or a "security deposit" that will tie up your funds until the transaction clears. Finally, while using a debit card is more fiscally responsible, it will not help build your credit, and without credit you won't be able to do things like get auto loans and mortgages.

Saving & Investing

Let's face it: there's a lot of concern that the U.S. Social Security system won't be able to support us when we're old geezers playing futuristic bingo and trying to pawn off our baseball card collections. Since the government can't be trusted, it's on us to make sure that we're bathing in the finest artisanal prune juices through our nineties. Even the smallest investment today (just $50 per month) can put you on course for a post-retirement summer house in Aruba—much better than porridge and terrestrial TV in a lonely bed-sit. Thank you power of compounding! Investing is so simple that the only excuse for you not to do it is if you're a modern-day James Dean who aspires to die young and leave a good-looking corpse. But that's just morbid and a bit small-minded. Let's stick to investing, shall we?

Whether you are buying a mattress or going to the movies, every decision you make with your money is an investment. At the heart of saving and investing is striking a balance between making the most of your money today and saving enough for tomorrow. Figuring out the investment horizon for different options is a good place to start—you can remain liquid while earning some interest with a savings account, put away money for 10 years with the hopes of buying a house in your thirties, or pad the coffers to make sure you are comfortable when retirement comes around. Here's a quick guide to these different approaches.

Believe It or Not, You Already Earn Enough to Invest

Irony of all ironies, suckas: just at the time in life when investing benefits you the most, it's also the most difficult. You're finally making some money to store up for future winters, but new responsibilities like rent, car payments, and groceries hit your bank account hard. And unlike student loans, credit cards, and utility bill payments, transferring funds to an investment account is optional, and thus usually ignored. But it's time to wake up and smell the money stacks. If you're able to contribute as little as $100 a month to an investment account, you'll have a sizable portfolio in no time. Coming up with $100 a month is as easy as skipping the daily latte, buying cheaper beers, or smoking less. With compounding interest, that $100 can go a long way.

Explaining the Power of Compounding

The sooner you start investing the better. As soon as you start investing, your own personal money tree will start sprouting new branches due to the fertilizing power of compounding. Check out this chart to see how it works:

Time Value of Money

Case 1: Investment is made now (at time zero), with an 8% interest rate:							
	Year 1	Year 2	Year 3	Year 4	Year 5	>>	Year 30
Investment	$1,000	$–	$–	$–	$–	>>	$–
Value @ Year End	$1,080	$1,166	$1,260	$1,360	$1,469	>>	$10,063
Case 2: Investment is made at the start of year four, with an 8% interest rate:							
	Year 1	Year 2	Year 3	Year 4	Year 5	>>	Year 30
Investment	$–	$–	$–	$1,000	$–	>>	$–
Value @ Year End	$–	$–	$–	$1,080	$1,166	>>	$7,988
Difference:	26%						

Conclusion: By investing the $1,000 today (year one) instead of waiting three years (start of year four), you earn an additional $2,000, or 26%, from your initial investment over 30 years. To earn the same return by investing in year four that you would have earned by starting in year one, you would need to invest an extra $260 ($1,260 total), or 26% more money. This is all due to the power of compounding: not only do you earn 8% interest on your initial investment, but as your investment grows each year (from the interest you receive), you also earn money on that interest. Now imagine if you'd been investing money every year. That's a lot of interest working for you. It's up to you whether you think you should start investing today (we clearly think you should), but by no means should you just have money sitting around. Take advantage of compounding and make your money work for you.

Starting Simple: Savings Account

Investing is the art of earning the highest return (or interest) on your money. For investment newbs, the easiest and least risky way to wrap your head around the concept is a savings account—money may not grow on trees, but it certainly does in banks. Determine a minimal amount of cash you can afford to stash away in a savings account each month (this can be $1, $50, $100, or even $1,000—whatever you can stomach). Now, sit back and watch it turn into a new flat-screen TV. Before you commit, however, be sure to shop around for the accounts that will pay the most interest with the fewest (or even no) fees. While savings accounts allow you to access your money at any time, many banks will charge a penalty for dipping below a minimum balance (see p. 150). As of today, the credit crunch has resulted in slightly lower returns (few acounts have rates above 3%)—still not bad for absolutely no work and the ability to withdraw your cash at anytime. That said, you can definitely get bigger returns elsewhere.

Beginner Investment Options

So you think you can make your money earn more than the 4% per year it could earn in an almost risk-free savings account? Then there is a world of options for you to consider: bonds, mutual funds, index funds, electronically traded funds (ETFs), and traditional stocks. (Of course, if you're really a high roller, there's also the lottery, but rumor has it your odds of being killed in a car accident on the way to purchase a lottery ticket are higher than the odds of actually winning.) The easiest way to get started is by opening an account with your bank or to use an online brokerage firm like E*Trade, Scottrade, or TD Ameritrade (be sure to check with your employer as they may have a deal with one). The problem with these services is they don't offer any individual advice, so you'll need to get familiar with the markets before diving in headfirst. A full-service brokerage form (e.g., Smith Barney) will charge a higher rate, but you will also receive as much guidance as you want on your investment decisions. Whichever route you choose, realize that the stock market provides an incentive for some degree of patience and stability. If you sell within a year of buying the stock you will be taxed 50% on your profits, whereas the tax rate drops to 15% after a year. Thus, when you buy stocks you are theoretically locking up your money for at least a few years.

Investing for Retirement: 401(k)s and IRAs

Of course, any of the investment vehicles we've mentioned thus far could be used to save money for retirement, but Uncle Sam has lent us a hand and set up special types of accounts for retirement planning. They're called 401(k)s and IRAs. These are the ultimate retirement savings/investment vehicles, and while it's tough to think that far ahead when you can't even decide what to have for lunch, we would recommend giving them some serious thought. Why? Social Security aside, statistics show that you'll need about 75% of your pre-retirement income to maintain a similar standard of living (and we do assume you don't want to retire in order to lower your standard of living). In other words, if you're making $150,000 a year, retire at age 60, and live to be 90, then you'll need to have saved over $3,000,000 (assuming you wanted all the money upfront). Plus, you'll probably want some extra padding in your pocket to sort out the grandkids. That may all seems like a lot, but you have the most important element of retirement savings on your side—youth. The sooner you start, the better.

A 401(k) is set up by your employer. The money that you contribute to the account comes straight from your salary and enters the 401(k) before being taxed. Thus, any contribution you make to it is tax-free. For example, if you make $45,000 a year, and contribute $2,000 of it to your 401(k), then you will only be taxed on $43,000 of your salary at year end. Taxes on the $2,000 are paid later when you withdraw the money during retirement. So why bother contributing now? Since your contribution is pre-tax, it means you have more money to contribute, and a larger account grows faster. In addition, instead of paying one-third of that money to the taxman today, why not invest it for your future? Furthermore, employers often "match" a portion of your contribution—all hail free money! You can invest up to $15,000 a year in a 401(k) and the only hitch is that you cannot withdraw the funds until you are 59.5 years old, unless you want to pay a 10% penalty. Although 401(k)s are set up by employers, there are no restrictions on moving it from one employer to the next. Just be sure you won't need any of the money contributed to this account for the next 40 years.

So if a 401(k) is so great, why even consider an IRA? If your employer doesn't offer a 401(k) or you freelance, IRAs are for you. They're set up by you, an individual (that's the "I" in the name). While contributions aren't tax free, withdrawals are (e.g., if you pay taxes on a small amount of cash today that will grow to be ten times its size tomorrow, then you won't pay any taxes on the increase). The icing on the cake is that if you need to withdraw funds before the age of 59.5, there is no 10% penalty. There are many different types of IRAs, but ROTH IRAs are the current cool kids on the block. You can set up ROTH IRAs through banks and brokerage firms.

Taxes

Before we even know what a receipt looks like, it is ingrained in our young minds that "Tax Day" is the worst day of the year—even worse than when your dental checkup fell on Halloween. However, you have to look around and tell yourself the same thing that I told myself when I ran a marathon: if all of these people can do it, then it can't be that hard. Oprah ran a marathon. Will Ferrell ran a marathon. And millions of Americans successfully file their tax returns every year without being incarcerated. So don't fret— not only are you smart enough to do your taxes, but you also have it easier than most given that you presumably have nothing more than a modest salary and a little bit of income from savings and investment accounts to declare. That said, don't treat your tax forms like a school assignment and start at midnight the night before they're due. This is more important than letter grades—it's about dollars and cents.

Basically, there are only two ways to tackle taxes: hire a professional or do them yourself. The D.I.Y. approach is not that taxing (pun intended!), but the problem is that screwing it up can garner you some annoying penalties and unwelcome attention from the IRS. Given that a professional at H&R Block can walk you through your tax return for as little as $75 (treat the fee like insurance against messing it up on your own), we suggest the following strategy: Hire a tax preparer for the first go around so you don't miss any major deductions, but pay attention to the process and take notes so that you can pick up the reins in subsequent years. Whichever route you choose, here are a few things to keep in mind.

Hiring a Professional

Sometimes you've got to spend money to save money. Such is the case when you buy one of those travel fanny packs that goes under your pants, and also when you pay a tax preparer to work his magic and reveal tax loopholes you never knew existed. Deductions come in all shapes and sizes, so it's worth poking around online to see if you might be

Tips & Tricks: Figuring Out Whom You Owe

For recent grads cutting ties with their parents' tax return and moving to new states, the question of whom you owe (and who is going to pay it) can be a tricky one. First and foremost, have a discussion with your parents to make sure they are not still claiming you as a dependent. You don't want to double-file, and they won't receive the W-2 form from your employer if you have started working. Next, think about where you have lived and worked in the past year. You will always have to pay Federal taxes, so that's a given. However, you also have to pay the state where you are a resident, as well as the state where you work (if they are the same, then clearly you only have to file once). Note that some states take no personal income tax from residents (e.g., Alaska, Florida, Washington). If you've moved around a lot, you may want to check in with an accountant or tax pro to make sure you're not leaving anyone out or double paying anything that's unnecessary.

eligible for any before deciding whether it's worth shelling out about $75-200 for a tax pro. To whet you're appetite, try this on for size: assuming your adjusted gross income is less than $65,000, you can deduct up to $2,500 in student-loan interest. Here's another: if you move a significant distance for a new job after graduation, the relocation expenses may be deductible. Good tax preparers should be well-versed in all of these tricks. However, you need to be sure to maintain a paper trail (e.g., check, receipt, e-mail) for anything you pay for that may be deductible. If you say you gave $1,000 in cash to a charity, for example, you need some way to verify that donation.

So, where can you find a pro? H&R Block is the go-to for most people who don't have exceptionally complicated tax returns—their people are affordable and reliable; they offer the flexibility to work online, on the phone; or in-person, and they should teach you all the tricks you need to go D.I.Y. with confidence next time. However, you can also check the Yellow Pages for tax preparers, or just hand everything off to your parents' accountant if you're really lucky. An added benefit of hiring a professional is that you're less likely to miss the dreaded April 15 deadline. Late payment penalties are 5% every month (max. 25%), so if you are low on fundage, arrange for a monthly payment plan with the IRS.

Do It Yourself

If you've just got a W-2 from work and a few 1099 forms from your savings and investment accounts, you might think you can handle your taxes on your own. More than likely you're right, but you probably still need a little more than a calculator and a pen. See if you can get a checklist of tax deductions from your parents' accountant or check out the latest edition of the *Master Tax Guide* so that you're aware of things to look out for. Then, make things easier on yourself by picking up some tax preparation software. It shouldn't run you more than $30 and will make the process much smoother and less shady. Turbo Tax by Quicken makes filing your taxes as easy as completing an online survey—fill in the blanks and let the computer go to work. TaxCut can be accessed via H&R Block's website and is the cheapest option (starting at $15), but it can be confusing for more involved returns. Whichever program you choose, make sure you get an edition that covers both Federal and state taxes.

Once you've got all your forms in order and you've fired up one of these programs, figure out what states you owe and you should be straight within a few hours (that said, don't leave it until the last minute). Before you wrap things up, sign up for electronic funds transfer with the IRS so that you get your money quicker and whatever you owe to the government doesn't get lost in the mail. Finally, remember that taxes are something that everyone has to battle with, so you're not alone: libraries, community centers, and college business departments often hold free Q&As and group help sessions. Just don't wander into AA accidentally...

Keep Good Records

A modicum of vigilance during the calendar year can go a long way toward making tax day manageable. Despite what you've seen in films, it is not wise to show up in an accountant's office with a duffle bag full of random receipts. Unless he is Lil Wayne, he will not say, "Go and get your money little duffle bag boy!" Either way, you're in trouble. So, what do you need to keep? First and foremost, your employer, as well as many of the organizations with which you do business (e.g., bank, brokerage firm), will send you forms at the end of the year that will be essential come tax time. But depending on your situation, you may need more than that as well. The following is a quick reference of the most relevant tax forms and where to get them.

Common Tax Forms & Deductions for Recent Grads

What	Who	Where to Get It
W2 Form from Employer (Annual Salary)	Anyone who is employed full time	Your company must provide this to you
1099 Misc (Freelance Earnings)	Anyone who has freelanced and earned an aggregate in excess of $600 from one source	Each entity who paid you more than $600 for the year must provide you with one
1099 Int (Investment Earnings)	Anyone who has a bank account, stock portfolio, or other investments	Your bank, investment company, and other institutions will each mail you one
1099 DIV (Dividend Earnings)	Anyone who owns an investment that pays dividends	The dividend payer will send this to you
W-2G (Gambling Earnings)	Anyone who struck it rich at the casino or in the lottery	All depends upon where you won, but you should receive this from the casino or lotto authority
1098-E (Student Debt Interest Payments)	Anyone who has student debt	Your lender should provide this to you
1098 (Mortgage Interest Payments)	Anyone who has taken out a mortgage	Your lender or mortgage agent will send this to you
Moving Expenses (can write off)	Anyone who has moved in the past year	You must keep your receipts
Medical Expenses (can write off)	Anyone who is paying for a deductible, COBRA, glasses, prescription drugs, or other medical expenses	You must maintain your own receipts
Job-Hunting Expenses (can write off)	Anyone who looked for a job	You must maintain your own receipts
Charitable Donations (can write off)	Anyone who has donated to a government-recognized charity organization	You will receive an official receipt from each recognized charity

Note: All tax documents that you are meant to receive should be mailed to you by January 31st. If you have not received any documents that you were expecting by the end of the first week in February, be sure to check with the companies who owe them to you. In addition, it is important to note that the information contained within this table refers to the most common tax forms required and deductions taken for recent grads. But every case is different, so consult with a tax professional to ensure you aren't missing out on any other forms or deductions.

Staying Healthy: Insurance, Doctors, and Dentists

Nothing puts a damper on a recent grad's day quite like a broken arm or a root canal that he can't afford. The Independent Insurance Agents and Brokers of America reports that young people age 18 to 24 are less likely to be insured than any other demographic—nearly one in three lacks coverage, and that statistic only improves to one in four for people age 25 to 34. But without good health (which often requires access to quality healthcare), all of the other issues that we discuss in this book fall by the wayside. For those of us fortunate enough to be covered by our parents' policies, health and dental insurance have never been a major concern—whenever we needed to go to the doctor, we did. The receptionist gave us lollipops and we got to play Pac-Man while mom paid the bill. Those were the days...

After graduation, however, you may have to take the reins on your own health and dental insurance. Maybe you feel like you're never going to get sick so you can just ignore the issue. But did you realize that insurance also covers your medication expenses, and if you don't have a doctor, you're never going to be able to refill that Ritalin prescription? Also, have you ever heard the expression "accidents happen"? Hopefully, you've found an employer who will take over your parents' role and pay your insurance, though you'll still have to navigate the issue of finding the right doctors and dentists to take care of you. But even if you are unemployed or work for a company with limited or no benefits, there are still ways to make sure you're not left in the lurch if you run into any problems. If you're confused about healthcare after college, don't worry—we've got the diagnosis right here.

Understanding Your Health Plan at Work

If you're lucky, you won't have an option when it comes to picking a health plan—you're going to take the one your employer offers. Since health insurance can cost upward of $500 per month, it's a big perk that should not be overlooked during the job-hunt. Instead of helping you select a specific plan, we want to run through the different types and what they all mean. That way, when you're handed a healthcare plan at work, you'll know how to decipher the acronyms and utilize it most effectively. However, we would also like to stress the importance of finding out exactly when your company benefits kick in—MSN Money notes that some companies have a probation period before coverage goes into effect. If this is the case, it might be worth talking to an insurance agent about an interim coverage policy.

All health insurance works basically as follows: in exchange for a monthly premium (i.e., what your bosses pay), you can visit doctors or specialists when issues arise, and the insurance companies will pay for what they think it should cost. Sometimes, insurance companies will cover the whole bill, but always keep in mind that they basically reserve the right to pay (or not as the case may be) for whatever part of the bill they want.

Let's take it to the next step. Most insurance plans also require a deductible, a co-pay, or both. A **deductible** is the predetermined amount that you have to spend on medical services in a given year before the insurance company starts to pony up. Then, even once you reach the deductible, the healthcare company might still ask you to pay a small fee (usually between $5-$50) for each visit, called a **co-pay**. And that's where the similarities end and the acronyms begin. Nowadays, almost every company or individual insurer offers a choice between a number of different plans called Managed Care, each of which has its own acronym that doesn't really correspond in any way to what it offers. Fortunately, we've provided a handy guide to acronymic decryption.

> ## Tips & Tricks: Work Freebies for Your Health
>
> Check with your employer to see if they provide free medical services. These don't usually include the type of medical services you'd get from your general practitioner, but rather services like massages or shrinks. Some companies also offer free gym membership (or at least a sizeable discount), and most should have sign-ups for free flu shots in the fall.

HMO. Health Maintenance Organizations (HMOs) place restrictions on the services a patient may receive. Under an HMO, the policyholder chooses a primary care physician (PCP) from the HMO's list. After you choose your PCP, you must visit him or her for any medical issue. The PCP then decides whether your ailment is bad enough to warrant visiting a specialist. But you are only covered if you see a specialist that is part of your plan. This system keeps costs (and the premium) low, but it can be annoying if you want to skip the step of visiting your PCP, or if you don't agree with the diagnosis.

PPO. Preferred Provider Organizations (PPOs) give you a choice of where to receive services, with the possibility of paying more out-of-pocket depending on where you choose to go. If you have a problem, you can go straight to a specialist without first getting approval from your PCP. And if the specialist is a member of the PPO, insurance covers a much higher percentage of the services rendered (up to 100%, depending on the plan). However, if you don't like the specialists on the list and just want to see the best orthopedic surgeon in the area (who happens not to be a member of the PPO), you will only be covered for a certain percentage of the visit.

POS. Point of Service (POS) plans are the beautiful lovechild of HMOs and PPOs. Like an HMO, you choose a PCP and visit him or her for referrals. Once a referral is made, you can choose to stay within the network, or venture outside and pay more out-of-pocket. Sometimes, you can even skip the visit to your PCP if you know the out-of-network specialist you would like to visit.

EPO. An easy way to understand an Exclusive Provider Organization (EPO) is to think of it as a PPO that just jumped into a really cold pool and is suffering from a serious case of shrinkage. The list of providers you can visit is much smaller than with a PPO, and if you go out-of-network, your services may not be covered at all (except in emergency cases).

Getting Healthcare on Your Own

What if you're unemployed, or your employer does not provide complimentary healthcare? While it may be easy to adhere to the "I'm young and healthy and never get sick" mode of thinking, the truth is that you are not invincible, no matter how many Echinacea tabs you pop to ward off colds, you can still cut your hand opening a can of Campbell's Chunky Soup. And, unfortunately, few hospitals will show any sympathy when you can't afford the bill. Basically, roaming around without health insurance is like signing up for a recreational Russian Roulette league. Even if nothing happens in the first few weeks, sooner or later someone's going down. Let's consider some ways to avoid a catastrophe:

Parents. If mom and dad can be convinced to help you out with one expense after college, it's probably healthcare—just use the argument that you "could die without it" and they should back down! Many states allow children to remain on their parents' plan until surprisingly old ages. The great state of New Jersey, for example, allows residents to ride their parents' coattails until the age of 30! This will cost you or your parents around $350/month, but it's cheaper than buying a new policy on your own.

Freelancer's Union. You might be making more than your friend who works for a Fortune 500 company, but you happen to be a freelance writer and you don't have benefits. Enter the Freelancer's Union (FreelancersUnion.org). Through the Union you can get discounted healthcare for as low as $130/month, but with annual deductibles as high as $10,000.

Short-term insurance. Short-term insurance is a nice option for individuals without a history of medical issues. "Emergency" coverage ranges from $40 to $70 per month for a generally healthy 25 year old. If necessary, check-ups and physicals come straight from your pocket, but they cost only a few hundred dollars and are worth the low monthly premium. Check out competitive quotes for short-term plans at eHealthInsurance. Companies like Standard Security Life Insurance of New York, Assurant, and HealthNet provide the best options for young people in need of health care.

> **Tips & Tricks:**
> **What's COBRA?**
>
> The Consolidated Omnibus Budget Reconciliation Act, better known as the semi-poisonous COBRA, enables you to continue health insurance after you have left an employer or after your parents have kicked you off of their plan. COBRA costs between $250 to $500 per month (depending on the cost of your original plan), and it can be utilized for up to 18 months after your old plan is discontinued.

Long-term coverage. This type of insurance is what an employer would purchase for you. Consider it as an option if you don't think you'll get benefits within the next year. Check out eHealthInsurance or Blue Cross Blue Shield to compare quotes. For healthy individuals, long-term insurance ranges from about $250 to $500 per month with a $1,000 annual deductible. (Note: if you have moved and are having trouble finding a doctor, ask around for recommendations, and remember that you can always go on your insurer's website to find a list of doctors who will accept your insurance.)

How to Choose a Doctor

Just because you have insurance doesn't mean you're out of the woods. Now the fun really begins: you get to pick a doctor. Generally, someone from HR will sit you down on your first day, hand you a book of 10,000 doctors, and ask you to pick one. It can feel like you are a teenage girl trying to pick a winner for March Madness—just, like, go with the one with the funnest name! Actually, it doesn't have to be that random, and there are a few simple ways to make an educated choice.

First and foremost, ask around. A good doctor embodies a perfect mix of professional know-how, geniality, and trustworthiness. So, while you can cast judgment on each candidate's med school degree if you want, the best way to find a good doctor is to talk to friends and colleagues to see if they can make a recommendation based on personal experience. Hopefully, any recommended doctors are included in your health plan (i.e., in that big blue book). If they aren't, it's not the end of the world—you can still go to them, you'll just have to pay extra. Only you can determine if you're willing to spend

Tips & Tricks: Flexible Spending Accounts (FSAs)

Another perk offered by some employers is a Flexible Spending Account, which allows you to deposit a portion of your salary, pre-tax, into a special account that can be used on certain expenditures. They include medical expenses and dependent care. Medical expenses include any bills that aren't paid by insurance companies, and dependent care could cover things like day care for all those kids of yours. However, bear in mind that the money you don't use will disappear at the end of the year. Nine out of ten recent grads have never even heard of an FSA, but who knows—maybe it makes sense for you.

more money to go to an "out-of-network" doctor when you can probably find one that is just as good "in-network".

What if you can't get any recommendations? No need to fret, there are other resources at your disposal. Major metropolitan areas usually have magazines (e.g., *New York* and *Philadelphia*) that release a "Best Doctors" report each year. If you aren't the magazine type, you can also browse WebMD and The American Medical Association's websites. Whatever you do, avoid the Yellow Pages—it's not a good sign if a doctor has to advertise to get patients.

Before committing to a doc, be sure to do a little digging first. Check the following background items by visiting the websites of WebMD, Castle Connolly, and The American Medial Association (don't use any pay-for services):

Education. If the doc holds a degree from The University of Phoenix Online, don't line up to see him. There's no need to be snooty and only see Harvard grads, but try to set a reasonable standard to narrow down the most qualified candidates.

Specialty and subspecialty. Find out what type of medicine the doctor specializes in to make sure you're not wasting your time by seeing a podiatrist for a sinus infection.

Membership and appointments. Take a look at what organizations different doctors belong to and what board positions they hold. The more they're involved in the medical community associated with their area of expertise, the more likely they are to be up-to-date with treatments and procedures.

Hospital/Med school affiliations. Top doctors work at top hospitals; top hospitals offer top resources; and top resources mean that you get top care. If you can't figure out which hospitals are the best, any hospital affiliated with a university that has a good med school should rank well.

Disciplinary action. A lawsuit or two may simply mean the physician is willing to attempt more risky procedures. Ten or twenty and you're venturing into dangerous territory. Make sure that he or she has not been charged with serious transgressions, such as sexual misconduct or narcotic offenses (search Castle Connolly). Also, check if the doctor has been fined or had his license suspended or revoked by contacting the respective state board of medicine.

Once you've found your doc and done your due diligence, there's one last step—call up the office and fire some questions at the secretary:

- Double-check that the practice does in fact accept your insurance.

- Ask if they are taking new patients and find out what the wait time for an appointment is. The best doctors are often busier than the police at Mardi Gras, but waiting too long can be hazardous to your health. One to four weeks is a normal wait time; one to four years is not.

- Pay attention to office hours. If the physician only sees patients two days a week for two hours each day, you may want to find someone with better availability.

- Ask how many patients are typically scheduled each hour. Three to five is a reasonable number. Leaving the office for an hour is acceptable, but leaving for four might get your boss asking questions.

- Inquire how after-hours calls are handled, and ask about the doc's availability in case of an emergency; check if any back-up physicians will be accessible if your main squeeze heads to the islands.

- Even if the main office is conveniently located, ask where they do their blood work, X-rays, or other tests so that you don't have to go to the end of the Earth for an endoscopy.

Finally, understand that just because you saw a doctor once doesn't mean you have to stick with him or her forever. By law, doctors' offices have to transfer your transcripts to the next physician. We like to compare finding your doctor to finding a true love: it might take some work, and the first one isn't always the best, but once you find one, you'll have a really beautiful (and healthy) future together.

How to Choose a Dentist

When most people think about setting up healthcare for themselves after college, managed care and general practitioners come to mind. But you can't forget the dentist, because otherwise your teeth will fall out, and then you will look sort of like that dude with "bitter beer face."

Finding a dentist isn't all that different from finding a general practitioner. The best bet is to ask coworkers, family, friends, and neighbors for referrals. Another option is to do some searching on the 'net and call a local periodontist (gums specialists) or a local dental lab to ask them for a recommendation. Finally, you can dig for a dentist's lab online and then call to do a background check. Don your two-brimmed hat for this process to feel like a modern-day Sherlock Holmes.

Once you think you've found a winning ticket, it's time to run it through the ringer. Look out for malpractice suits, and call the state board of consumer affairs to find out if there are any records of actions against the dentist. Has the dentist's license ever been revoked or suspended? Do some Googling to find lawsuits and any other dirt. In this case, no results are a good result. You can also see if the dentist is rated on Dr. Oogle.

Next, it's time to grill the dentist's office. Ask if it's the dentist owns the practice or if someone else owns it. If the dentist is an owner or co-owner, chances are he's more invested in his work and reputation. Also, find out how long he's been practicing. Don't sign up with a new dentist—it takes more than two years for a good dentist to really know what he's doing.

As with general practitioners, you don't have to stick with a dentist just because you go there once. Here are red flags to look out for on your first visit:

- You haven't had a filling in years, yet the dentist insists you need several fillings. (Bear in mind that if you've been sucking down six Cokes a day and you never brush your teeth, maybe he's right.)

- The dentist says you need to replace your silver fillings with plastic or "white composite" ones. Silver fillings last three times as long as plastic ones. And though silver fillings contain mercury, there's little scientific evidence that the mercury content in them is toxic to your body.

- The dentist says your gums aren't healthy and you need "root planing"— a deep-cleaning of tartar in hard-to-reach spots. Few healthy recent grads need such an intensive service.

- The dentist claims you need a crown or multiple crowns.

- Be wary of a zillion dental plans or tons of advertising: a good dentist doesn't need to advertise for patients.

Chapter VI: Cars & Commuting

Cars & Commuting

In order to be the consummate grad about town, it is sometimes necessary to have a car. How else are you going to get to work, pick up your furniture at Ikea, and still make an 8:30 rez at California Pizza Kitchen? Without a ride, it can be difficult to achieve this type of mobility, but sometimes that's the way the cookie doth crumble. Cars are a major additional expense for the fledgling graduate, so make sure you assess your needs and know all your options before throwing your life savings into that Mini Cooper.

Oftentimes, the post-college city that you choose will determine whether or not a car is in the cards. Atlanta, Houston, and L.A. are typical "car towns," and they've got the traffic jams to prove it. Meanwhile, owning a car in Manhattan is a huge extravagance, and you may quickly discover that exorbitant parking fees and the fact that you never actually drive anywhere defeat the purpose of the investment. So, do you really need one? This decision is sort of like one of those "choose your own adventure" books: if you say, "No, I definitely don't need a car," then you can check out our tips for getting around without one (see p. 178) and then skip straight to the end (or to the next chapter, in this case). If you choose, "Yes, I think I need a car," however, you've got quite the adventure in front of you (keep reading). But don't worry—we'll try to make sure there aren't too many unpleasant surprises.

If you decide to go the car route, the first step is to think about whether you are going to buy or lease, what type of insurance policy you need, and where you're going to put the damn thing when you're not out rolling. And what about the thorny issue of financing? Presumably you are past the age where it is appropriate to have a bar mitzvah or apply to be on *My Super Sweet 16*. So, unless someone gets extra generous with the graduation gift, you'll probably have to throw down some money of your own. And if you are already paying rent, a car might just be the straw that broke the bank account. Let's break down the math: a typical month of car ownership can run well in excess of $600 once you add up the car payment ($350), a few gas fill-ups ($100), insurance costs ($150), miscellaneous maintenance (a bunch), and novelty air fresheners ($5). That's a lot of dough that could be put into different pastures, like your savings or videogame consoles.

Still, in spite of the financial drain associated with a good old-fashioned gas-guzzler, we can't deny the pleasure of rolling down the freeway at 66mph in a 65mph zone, bumping Vanessa Carlton and screaming into a Bluetooth receiver. We also can't deny that it's sometimes flat-out necessary to have a car.

In this chapter, we'll cover all the car basics you need to know in order to make an informed decision about riding dirty as a recent grad.[1] From getting around town with-

---

1 Don't actually ride dirty—we just like saying that. "Riding dirty" means driving in an illegal fashion, generally without registration and/or with narcotics in the glove compartment. *See: Chamillionaire.*

out a whip to looking for new and used cars, comparing insurance policies, and staying safe on the road, we've got the car game covered. We understand that for some people, cars are more than just a way of getting from place to place—if there's car you know you want to drive no matter what, then by all means do whatever you can (within the law) to make it happen. But for the most part, we encourage taking some time to find a solution that is as safe and affordable as possible. And that may mean not getting a car at all, so keep an open mind.

Getting Around Without a Car

Not having a car means less worry and more money saved. And, in some cities, it just makes more sense not to have one. But how are you going to "get around 'round 'round 'round" like the Beach Boys if you don't have a whip? Let's consider the alternatives.

Commuting to Work Without a Car

Work days can be trying enough without traffic to contend with, so that's at least one silver lining to a car-less commute. And trust us, there are many others. Here are some other transportation options to explore:

Public transportation. Given NYC's ridiculous traffic, ridiculous parking fees, and excellent subway system, being a "straphanger" in Manhattan is a no-brainer. But even in car-dependent regions like Los Angeles, there are train lines and buses galore. As noted Chapter 2, you may have to make some deliberate choices about where you live if you want to take advantage of public transportation. But remember that in most major cities, a bus is never that far away. Even if they don't go all the way to your office, buses should at least provide an easy way to get to mass transit stations.

By bike, by foot, or by roller-blade. We know all the stereotypes about rollerbladers—neon spandex, old-school Walkmans... propensity to call *Starlight Express* "Andrew Lloyd Webber's best work." But we never let a little ribbing get in the way of an economical commute. There are many ways to get around under your own power, and they have the added benefit of providing a little exercise. A twenty-five minute stroll to work in the morning can really get the blood flowing and foster a much sunnier disposition than implanting your nose in the next man's armpit on the subway. If you live close enough to work to pull this off, the two other factors to consider are weather and hygiene. If you live in a place with extreme heat or cold during certain parts of the year, do you have a viable alternative for those days when even Lance Armstrong would rather drive? Also, if the walk/ride is arduous enough for you to break a sweat, are there facilities at your workplace for you to shower? B.O. will make you the office pariah quicker than hanging a poster of Mussolini in your cubicle.

Carpools. Zipping around in diamond lanes, reading the paper, sipping a fresh Dunkin' Donuts coffee—talk about the life! Websites like RideAmigos, iCarpool, and CarpoolConnect match up commuters with compatible routes and schedules. The "casual carpool" is an intriguing idea that is becoming more common in the United States. It's like Craigslist's "Casual Encounters," only, instead of sexual deviance, complete strangers offer you a ride in their car so they can use the carpool lane. Casual carpools are most prominent in the Washington D.C. area, but they are also found in San Francisco, Pittsburgh, Seattle, and many other cities.

> **Tips & Tricks:**
> **How to Sell Your Car**
>
> If you are moving to a new city or just can't afford the cost of ownership anymore, you may be looking to sell your car. For some people, this maneuver might even be a necessary step toward funding a move. But before you write "For Sale" in dirt on your windshield, do some research to figure out how to keep things kosher and how to make the biggest profit from the sale of your ride. Contact the DMV to find out about transfer of title, registration, and all that good stuff. Then research how much models from the same year with similar mileage are going for in order to price your car correctly (try Edmunds' "True Market Value" pricing tool). Finally, advertise it on Craigslist, AutoTrader.com, and in front of your house. Then sell to the highest bidder. Once you get paid, head straight for the border! (Or wherever it was that you were going).

Cars & Commuting

Joy Riding and Weekend Trips

Sometimes the weekday commute from your house only involves a hop, skip, and a jump, but you still want the flexibility to cruise to the strip mall, hit up an amusement park, or visit your boyfriend every weekend. If your leisure car use is exceptionally sporadic, here are a few alternatives to leasing and buying:

Car rentals. Although the costs of renting a car can add up quickly, it is a viable option for the occasional three-day weekend getaway. If you need wheels, try Thrifty, Enterprise, or Dollar Rent-a-Car. Most major rental agencies have a hefty surcharge for drivers under 24 or 25, which can really hurt a budget-conscious grad. Call ahead before booking to find out what the real rate will be and to inquire about insurance options. Rent-a-Wreck waves the underage surcharge, but don't be surprised if you get a car that Xzibit would laugh at on *Pimp My Ride*. Finally, check to see if your employer gets special rates with any car rental companies.

Car sharing. In a perfect world, you would be able to "own" a car for the few days a month when you need it and you would never have to worry about parking or maintenance. This is exactly the idea behind car sharing companies like Zipcar and Flexcar, which offer access to a huge fleet of autos positioned around most major cities. Monthly memberships start at around $50, and an hour of car use runs less than $10. Before committing, check the sites to see if you live in an area with a high density of cars. When you need one, you just find out where it's parked and then use the access card provided by the company to get into the car. Note that while the hourly rates are low, Zipcars are best used for short drives and errands of a few hours. If you are going away for the weekend, a traditional rental is more economical.

Trains, planes, and buses. They may not be glamorous, but Amtrak trains and Greyhound buses are two convenient, affordable options for getting where you need to go. Also, check for other regional bus services, like the (in)famous "Chinatown" service connecting DC, Baltimore, Philly, New York, and Boston. Many cities are serviced by affordable shuttle flights that run on the hour, so don't rule out flying, either. (See p. 34 for more on finding cheap flights.)

Buying Versus Leasing

While your investment banker friends will probably create models and Excel spreadsheets to determine whether they should lease or buy a car, the decision is not a complex one. You need to consider two factors: 1) How much money can you spend each month on a car (and how much do you expect to be able to spend over the next several years), and 2) Are you the type of person who would be content owning a car for a long time, or are you an A.D.D. type who would rather "try" a new car every few years without the "hassle" of ownership? As far as monthly expenses go, buying a new car is the most expensive option (~$600/month assuming a $20k car and a 6% loan), followed by leasing a car (~$350 for the same car/loan), and finally buying a used car (~$280/month assuming a $10k purchase price and an 8% loan). But here's the kicker: at the end of a lease, you can't sell the car, thus you can't recoup any money—all the dough spent leasing it goes down the drain. After you're finished with a new or used car (5-10 years), however, you can resell it to earn a cash back bonus. Theoretically, if you purchased a car and then sold it at the end of your loan period, the total expense may be cheaper than the aggregate of the monthly lease payments on multiple vehicles over the same time period (but we urge you to do the math on this one before assuming it to be true in all cases). As for what type of consumer you are, only you can really tell—if you preordered the iPhone and own an XBox 360, a Playstation 3, and a Wii, then you clearly like having the newest things and may be a leaser. While we genuinely think the "buy or lease?" question is relatively straightforward, there are a few other things to consider when making this decision. For example, when you lease, all repairs will be under warranty for the term of your lease, whereas when you buy a car, all damage beyond the manufacturers warranty is an out-of-pocket expense. In addition, there may be yearly mileage limits on a leased vehicle, but you'd only really hit those if you had a long commute or took road trips every weekend. If you buy a car, you'll have to lend special attention to maintaining it in order to preserve its resale value (e.g., regularly wash and wax it, park it in the shade, change the oil regularly). And finally, regardless of whether you lease or buy, you still have to purchase insurance, pay DMV fees, and cover all of the other costs associated with driving.

> **Tips & Tricks:**
> **Car Loans & Leases**
>
> Leasing a car is a straightforward process; you get your lease from the car dealership. However, where do you get a new or used car loan from? Check with your local bank, Edmunds online, or Bankrate.com to find a good starting point. However, whether you're leasing or buying, realize that you'll get different terms depending on your credit and income level. (Note: a used car loan will always carry a higher interest rate than a new car loan.)

Cars & Commuting

Choosing a Car

After you've decided to lease or buy, it's time to hone in on the lot and see what kind of steel horse strikes your fancy. When it comes to cars, the choice can be overwhelming—everybody knows that dogs love trucks, but humans often wonder if maybe a sedan or coupe might fit the bill a little better.

As is often the case, the first consideration will probably be cost. Monthly car payments should not exceed 12-15% of your after-tax income, so break out the calculator and figure out a reasonable price range (or use an online car payment calculator). After you've completed that step, assessing the realities of your car needs and wants should help to narrow down the field. Are you going to be stranded in the winter without four-wheel drive? Do you want enough space to handle weekend trips with friends or are you more of a solo road warrior? What standards do you hold for gas mileage and safety features?

Finally, you are definitely going to have to get insurance. And while you probably don't plan to choose a policy until after you've sealed the deal on a car, it should factor into your choice rather significantly. Insurance fees are not based solely on you as a driver, but also on the specific car you own. Vehicles with higher horsepower or cars that have a greater probability of being stolen will draw higher premiums from insurance companies.

So where does that leave us? With a lot of choices is where. But don't worry—this is going to be fun (sort of). Let's break it down.

Purchasing a Used Car

The main reasons for buying a used car are either to save money or to achieve a little retro chic on the road. The two things to remember when jumping into the fray are 1) Used car salesmen have a bad reputation for a reason, and 2) An unreliable used car could end up draining more cash in maintenance and repair fees than a new one. However, not all used cars are jalopies, and when they work out, they are definitely the cheapest option. Shop around at car dealerships (watch enough local network broadcasts and you'll see the commercials), peruse Craigslist and print classifieds, and check out websites like Carmax, ConsumerGuide, and AutoTrader. In addition to accident history, you should research the number of previous owners, past mechanical problems, and maintenance history. Also, find out if the car has ever failed inspection. Run a vehicle history report at AutoCheck.com using the Vehicle Identification Number (see Tips & Tricks on the next page). Once you've poked around a bit, you'll begin to get a sense of the price range on different models and years. However, remember that when buying used cars, it is also important to assess the condition and mileage of the car before determining a fair price. Look for cars that are Certified Pre-Owned (CPO), which means they have been inspected rigorously and are usually covered by a warranty from the manufacturer. CPO cars cost a bit more, but the added warranty

and reliability may justify the cost. Once you've made a decision, don't agree to sign an "as is" statement, which means that as soon as you leave the lot the car is solely your responsibility. Instead, you should be given at least 30 days to make sure the car is in good condition.

Purchasing a New Car

These days, any good car search begins with some rigorous online research, which is a lot more pleasant than traipsing around talking to sleazy salespeople. Start off at the manufacturers' websites to check out cars and options, usually accompanied by slick videos and other digital flourishes. Once you've settled on a few possibilities, check out pricing at Autoweb, Car.com, or ConsumerGuide, then read reviews at *Car and Driver* and Edmunds. If you are considering two options that are similar in price, bear in mind that while one car is cheaper to buy, it may still be more expensive to own. Edmunds offers a "True Cost of Ownership" calculator that accounts for depreciation, financing, insurance, taxes and fees, fuel, maintenance, and repairs over a given time period.

> ### Tips & Tricks: How to Find the Vehicle Identification Number (VIN)
>
> This useful number can be found in the following places: the previous driver's insurance card, the car registration, the VIN plate on the driver's side dashboard, and the certificate label on the driver's side doorjamb.

Hitting the Dealership

The Internet is only a means to an end—eventually you are going to have to get off your butt and get up close and personal with some cars. But beware: the only people who hate window shoppers more than 50 Cent are car salesmen. As soon as you set foot on the dealership lot, be prepared to get pitched to harder than Barry Bonds with the bases loaded (no one will try to intentionally walk you—the one and only thing they want is to have you *driving* out of there).

Because car salespeople are not always the most scrupulous individuals, it is best to come prepared and know exactly what you want. Once you've done your research and picked out a few favorites, take a preliminary trip to the dealership(s) for the purpose of taking some test drives. Never buy a car without a test drive, unless you are the "saving yourself for marriage" type. Call ahead to schedule an appointment and make sure the dealership knows exactly what you want to see. Take a ride that involves a variety of driving situations (e.g., stop and go traffic, tight turns, highway), then gather all the necessary information and get out of there before a wheel falls off the "straight-talk express." The dealer may try to "lowball" you just to get you to come back, but realize

Tips & Tricks:
When to Car Shop

Knowing the ins-and-outs of an enemy organization is a key to success in consumer battles. In terms of cars, this means realizing that most car dealerships impose monthly quotas on their salespeople, so if you go in at the end of the month you might find yourself the happy beneficiary of some desperate deal-making. The same goes for any day that will clearly be a slow one for sales on the car lot. Check the forecast for blizzards, hail storms, hurricanes, and tornadoes—the worse the weather, the better your chances of saving money on a car.

that he or she has no intention of actually selling at this tantalizing price.

Next, head back to the lab and run the numbers on financing options. Look up incentives and rebates to see specials in your area and deals geared specifically at recent grads. Often, you will be offered either a cash rebate or low-interest financing options. Before grabbing the cash, use an online "rebate versus interest" tool to figure out which is the better deal (Edmunds.com has a good one). You can then either call or e-mail local dealers for price comparisons, or get multiple quotes at the same time using Edmunds' "Dealer Locator." Ultimately, take the lowest bidder and then call around to see if any others will meet the price. Once you get a good offer, ask the dealer to fax over a worksheet with all prices, taxes, and fees.

Sealing the Deal

Round One... Fight! When it finally comes time for a purchase, lace up your sparring gloves and get ready to deflect all of the BS that the car salesman is likely to throw your way. Here are some potential scams to avoid:

- **Beware of extras.** Know exactly what features you want, because the salesman will try to throw in as many unnecessary extras as possible.

- **Know your credit.** Don't allow the dealership to run a credit check using your license or Social Security number before settling on a price, as this information may be used to screw you on incentives and interest rates. When it comes to financing, dealers will try to get you to go through their finance department, but the "low APRs" (Annual Percentage Rates) that you heard about on the commercial generally apply only to people with perfect credit or first-time buyers. As a recent grad, you may fit the bill, but it's still worth checking to see if you can get a lower interest rate through a bank. Check

E-LOAN and Lending Tree, or compare loan rates from multiple area banks on Bankrate.

- **Factory fib.** Cars ordered from the factory should not cost more than those in the lot. Also, be careful about letting the salesman locate the car at another dealership; they often charge an unnecessary fee.

- **Signing.** Once the papers have been drawn up, feel free to take them away so that you can review them with a fine-toothed comb. Like Congressmen, car salesmen have been known to "earmark" a few extra clauses in the final copy.

> **Tips & Tricks:**
> ## Car Deals for Recent Grads
>
> In the hopes of building brand loyalty from the get-go, many car companies offer purchasing and leasing incentives to recent grads. All you need to do is to prove your graduate status from an accredited university (depending on how restrictive the program is) and the car companies will offer rebates, special financing rates, and a delayed first payment. Almost all companies offer incentives, so shop around before making a purchase.

Cars & Commuting

Congratulations, you are now a car owner! You are probably feeling very protective, and maybe you have even named your car something like "Don Juan DeMarco" or "Desert Storm." But before you put the pedal to the metal, you've got a few more things to sort out, so keep reading!

Car Insurance

Auto insurance is required by law in almost every state, so dealing with it is less an option than an obligation. There are two main aspects of car insurance—protecting your car and protecting yourself. Whether your car gets jacked from the car lot or you get into an accident that dents both your fender and your forehead, you are going to be glad you're covered. Indeed, driving without insurance is one of the least intelligent things you can do—if you get caught (or worse still, you get hurt), you may incur heavy fines and bills, lose your license, or even go to jail. So, put that college-educated brain to use and do some research to find a policy that works best for you.

When it comes to car insurance, comparison shopping is absolutely essential. Standards for calculating premiums vary considerably across different providers—in *The Quarterlifer's Companion*, Todd Morgano of Progressive Auto Insurance points out that "the cost of a six-month auto insurance policy for the same driver with comparable coverage varies from company to company by an average of $586." That's pretty insane, and it should provide plenty of incentive to consider all the options. For example, can you get onto your parents' policy? This setup is required if the car is registered in their name, but it may also be a good idea if they receive a multi-car or multi-policy discount. Furthermore, if you already have a policy, make sure that you are not wasting money by leaving it unchanged. First of all, it's more expensive to insure a 16-year-old Tyrese wannabe than a 23-year-old with a clean license. Moreover, premium prices tend to fluctuate yearly no matter who you are—if a large number of people in a given group (e.g., age, type of vehicle, number of accidents) files claims in a given year, everyone's rates rise. Thus, you may be able to find lower overall premiums or discounts elsewhere due to changes in age, location, and other factors that determine your rates.

If you do decide to make a change or go it on your own, here are some things to consider.

The Bare Bones Basics

Before picking up the phone for a "15 minute" call to Geico, take some time to familiarize yourself with the different types of coverage.

- **Liability.** Required by 47 states, liability covers accidental bodily injury and property damages caused by an accident (e.g., the woman in the other car's broken butt bone and the neighbor's flattened fence).

- **Collision.** Not mandatory (but purchased by most), collision pays for any repairs to your car after an accident, from a bruised bumper to a busted trunk. It does not pay for damage to the other person's car.

- **Comprehensive.** Also optional but popular (like parmesan cheese or pants), comprehensive pays for losses that are not the result of a collision, such as fire or theft.

- **Medical.** Pays all medical expenses of those in the car regardless of fault.

- **Emergency Roadside Service.** Covers situations like fixing a flat, getting keys out of a locked car, running out of gas, or using a tow truck. Some providers will even pay a bond if you get sent to the big house for a traffic violation.

- **Gap Insurance.** As soon as a car is driven off the lot, its market value depreciates 20-30%. In the case of an accident or theft, gap insurance pays the difference between what you owe (the actual market price) and what the insurance company says the car is worth. For example, if a $25,000 car is totaled and you have collision but no gap insurance, the insurance company will pay $20,000 rather than the full $25,000 that you paid for it. It is generally offered only on new cars.

> **Tips & Tricks: Double Coverage = Double Payment**
>
> Before perusing prices, check any other insurance policies that you hold (e.g., health insurance, renter's insurance); you may already be covered for certain aspects of a car insurance policy. For example, a person with comprehensive health insurance would probably only need to purchase the minimum personal injury protection (PIP) coverage.

- **Personal Injury Protection (PIP).** Being a PIMP is illegal in all states except Nevada, but having PIP is required by some. It covers medical expenses and lost wages for insured drivers regardless of fault.

- **Uninsured Motorists.** Pays for car damage when an accident is caused by someone without liability insurance.

- **Underinsured Motorists.** Pays for car damage when an accident is caused by someone with insufficient liability insurance.

- **Rental Reimbursement.** Dinero for a rental if the wheels on the car can't go 'round and 'round.

Figuring Out What to Expect

The average policy containing liability, collision, and comprehensive coverage costs about $775 per year. However, that figure is dependent on a number of things:

- **Type of car.** Sports cars, large SUVs, and really small cars like the Mini Cooper may be the jam, but beware the higher premiums that accompany these types of automobiles.

- **Car features.** Anti-theft devices, airbags, anti-lock brakes, and automatic seatbelts warrant an automatic price reduction.

- **Theft history.** Models with bad reps get bad rates. Check out theft history to get an idea of how a car will fare on the street. (According to the National Insurance Crime Bureau, the "most stolen cars" in 2006 were the '95 Honda Civic, the '91 Honda Accord, and the '89 Toyota Camry.)

- **Location.** Areas with high accident rates or incidents of larceny raise prices. (We know what you're thinking, but don't do it. Lying about where you live will allow the insurance company to screw you down the line.)

- **You.** Not all drivers are treated the same. For example, young single males can expect to pay more just for being young, single, and male. At least you can't get pregnant!

- **How often you drive.** Long commute? Price increase is absolute.

- **Credit report.** If you missed your last two card payments due to a drunken visit to the L.L. Bean website, it could increase your premium by hundreds.

- **Driving record.** Clean licenses warrant lower premiums.

- **Discounts.** Most companies offer sizable student discounts to those who maintain certain grades. You can also save if you have multiple cars insured (unlikely) or if you hold a renter's insurance policy with the same company.

- **Deductible.** A deductible is the amount paid out-of-pocket before the insurance company kicks in cash. A higher deductible will mean a lower premium price, but it also means that you must fork over more of your own money in the case of a calamity. Deductibles are usually offered in amounts of $100, $250, $500, or $1,000.

Finding a Policy

The first step in the search for auto insurance is learning your state's minimum requirements. Since safe is always better than sorry, most people go beyond the minimum to ensure coverage for a variety of problems. Initially, getting quotes online is a quick and easy way to make comparisons without the pressure of an agent. Have on hand your driver's license number; the year, make, and model of the vehicle; and the vehicle identification number (VIN). Geico, Allstate, Progressive, and all the other companies you've seen on TV are worth checking out, but be sure to do as much comparison shopping as possible. Use Esurance.com to get quotes and compare company ratings, and gauge the level of coverage provided by each policy against these recommendations from About.com:

- Bodily Injury Liability: $300,000 per occurrence
- Property Damage Liability: $100,000 per occurrence
- Medical Payments: $10,000 per person
- Uninsured Motorist Bodily Injury: $300,000 per accident
- Uninsured Motorist Property Damage: $10,000 per accident
- Collision Deductible: $500
- Comprehensive Deductible: $0-100

Insurance lingo to a recent grad can be like AIM-speak to your grandmother, so you may want someone who can answer questions and walk you through the process. If this is the case, consider getting off the 'net and into an insurance agent's office (locate agents in your area by going to company websites or using Automotive.com's "Agent Locator"). When you finally make a decision, don't get off the phone or leave the agency without knowing exactly what you're getting (i.e., how much are you paying, what is your deductible, and where are you covered). Finally, familiarize yourself with the correct protocol should anything go wrong. How you handle the scene of an accident can make a huge difference in whether or not your claim is accepted.

Mileage Chart: How Much Do You Need for Gas?

Even once you have a car, the cost of gas can really add up from month to month. Assess your commuting patterns and then use this chart to determine how much you should expect to spend filling up each week:

Miles driven per week ▶	100	125	150	175	200	225	250
Miles per gallon ▼	Cost per week (assuming $3/gallon)						
10 MPG	$ 30.0	$ 37.5	$ 45.0	$ 52.5	$ 60.0	$ 67.5	$ 75.0
15 MPG	$ 20.0	$ 25.0	$ 30.0	$ 35.0	$ 40.0	$ 45.0	$ 50.0
20 MPG	$ 15.0	$ 18.8	$ 22.5	$ 26.3	$ 30.0	$ 33.8	$ 37.5
25 MPG	$ 12.0	$ 15.0	$ 18.0	$ 21.0	$ 24.0	$ 27.0	$ 30.0
30 MPG	$ 10.0	$ 12.5	$ 15.0	$ 17.5	$ 20.0	$ 22.5	$ 25.0
35 MPG	$ 8.6	$ 10.7	$ 12.9	$ 15.0	$ 17.1	$ 19.3	$ 21.4
40 MPG	$ 7.5	$ 9.4	$ 13.1	$ 13.1	$ 15.0	$ 16.9	$ 18.8

Cars & Commuting

Car Checklist

"License and registration, now step out of the car. Are you carryin' booze on you? I know a lot of grads are..." Okay, maybe that's not how the song goes. But at any rate, we hope that if you've still got "99 Problems," at least walking to work ain't one.

Just to make sure you are completely road-ready, we've compiled a quick checklist of car issues to deal with before driving. However, be aware that each state has its own unique regulations and standards (i.e., you may need to get a safety inspection in addition to an emissions test), so it's always a good idea to visit the Department of Motor Vehicles to make sure that everything is ready to go. Also, as a general rule, just make sure your tags, insurance, and registration are up-to-date and you should be fine.

- **Driver's license.** Presumably you didn't forget this little detail. Hit the Department of Motor Vehicles if your license has expired or if you need a new one. Remember, if you have moved you can get a driver's license in your new state of residence (which in turn can help you register to vote there, but is not always a requirement).

- **Camera.** Get your "citizen journalist" on and start carry- ing a disposable camera in your glove compartment. Photos from the scene of an accident could be clutch when it comes time to file a claim or dispute a parking ticket.

- **Cell phones.** Find out if it's legal to operate a cell phone while driving in your state before you get caught looking like an a-hole.

- **Emissions.** There should be a little sticker on your windshield that says your vehicle fulfills the state's emissions standards. If not, or if the expiration date on the sticker has passed, you need to contact the DMV to find your local emissions testing station. Ask about exemptions (some states exempt new vehicles), and make sure you don't get caught driving with an out-of-date sticker.

- **Insurance.** Don't get on the road without insurance—it is illegal and dangerous. See page 185 to learn about choosing a policy.

- **License plates.** Having license plates is necessary. Get them from the DMV for $25-50, but be prepared to pay extra if you want them to say "UR PWNED" or "LOL WTF." If you re-register in a new state (see next page) and receive new plates, make sure you send the old ones back and notify the tax collector in the town where the car was originally registered—some states charge property tax on cars, so you want to avoiding paying if you don't actually live there anymore.

- **Oil changes.** Again, there should be a sticker on the windshield telling you the mileage mark at which you should get your next oil change. Keep an eye on the odometer and don't go too far over this mark. Midas, Jiffy Lube, and local garages can all handle this task, so don't be afraid to shop around. Also, be wary when they tell you about the five other things that they can do to fix up your car while you're there.

- **Parking.** Make sure you have a reasonable and secure place to keep your car, both at home and at work. Some cities and neighborhoods require resident parking permits for street parking. If so, you will need to contact City Hall and apply for a permit, a process that generally requires a driver's license from the state you're in and proof of residency (e.g., gas/electric bill, bank statement, cable bill). Pay all parking tickets on time to avoid getting clamped by "the boot."

- **Miscellaneous.** Do you have enough windshield washer fluid? What about antifreeze?

- **Registration.** Hit the DMV to register your vehicle, and keep the registration with you in the car at all times. Registration is required every year, so if you move and have a permanent address in your new post-college city, you may want to register in that state. However, if you still have an address in the state where you came from (e.g., mom and dad's house), you can also continue to register there.

- **Seatbelt.** Are you wearing your seatbelt!?!?

Top 10 Ways to Be a Green Driver

According to the U.S. Environmental Protection Agency, driving a car is the worst thing that most people do for the environment during their lifetime. (Yes, even worse than using aerosol deodorants!) Here are ten easy ways to reduce the harm of riding:

1) **Drive less.** Use public transportation or carpool. Better yet, take a walk or hop on your bike.

Top 10 Ways to Be a Green Driver Continued...

2) **Drive smart.** Speeding not only gets the cops on your tail, but it also attracts the wrath of Captain Planet because high speeds produce greater emissions. Heavy breaking and rapid acceleration also reduce fuel economy, so try to develop a smoother driving style.

3) **Don't "top off."** When you fill up a tank of gas, don't give it that extra little pump at the end—oil spillage is not a good look. Also, always make sure the gas cap is secured tightly.

4) **Regular maintenance.** Another factoid, courtesy of the National Safety Council: poorly-maintained vehicles can release ten times the emissions of well-maintained ones. Follow the manufacturer's instructions for routine maintenance and look out for red flags like reduced fuel efficiency, leaks, and black exhaust billowing out of the back of your whip.

5) **Get an eco-friendly car.** Newer cars are better for the environment than older ones. Check the fuel efficiency rating and look into trendy cars that people like Larry David drive. (As a bonus, these "green" cars are often cheaper than their competitors.)

6) **Use clean fuels.** Using "oxygenated gasoline" and alternative energy sources like ethanol and electricity is way better than burning through tanks of premium unleaded in your Hummer.

7) **Cool it on the AC.** Pumping the air-conditioning while crawling through city traffic can increase fuel consumption by over 20%.

8) **Avoid idling.** Idling is wasteful, so avoid the Wendy's drive-thru and L.A. traffic jams. Also, don't sit around in parking lots bumping Joan Jett like a chach.

9) **Get good tires.** If you want to floss, cop 22-inch rims. If you want to make the world a better place, use radial tires because they offer less rolling resistance and thus improve fuel efficiency. Also, make sure tires are properly inflated at all times.

10) **Cut the dead weight.** Have you driven around with golf clubs and an old bag of cement in your trunk for the past nine months? Extra weight means reduced efficiency, so treat your car like a professional athlete and shed those pounds.

Chapter VII: The Grad 2.0 Plan

The Grad 2.0 Plan

Grad 2.0 \ *grād too point ō* \, *noun:*

(1) A college graduate who exceeds the minimum requirements of life after college. Interests may include cooking, dating, and self-education.

(2) A well-rounded, engaged twentysomething who evokes the traditional qualities of Homo Universalis (i.e., the Renaissance man).

During the 15th century, there were men in Italy who were good at everything: sculpture, painting, rowing boats, extemporaneous speaking... the list goes on to include most activities. They were called Renaissance men, and they were so remarkable that the entire century was named after them.

There are many lessons we can learn from these historical figures. But one stands out: the path to enlightenment is not found through narrow focus, but rather through well-roundedness. This perspective is what galvanized Renaissance men as the preeminent humans of all-time.

Of course, we all know today that too much of one thing doesn't do a body good when it comes to booze and snack foods. But what about things that are supposed to be good for us? Take careers, for example—they are generally cast in a positive light, but if you are not careful, you'll suddenly find yourself 30 years down the line with high blood pressure, a sexless marriage, and a boatload of regret. Indeed, even in the first year out of college, many recent grads obsess painfully (and unnecessarily) over jobs, apartments, and all the other issues discussed thus far, sometimes even falling victim to a "One-Year Rut." Those things are important, no doubt. But there's got to be more to life after college than work and bills, right?

Of course there is. All that effort "setting up your life" is just a launching pad for actually enjoying it. It's easy to get tunnel vision and miss the fun and fulfilling aspects of graduate life, but that would be a grave mistake. At the root of the recent grad experience is freedom—the ability to make your own decisions, own your free time, and pursue your interests beyond the confines of a syllabus. Just imagine what sort of hijinks Leonardo Da Vinci would get up to in the new millennium!

The point is that being in your twenties is supposed to be awesome, not stressful and depressing. As such, taking advantage of life beyond the office should be par for the post-college links rather than an anomaly. Staying in touch with friends—whether at a bar, through reunions, or on Facebook—is just fun, while other activities like reading, cooking, and checking out your city's cultural offerings can accrue fringe benefits in your professional, social, and romantic life. It's now up to you to find all those things that were served up on a platter in college (e.g., knowledge, food, and a well-stocked dating pool).

Clearly, there's no need to become a whole new person. Nor should you feel pressure to be "highbrow," whatever that even means. As much as we think Tony Robbins is weirdly handsome, we certainly don't want this chapter to sound like self-help. Approach it more as a collection of things that it took us a while to appreciate after graduating—a head start, if you will. At the end of the day, the "Grad 2.0" plan is really just about branching out, having fun, and generally fostering a nice *espirit de corps* within the recent grad community. Just as with extracurriculars at school, the idea is to choose the things that appeal to you rather than doing everything.

In this chapter, we will provide you with the crampons to avoid the most common pitfalls of the one-dimensional grad. There are many years of growth, change, and enjoyment ahead of you, but here we focus on a preliminary "7-step" program for the post-grad transformation. This crash course covers getting cultured, staying informed, dating, cooking, navigating reunions, reassessing your Facebook profile, and—perhaps most importantly—keeping it real. The main theme is balance: the Tao of Grad 2.0ism is all about being well-rounded and making sure that the pressures of the "transition" don't make you blind to all the sweet stuff that graduate life has to offer.

The Cultured Grad

Recent grads who spend all of their time stressing about jobs, apartments, and credit card bills are sort of like those kids who spent all four years of college cloistered away in the math library. But while it's taboo to hate on huge nerds, transition-obsessed

grads definitely get no love. After all, the newfound freedom of post-grad life should *expand* your capacity to pursue cultural endeavors, not limit it. No matter how brilliant and interesting the students were at your alma mater, college was probably a bit culturally insular since studying and partying trumped all other activities. Even though you probably have less free time now than you did in school, you may find that you have more flexibility in deciding how to use it. Now is the time to finally dig into new topics, not because they'll help your GPA or career prospects, but just because they interest you.

Oftentimes, the term *cultured* carries a lot of implicit value judgments about what counts as "culture." But as we like to say, "He who likes Nick Cannon movies shall not throw stones." If you are into classical music, Impressionism, and ballet, then by all means foster those interests. However, if you're into German graffiti and late-eighties heavy metal, then don't feel you have to get into Handel. Of course, no one should be afraid to branch out and try something new from time to time, but at the end of the day, upgrading to Grad 2.0 is really just about doing things that *aren't* work. And while it's nice to go a step beyond *US Weekly* and *High School Musical* from time to time, don't feel that traditional "high culture" is the only Holy Grail worth pursuing.

Things to Do

There are countless ways to be a cultured grad, and they don't all include looking at an upside-down urinal and pretending it's a magnificent *object d'art*. From museums to organizations and bar events, there are tons of places to see and things to do other than getting drunk (although sometimes you can get drunk at the same time—cash back!).

Museums & art galleries. Appreciating art does not have to involve flipping through flashcards and pouring through semi-illegible notes. Why not get out there and enjoy it on your own terms? (As you know, it always looks better in real life than it does in the textbook.) A lot of museums are free (or free to the employees of many major corporations if you show your ID), and new exhibitions rotate through the halls several times a year. Many museums also offer free or very inexpensive lectures on topics ranging from the Renaissance masters to Pixar animation, or weekly classes taught by professors and historians. *But hey, I thought you said no more "learning"!?* In an attempt to get us twentysomethings through the doors, many museums offer monthly parties (e.g., First Fridays at the Guggenheim in New York City) where you can appreciate art, grab a drink, and maybe even find a date. If you are really into the scene, you can also get on the art gallery circuit. Better yet, stop by openings, where you'll often find an open bar and hors d'oeuvres, not to mention a lot of interesting and/or hilariously pretentious people. It's a great place to socialize or bring a date. To stay abreast of openings, just sign up for a gallery's newsletter, usually on its website.

Events at bars. Bars aren't just places to drink and pretend to watch sports while staring at people lecherously; many bars also hold monthly events such as poetry readings, art shows, trivia nights, and discussions on prearranged topics (e.g., time travel at a meeting of The Secret Science Club). The best way to find out about these types of events is by reading blogs, local magazines, and newspapers. You can even check to see if your favorite bars have websites with event calendars.

Organizations/Charities. Many charity events (particularly the ones called "galas" or "balls") have the reputation of being overly ostentatious, but it's important not to let the

The Grad 2.0 Plan

Tips & Tricks:
How to Find Things to Do

Finding interesting things to do around your city is not as difficult as it seems—you just need to know where to look. Start where our generation always starts, on the 'net. Browse local blogs (e.g., the Gothamist blog network), and sign up for e-mail lists from your favorite institutions (e.g., bars, museums, concert venues). If you're brave enough to venture offline, check out the events section of the free local papers that are handed out at delis, coffeeshops, and bars, or pick up local magazines with cultural listings (e.g., *TimeOut*).

snootiness of some attendees overshadow the objective. Even though attending may cost more than a regular night out at a bar, at least you're supporting a good cause. In addition, everyone will be dressed to the nines and it's a nice place to meet people if packed dive bars and dance floor conversations aren't your style. If you're more interested in the cause than the party, why not go ahead and volunteer for the charity? There are a range of charities that fit anyone's interests, from working for a religious center to supporting the local public library or children with terminal illnesses.

Concerts/Operas. You probably won't forget to see your favorite band's concerts, but don't rule out shows at smaller venues and local music festivals (every city's got one). Want a classy night out? Consider visiting the local Philharmonic/Symphony or Opera. While ticket prices can hurt your bank account, rehearsals are usually free, and venues tend to sell tickets at highly discounted prices the day of the performance (check each venue's website for details). Also, it never hurts to flash a student ID if you've still got one.

Film. There's more to film than Will Ferrell and torture porn. Museums often show an interesting lineup of documentaries and other special-interest films that don't make it to the major cineplexes, and smaller independent theaters will give you a chance to brush up on your French (or your reading, as the case may be). Furthermore, if your city has a science center, you may be in for the audio-visual treat that is an IMAX movie. If you're really lucky, it has an OMNI cinema—those are the jam!

Sports/Parks. The fact that we now spend the majority of our days in stale, climate-controlled environments is all the more incentive to get out and enjoy the outdoor public spaces that your city has to offer. Watch street performers, bang a congo in a drum circle, or just enjoy nature. Many parks also have sports leagues, courts, and fields that can be rented out by individuals or teams. There's always a range of leagues for everyone from novices to wanna-be pro athletes, so make sure to check out local rags, league websites, and gyms.

Things to Read

A bizarre thing happens when you leave school—suddenly, you actually want to read all those novels and articles you were assigned in college, rather than skimming them before class and stopping after the first 25 pages (or renting the movie). I guess that in spite of ourselves, we all have that little rebellious streak in our minds telling us not to take orders. Unfortunately, we also have that little voice that says, "Don't pick up that book. *Flavor of Love* is on and it's going to be really funny!" Thankfully, you don't have to sacrifice "TV time" (or "social time") for "reading time" anymore. Pick up a newspaper before work, browse some blogs during your lunch break, or bring a book on your daily commute. Here are some ways to stay on top of the things that interest you most:

Blogs & zines. No matter how esoteric your interests may be, you'll always be able to find content providers who cater to them, usually in the form of a blog or a zine. (And if you can't, maybe you have a business on your hands!) You can find blogs through a simple Google search, check out Technorati to browse by topic, or figure out where your favorite blogs are linking to in order to find more reading options. Once you find your favorite blogs, you can of course check the pages day-in and day-out. Alternatively, you can use a magical little tool called an RSS reader. Essentially, RSS is a rudimentary version of a website that contains only titles and teaser text in digest format. Each title also links to the actual article on the blog/zine. A user can then subscribe to the RSS feed using a feed reader (e.g., reader.google.com or Bloglines). This will enable you to check just one location (your feed reader) and see all of the new postings on all of your favorite blogs. It might take a few days to get used to, but once you do, you'll never turn back. The wild, wild west of blogs just got a lot tamer—Will Smith was clearly using an RSS feeder when he said, "I'm the slickest they is. I'm the quickest they is... did I say I'm the slickest they is?"

Magazines/Industry rags. Second only to *Uncle John's Bathroom Reader*, magazines and industry rags are ideal reading materials for short spans of time. Stop by a local newsstand to find something that piques your interest or check online. In addition, once you've begun your job, see if you can find the relevant industry paper (e.g., *The Deal* for the investment banking industry). While the annual subscriptions rate might be steeper than that of *People*, having a subscription to an industry-specific publication will keep you in the know and possibly even give you a leg up on your coworkers.

Books. Sometimes life seems too busy to sit down with a good book, but try to make time. Books aren't always cheap, but there are ways to purchase them inexpensively. (There's also a little thing called the public library, should you deign to get reacquainted.) Find used editions of the books that interest you on Barnes & Noble's website, Amazon.com, Half.com, and second-hand stores. However, remember to factor in the shipping costs when considering buying used versus new books online. If you're buying several books at a time, buying the new ones and having them shipped in one box from Amazon.com may be cheaper than buying each from a different used-book seller with its own shipping fees. Finally, don't forget about audiobooks—if reading on the go makes you nauseous, listen in the car or throw them on your MP3 player for the subway ride.

News. And last but not least, don't forget about the daily news. In fact, we think the news is so important that we've dedicated an entire section to it—just keep on reading!

The Informed Grad

Being at school can put you in a bit of a cultural bubble where information from the outside world rarely registers on your radar. For a time, subjects like "the racial politics of cricket in neo-colonial India" take precedence over the Iraq War. But after graduation, new issues can be just as distracting—between work, cooking your own food, paying the bills, and trying to do something fun once in a while, it is difficult to stay on top of current affairs. But no matter how much we like to rail against the shortcomings of Fox News, CNN, and the sensationalism of the 24-hour news cycle, the fact remains that having a basic grasp on what's going on in the world can have many auxiliary benefits. It will improve your conversational skills, help you impress older colleagues who think our generation doesn't care about anything, and maybe even give you added insight into the broader implications of the things you work on. Beyond that, issues that used to feel very remote now actually affect you—social security, rising property prices, taxes, intrest rates, etc. The more engaged you are with the realities of civic life, the more the news will resonate with your experience and become relevant to you.

There are an unlimited number of news sources and tons of ways to get your information. Part of the process involves figuring out what is important to you and tracking down the outlets that cater to your interests. However, the most important thing is that you develop a habit of checking the news that fits into your week, engages you, and doesn't feel like a chore. Try to maintain an outward-looking view, but don't neglect to read into what piques your curiosity most. If your first inclination is to breeze past the front page and go straight to the arts section, then don't feel bad. (Just try to go back to the headlines before you're done.)

Bow Down to the Interweb

Even though you look the part with the *Wall Street Journal* tucked under your arm or a printed copy of *Times Digest* poking out the pocket of your overcoat, there's really no need to pay for quality news in this day and age. With every major news source around the world battling for a Web presence, there is not only an overwhelming amount of choice, but also a great opportunity to get a well-rounded set of viewpoints. Find a few sites that will cover a range of opinions and make a point of surveying the headlines and the stories that jump out at you whenever you have time.

Podcasts and Magazines

The problem with reading news online is two-fold: firstly, it involves being at the computer every day, which for some people might not be a reality (though we hope you can at least check Gradspot.com). Secondly, it's easy to be dragged into the 24-hour "breaking news" culture where every five seconds something else emerges to threaten the tenuous balance of life on Earth. Of course, the more important stories will stick for a longer period of time, but it's still difficult to keep track of the deluge of information and put it in perspective. Podcasts and weekly news magazines can help lighten the burden.

The Grad 2.0 Plan

Podcasts. If you have an MP3 player, subscribing to a free podcast is a great way to get news while multi-tasking. *The New York Times* has a whole slew of options, including one called "Front Page" that summarizes the major headlines every morning in about five minutes. *The Wall Street Journal*, BBC, and CNN all offer a large lineup as well, though if you want to put your trust in some people who really know radio, NPR has the podcast game on lock. Getting a longer, weekly show like *Weekend Edition* and trying to listen to it in segments at the gym or during your commute will keep you well-informed, as well. Depending on what your job entails, you could even listen at your work station while filling in Excel spreadsheets or mindlessly entering data.

Magazines. Weekly news and opinion podcasts can put the week's events in perspective, but sometimes you just want to grab a magazine, get comfortable on the toilet, and learn as much as you can before all is said and done. If you are willing to shell out a little *dinero* for the privilege of being worldly, we highly recommend a subscription to *The Week*, which offers a roundup of the best in US and international media. If you want to make your "7 Days" more Craig David-like, you could even shell out for the British edition. *The Economist* is another good option for a world perspective, though obviously you're getting a certain bias toward what is and is not newsworthy.

Front Page Flash

We at Gradspot.com know how hard it is to stay on top of what's going on in the world. In order to help you out, we created *Front Page Flash*, a weekly roundup of the most conversation-worthy news stories that we think you should know about. Check the site every week, or sign up for the *FPF Newsletter* to have it delivered straight to your inbox. We want to make it simple to soak up the top stories and we hope you find it useful. This shouldn't be the sum of all your news consumption, but during a busy week it should help you get by. *Front Page Flash—we don't report the news, we link to it.*

Dating

In many ways, dating will never be as easy as it was in college. A combination of raging hormones, close quarters, and socially acceptable binge drinking meant that meeting people was rarely an issue. But as a result, dating in college could be a bit like eating fast food—a preference for convenience led to lowered standards, so even though you really liked Wendy's, you might have been willing to settle for Dairy Queen if it was closer.

To say that college cheapens the meaning of dating is an insult to the many fulfilling relationships that blossom in dorm rooms around the country. However, there is some truth to the notion that college life breeds more of a "hook-up" culture than a traditional "dating" one. Because people live so close to one another and often have very

little to do, relationships can easily remain casual, and the concept of an actual "date" is rarely stretched beyond watching *Hitch* in a soiled common room or eating at one of the more moderately priced restaurants around campus.

Dating in the "real world" can be a rude awakening for some, while others find it to be a breath of fresh air. The important thing to remember is that dating can still be casual—just because you've graduated doesn't mean you have to immediately find a husband or wife. Wait until you are at least 30 for that crisis. For now, here are some more pertinent things to consider before diving into the post-college dating scene.

Expanding the Dating Pool

In college, almost every class, party, and trip to the dining hall is a chance to meet a date for the weekend. Indeed, some people don't even need to venture outside the dorm to get it cracking. In the post-college world, the demanding schedules of working life and the lack of communal living spaces can make it much harder to meet potential mates. The upside, however, is that you are likely to meet a broader range of people outside of the confines of campus life, where—in a very general sense—everyone is at a very similar stage in life. Take advantage of the opportunity to date outside your age and type. At the very least, you'll expand your horizons and learn a thing or two about your preferences. Just try to avoid going too young or too old—one is illegal, and the other is just a bit odd.

Prepare to Get Burned

One of the things that's difficult about dating outside of college is you lack the social network and shared community that not only make it easier to meet people, but also ensure that accountability remains high. In college, everyone knows everyone else and the gossip mill is exceedingly well-oiled. This means your dirty laundry will get aired out worse than Lindsay Lohan's, but it also means

Tips & Tricks:
For Guys—Should I Pay on a First Date?

In spite of all the fuss about "equal rights," it turns out that most girls still expect dudes to pay for them on first dates. Trying to split the bill might be acceptable, but you have to know how to approach the issue. If you advocate "going Dutch," your date might think you are proposing some sort of despicable Flemish sex act and slap you in the face. Asking to "go halvsies" will make her think that you are into men (though maybe that's the vibe you are trying to give off), and suggesting that you each pay for your own order is awkward and probably won't work out in your favor. Worst of all, she may interpret your negotiations as evidence that you just want to be "friends," because if you really wanted to get it cracking obviously you would try to buy your way into her pants! The best bet is to ask for the check at the appropriate moment and then make the motions toward settling it on your own. If your date protests, offer mild resistance and continue. If she protests further, she probably actually means it, so you can give in and split the bill. Problem solved!

you are more likely to run into hook-ups on campus or have friends who have friends who know the person you dry-humped on Saturday night. Out in the wider world, it becomes easier to treat people horribly and disappear off the face of the Earth when you no longer want to see them. That's not meant to be a depressing revelation, but rather a caveat for those who are used to a more insular dating pool. If he or she doesn't

Tips & Tricks: Office Romance

Now that you're out of college, office romance is no longer something that only happens on TV and in the movies. You might walk in on some risky biz in the copy room, or you might be the one who gets walked in on. Before you dip your hand into that honey jar, however, make sure you are familiar with all the consequences by turning to page 124.

call back, you may never know why. In this case, you've got to just keep it moving and assume it's for the best.

Where to Meet People

Many recent graduates say the hardest part about post-college dating is figuring out how to meet people. Let's face it, not everyone is adept at picking up strangers in bars, and some people require a more structured social scenario to feel comfortable striking up conversations with new people. Without a built-in social scene at your disposal, you might have to think outside of the box when on the prowl. The key is to take every opportunity you're given to meet someone new, because you don't know when you might get another. Try attending alumni events in your city, joining co-ed sports leagues, or even perusing dating websites like Match, eHarmony, and PerfectMatch (see next page for "Confessions of a Match.com User"). Attend cultural events (see p. 197) where you are likely to meet people with similar interests. It can be intimidating to put yourself out there in these types of situations, but keep in mind that those efforts that aren't blessed by Cupid's arrow should at least become stories worth telling your friends.

The Importance of Matchmaking

Just as networking for a job is made exponentially easier if you have a connection to the person you are talking to, being "set up" for a date takes some of the pressure off by providing a foundation for conversation. Go out with your coworkers and meet their college friends, or ask your friends if they have met anyone interesting through their jobs. If you are doing the matchmaking, don't be too heavy-handed about it. Instead of just sending two people off on a blind date (though this might work if they are interested), try inviting them both to a party at your apartment or a group dinner to see if they hit it off. Believe it or not, this is how many fruitful relationships are spawned. And if love does blossom, the couple will probably make you the best man or bridesmaid at the wedding. Or, if things go sour, they may stop being friends with you altogether. It's touch and go!

Long-distance Relationships

If you graduated in love or somewhere close to it, you may find yourself in the extremely difficult situation of dating long-distance. Maybe your beau has yet to graduate, or maybe you and your mate have decided to pursue opportunities in different cities. There's no magic formula for a successful "LDR," but start off on the right foot by installing a webcam or subscribing to a "quality" website to help get you through the sexless days. Next, have a candid conversation about your expectations and set a realistic timeframe for how long you will remain apart. If neither of you is sure how long it will be, cut it off when you can no longer afford the $14.99/month for that website. Another thing to discuss is whether you are going to have an open or closed relationship. If it's the former, will you be expected to disclose your extracurricular activities or keep them to yourself? Going with the "let's see what happens" approach might work for some couples, but it also breeds suspicion—presumably one or both of you is moving to a new place and meeting lots of new people, so long periods of "radio silence" might not go over well. Realistically speaking, however, these are all just things to think about. There is no set rulebook for LDRs, so the real key is just to be honest with yourself about your motivations and feelings. If you feel dissatisfied, is it because you wish you could be with your boyfriend or girlfriend, or because you wish you could see other people? Follow your gut rather than intellectualizing the situation to death, because there are few ways to rationalize a $500 phone bill and months of loneliness.

The Grad 2.0 Plan

Confessions of a Match.com User, by Nick Schonberger

In an effort to meet women and expand my daily activities beyond reading, writing, rap concerts, and basketball games, I have joined Match.com. I have high hopes… well, not really. DC was recently voted as having an only slightly less unattractive population than Philadelphia, where most people look like Rocky Balboa used their face as a punching bag. Now, I am certainly no Fabio, but I am reasonably handsome. A few women have "winked" at me. I have "winked" back at some. I have even sent some introductory e-mails, which, for the most part, have yielded no response.

Could it be my tag line, "Moderately Interesting Man Seeks More Interesting Woman"? Could it be that I list my occupation as "Very Minor Internet Celebrity"? I mean come on—my blog on SocialConsumer.com is massive (at least in a very small niche). Perhaps it is just that I have uploaded only one picture.

Confessions of a Match.com User Continued...

Speaking of pictures, I find it troubling that, on a dating site, women post pictures of themselves hanging on OTHER MEN. Is this supposed to attract me? I am not interested in threesomes! (Not that kind, at least.) I will also judge a lady based on whom I perceive her to have been with in the past. Greasy-haired dude with striped shirt and black shoes? I will flat out assume she has questionable taste.

Another odd feature of these pictures is the preponderance of vacation shots. They are always of a beach. Do these women ever go anywhere interesting? They always list "travel" as a favorite hobby, yet they all seem to have been to Italy, the beach, and the beach. Personally, I would never list "travel" as a hobby. It seems ridiculous. And, I am convinced that if I list the places I have visited in the last year (Memphis, Vegas, Little Rock, Charleston, Boston, London, Oxford, Atlanta, New York, etc.) it would just make me look like I sell some weird s—t.

Most of the women list their drinking habits as "Social, one or two," and then have loads of pictures of themselves drinking giant margaritas that are in fact four or five drinks. As someone who has spent the last 18 months transitioning from an antisocial alcoholic man to an antisocial sober man, I find this troubling.

Selecting "turn ons" from a finite list has also distressed me. Can I only be excited by flirting, public displays of affection, money, power, body piercing, and skinny dipping? Coincidentally, the first time I made out with a girl, she suggested skinny dipping and I said, "Why don't we just get naked here?" Then we awkwardly fooled around on a lakeside dock. I guess that is another story altogether and I suppose skinny dipping means that you are interested in risk-taking. On the whole, this is a pretty good trait.

Turn offs are basically chosen from the same list. I simply selected body piercing, and then realized that on Match, all piercing (including ear) is considered body piercing. "Eating with one's mouth full" was not an option and neither was "wearing Ugg boots." The limits of Match are indeed frustrating. For body art you can select "none," "strategically placed tattoo," or "visible tattoo." Well, in my mind, all good tattoos are strategically placed. The logic behind this wording not withstanding, the tattoo options are a prime example of Match using useless categories in an effort to define compatibility.

The Grad 2.0 Plan

The Reunion Grad

After college, one of the major changes to your social calendar will be the preponderance of reunion-oriented events that begin to crop up. Beyond the unforgettable Fifth Year High School Reunion, there's the football rivalry weekend, the freshman dorm get-together, the model congress rendezvous, and quality time with that family you started during your year abroad in Brazil. All of these reunions present a potential viper's nest of awkward situations and uncomfortable conversations. To keep your head above the fray, be sure to heed:

Gradspot's Reunion Commandments

Thou shalt not be the first to ask, "What are you up to now?" It's inevitable. You know it's coming. But you still don't want to be the one to admit you have nothing else to say. If someone asks you, then you are sort of obliged to reciprocate, but at least you can join in with the knowledge that you held out for a higher ground. A good tactic is to find an odd feature of the surroundings and comment on it—"James, look up there. Did you ever notice that remarkable gargoyle in all our years here!?" If you walk away soon after, you will leave the impression that you are now hilarious and maybe slightly insane.

Thou shalt not talk about thy job for over 60 seconds. It's amazing to me that when it comes down to it, people barely know what their best friends do at work. No matter how much they try, no one truly cares enough to figure it out. So the chance of giving even the remotest s–t about what a casual acquaintance does is highly unlikely–keep this truth in mind. As a corollary, it is reasonable to make up stories and spread various falsehoods about your life to spice up the proceedings.

Thou shalt not treat reunion as therapy. Apologizing for something that happened years ago is mad awkward, as is telling people in intimate detail about how depressed you are. Keep it light–reunions are long and you can't really afford to drag the mood down.

Thou shalt not get blackout drunk. This is controversial, but hear me out. There are some people you expect to wild out, and when you see them you'll laugh and say, "That dude is so good at partying!" But you don't want to be that dude. To most people, getting insanely wasted suggests that you are depressed and have adjusted horribly to life after college. Not a good look.

Thou shalt not blow up other people's spots. A lot of drunk people with very little to talk about are the WD-40 that keeps the gossip mill running. "Is your old roommate and best friend still addicted to heroin?" "Did you hear that James is a convicted sex offender?" People will pry at you for information about others, and you may even let things slip unwittingly amidst the mayhem, but it's a losing game. Better to just say that everyone's "doing great" and leave it at that.

Thou shalt not assume that everyone is the same as they used to be. Some guys who used to be complete a-holes may very well still be a-holes, but at least give them a shot at redemption. This works best for high school, especially once the open bar kicks in–the biggest chaches probably drank a lot in high school, but now they've had at least five years to reign themselves in. Meanwhile, the dorkier kids probably started drinking when they were in college, so it can be shocking to see them pound a mixed drink. But hey, everyone's got to grow on his own terms.

This final commandment also holds true when it comes down to getting down–the nerdiest girls from school, according to my brother, are the ones who will jump you the hardest at the reunion. On the flip side, if you are a huge dorkus malorkus and think you might be able to rekindle something with your high school sweetheart, be prepared to see her skipping into the woods by the football field with a "high school hero."

The Grad 2.0 Plan

The Post-grad Facebooker

What NOT to Do on Your Facebook Profile

Danny Danger may be the man, but he's still lonely. Friend him on Facebook now!

As discussed in Chapter 3, making your Facebook profile work-appropriate is a pretty simple task: change your privacy settings and try to avoid obvious red flags like bad-mouthing of employers, drug use, and racism. Gaining Facebook acceptance amongst your peers, on the other hand, is a complex and nuanced subject worthy of careful consideration. After graduation, many of the most "college" activities lose their cachet among more refined grads. By the same token, aggressive leaps into "adult" activities— e.g., getting married and having extravagant dinner parties—can be just as suspect to prying eyes. To date, I've never seen a Facebook profile that perfectly balances professional and social demands, but here are a few pervasive social networking faux pas that everyone should try to avoid:

Posting your own wedding pictures. Similarly, don't put "engaged" or "married" for relationship status, and certainly don't send out wedding invitations via the 'book. This type of thing really seems to freak people out. Wedding photos are probably best on ShutterFly... maybe Flickr at a stretch. The problem is that deep down, Facebook still breeds the subconscious allure of juvenile behavior and "random play." Within this context, life-long bonds of love throw people off and make them uncomfortable. It's like those people who bring their children to bars—they think everything is still all good but they just end up pissing everyone off.

Joining Facebook after graduating. This is such a cry for help that it is actually disconcerting. Another related issue is late-blooming. We see this when a person displays a post-graduation surge in Facebook activity, furiously entering the public sphere under the guise of being an incredibly social and fun-loving person. This is evidenced by a multitude of tagged photos from various sources and excessive wall-posting. Late-blooming appears a bit alarming because in post-college life, it is almost impossible to party at such a high clip without the aid of drugs. Overall, this behavior is indicative of a person who has serious regrets and forgot to showcase her exceptional partying and socializing skills at the appropriate time.

Putting up an album for every weekend of the year. Much like *Real World* cast members, some people go to the same bar every weekend and apparently have an awesome time. Because the rest of us are very bored and voyeuristic, we will be forced to click through all 47 pictures of every album, even though they fill us with revulsion and acrimony.

Using the wall for private correspondence. Since its inception, the wall has been the cause of many of Facebook's most egregious faux pas. In post-grad life, walling what should be messaged remains an epidemic. Doing this is the online equivalent of shouting across the table. Even the notion of saying happy birthday publicly is self-congratulatory. It says, "Look at me everyone, I'm a good friend!" Use messages for private correspondence and use the wall to publicly roast people. Because that's what it's for!

Joining a disingenuous network. Hanging out in New York a couple of weekends a month does not make you eligible for the New York network. Nor does having a grandmother that lives in Santa Monica validate your inclusion in the L.A. network. In many ways, joining a non-school affiliated network is useless enough as it is, but trying to fake the funk in a network that's a stretch is just dishonest. A lie is a lie.

Posting uninteresting links. With the advent of the news feed, Facebook users are able to push their agendas on you like never before. Posting an interesting link, or even a self-serving one, is not such a crime, but incessantly linking front page news is offensive. If you are trying to prove that you are informed, that is obnoxious. If you think your friends need you to keep them informed, that is even more obnoxious.

Posting Facebook videos. This isn't really a faux pas, but has anyone ever seen a good Facebook video? I reckon the answer is "no," because they are all terrible. This is a bizarre phenomenon, and it just goes to prove that no one on YouTube is actually an amateur. What a sham! At least YouPorn keeps it real.

Including your entire CV under "Work Info." I've heard other people complain about this maneuver, and I can see how it might get one's goat. It is the most clear and distressing indicator of the transformation of Facebook from hilarious free-for-all to lame career networking tool.

Cooking

One of the harshest realities of living independently is dealing with the necessity of feeding yourself. For many of us, dining hall meal plans only reinforced a lifetime of culinary ineptitude. Maybe you mixed a nice salad or figured out that making *matzo pizza* was not as disgusting as expected, but beyond these trial-by-fire experiments most college students graduate with no basic grasp of how to buy, store, and prepare food. "Home economics" isn't at the top of the curriculum anymore and, let's face the facts: some parents are horrible in the kitchen, as well.

One thing is for sure: you watched the Food Network. And it turns out that after watching over 1,000 hours of programming, you know how to properly remove the meat from a snow crab yet you still don't know how to boil an egg. There's no real shame in that—any self-respecting person would rather watch Gordon Ramsay tell someone to go f–k himself than write down a Rachael Ray recipe. But a rotation of simple, quick recipes is essential to any budget- and body-conscious grad. This talent, in turn, has a trickle down effect into your broader life, allowing you to impress friends, dates, and colleagues with your culinary acumen.

The Grad 2.0 Plan

Tips & Tricks:
The Price of Eating Out

Take-out and delivery 'straunts fuel the recent grad community, but they are also a severe drain on our collective wealth. Between work, seeing friends, and running errands, many people don't think they have time to prepare their own meals. And with online and even text-message ordering becoming easier than ever, they end up eating out for lunch five days a week, grabbing something most nights on the way home, and going to restaurants on the weekends. Even if you have a corporate account to cover the meals you eat in the office, this behavior can really hurt your bottom line—"A burrito a day keeps the savings at bay," as they say. But while grabbing a Philly cheese steak from the corner store is a "kickable" habit, we realize that going to dinner with friends is about more than just the food. However, you need to make it affordable. If you are a barista and your friend is a hedge-fund analyst, make sure she knows that you don't want to go to $100-a-head dinners (unless she's paying). Don't get suckered into paying above your means out of pride, because the fact is that every American city has amazing food for cheap if you know where to look. Choose your battles wisely, and find ways to cut costs, such as skipping appetizers and desserts or going to BYOB establishments.

Kitchen 101

More than likely, your kitchen looks more like a small closet than the *Iron Chef*'s Kitchen Stadium. But that doesn't mean you can't whip up a few well-practiced dishes. Before you get started, it's important to make sure your cooking area is clean. At the end of the day, *Ratatouille* is still a bit unrealistic, and having a rat infestation is not going to make you into a master chef. Use a disinfectant to wipe down surfaces, especially after handling raw chicken. Clean all your cookware and utensils to avoid germs and food that always tastes like the *last* thing you cooked. ("I really want stir-fry on Thursday, so let's have it on Wednesday, shall we?") As annoying as it may sound, it really is easier to give things a quick rinse and scrub immediately after using them than battling with a dried-up, filth-encrusted mound of dirty dishes at the end of each month.

All clean? Okay, let's proceed. Hopefully you have a stove-top, oven, sink, and refrigerator. If you're lucky you have a microwave and a coffee-maker, but those are luxuries. When push comes to shove, you can do most cooking with some pretty simple tools—don't be lured by the stainless steel pairing knife and the fresh yogurt maker when you reach the checkout at William-Sonoma. Here are a few essentials that should serve you well:

- Pots
- Pans
- Colander
- Cutting board (plastic is easier to clean)
- Baking sheet
- Spatula
- Ladle or large wooden spoon
- Cutting knives
- Knives, forks, and spoons
- Glasses and mugs
- Plates and bowls
- Tupperware (for leftovers)
- Can and bottle openers

Tips & Tricks: Finding Recipes

Along with Gradspot.com's "Recipe of the Week," check out these sites for recipes, tips, and cooking inspiration:

- Chowhound.com
- CookThink.com
- FoodNetwork.com
- Recipes.com
- Epicurious.com

Learning to Shop and Cook

Stocking "the pantry" (or the mini-fridge and cupboard, as the case may be) can be an inordinately onerous task for recent grads with no kitchen know-how. When you do a lap around the supermarket and end up with cereal straws, a steak, Kool-Aid mix, Double Stuf Oreos, Dave's Insanity hot sauce, and some Kraft Singles, you know you've got a little work to do. Putting some thought into your purchases beforehand (or even bringing—dare I say it—a *shopping list!?*) can help cut down on impulse buys and produce a more useful end result. So, what should you look for?

Beyond the obligatory salt-pepper-olive oil triumvirate, take stock of what you like to eat and build your pantry based on your preferences. Do you like hummus? You probably do. But did you realize that keeping garlic, oil, a few spices, and a can of chickpeas around will help you to make it whenever you want? The fun of learning to make your favorite foods from a few staple ingredients is two-fold: 1) You can experiment with a food that you already know, or 2) You can create a personalized version of a favorite dish that will wow your guests.

Pasta, polenta, and oatmeal are other good stock items; they will never leave you hungry and they are extremely versatile. Frozen chicken, pork, or sausage all serve a similar purpose in the kitchen—they provide a good base protein and can be deployed in a wide range of dishes. Pasta is also a major staple for the young adult, but unfortunately most pre-made sauces are gross. We recommend keeping a can of crushed tomatoes around at all times to make a quick sauce from scratch. Over time you will develop a "signature" sauce, and everyone will think you are either a) of Italian ancestry, b) the jam, or c) both. A basic tomato sauce is the perfect base for a variety of add-ons, and it requires only minimal cooking time. After you get a great multi-use sauce going, make a big batch and save it for pastas, pizzas, or whatever else you dream up.

At the end of the day, it's important to remember that "when you're hungry" is not the only time of day to cook. Take an hour on the weekend to make a large casserole or chili that you can eat throughout the week. If you have roommates who are also interested in eating at home more, set up a rotation where you cook for one another. Finally, don't be intimidated—with basic ingredients it is hard to make food that is inedible, and remember that, these days, you've always got the Internet as a resource to tell you the difference between frying and sautéing, or to provide simple recipes for almost anything.

The One-year Rut

No matter what stage of the post-college transition you find yourself at, it's almost inevitable for a "grass is always greener" mentality to creep into play at some point in the first year after graduation. Missing college is normal, but there are a lot of reasons for hitting a rut beyond a simple dorm party jones. The people who have been working begin to feel burnt out and wonder if they should have taken time off. The ones who took time off fear that they have fallen behind. And the rest feel like they have toed the line between work and relaxation without fully accruing the benefits of either. The fact is that, to a certain extent, every recent grad is at the bottom of the totem pole, and that can suck. It can also be intimidating to adapt to environments populated primarily by older, more experienced people rather than by your peers. As a result, some grads even fall victim to "Imposter Syndrome": feelings of fraudulence and an irrational fear of being "exposed" as inept or incapable (see p. 136).

If you are suffering an extended malaise, you are certainly not alone—whether they are willing to admit it or not, most grads experience some degree of discontentment around the 12-month mark. It's easy to become overwhelmed with the responsibilities and choices of post-college life, and these concerns can lead to exaggerated fears about the future. If you can barely juggle a boyfriend, an internship, and an apartment, how are you ever going to be able to handle marriage, kids, and mortgages? People do it, and so will you (if that's what you want). But you are probably not at that stage in your life yet, so why worry? Getting bogged down in the small stuff will only drive you crazy, as will thinking too far ahead. Instead, try focusing on means rather than ends and setting practical, achievable benchmarks for yourself (e.g., "How can I get my next story published?" rather than "Why am I not the editor of *The New Yorker*?")

The Grad 2.0 Plan

Socially, the reality of post-grad life begins to sink in as it grows harder to stay in touch with friends, and demanding work schedules make dating and hanging out much more difficult than they were in college. Jealousy can also rear its ugly head, and it's definitely worth keeping that in check—just because your friend in a different industry got her first promotion already doesn't mean that you should have done the same. Rather than bemoaning this state of affairs, make a concerted effort to reconnect with old friends or go visit them in the cities where they've settled. Friendships and romantic relationships may require more work than they used to, but they can also be more rewarding as a result.

> ### Tips & Tricks: When to Admit You Hate Your Job
>
> Does it feel like work is throwing you into an emotional rut? Be sure to assess the source of any negative feelings about your job—if you are just frustrated because you think you should be running a company, dating a model, and vacationing in Bora Bora, then give yourself time. However, if every day fills you with dread and you often consider staying in bed instead of going to work, maybe you are in the wrong job. If you've been there a year and feel discontent, now is the perfect time for a change. For tips on switching jobs, see page 137.

We won't lie: post-college life isn't all fun and games. But remember that it's a time of *transition*. Embracing your "Grad 2.0" potential will definitely help you to enjoy yourself and take some of the attention off work, roommate problems, and anything else that's getting you down. Moreover, rest assured that people bounce back from the struggles of this transitional phase, often with a new sense of purpose and recalibrated goals. How do we know this? Because we went through it ourselves, as did most of our friends. And you and your friends probably will as well. That's the point—it's nothing new and just like everyone before you, you'll bounce back. The important thing is that during "The Rut" you maintain the perspective that you are not the victim of a massive anti-recent grad conspiracy—"The Rut" is normal and you're in control of your own life, so go out and get what you want!

The Golden Rule of Grad 2.0

Alas, fair graduates, we've come to the end of the road. We've talked about jobs and apartments, student debt and Facebook etiquette. Of course, there are many more issues that you'll encounter in your post-college life, but we can save those for another time and place (i.e., Gradspot.com). Hopefully, you've now got all the tools you need to lay a foundation for your new life of independence. Before we say farewell, however, we'd like to impart one last piece of advice that we hope you'll keep with you wherever

The Grad 2.0 Plan

you go: No matter what happens, always remember to keep it real. It may sound clichéd, but bear with us for a second.

"Keeping it real" lies at the very crux of the Grad 2.0 dilemma. The first few years out of college are a roller coaster of emotions and doubts, and it's incredibly easy to lose track of what's important. In an attempt to fit in, many working n00bs have the tendency to conform to the stereotypes promoted by their jobs. For example, i-bankers talk about being "bullish on big boobs" and fashionistas try to model their lives on the girls from *The Hills*, even though the girls on *The Hills* are barely old enough to drink.

The new emphasis on money and salaries can make even the most down-to-Earth grads begin to doubt themselves. And in some ways, the desire to assimilate is an inevitable byproduct of being at the bottom of the totem pole. But in the long-run, compromising the person you really are will only draw you further and further away from the people and places that will make you happy. So how do you keep it real?

In his remarkable book *Reallionaire*, Dr. Farrah Gray details the amazing combination of positive thinking and entrepreneurial gusto that made him a millionaire by the age of fourteen. Starting out selling moisturizer on the street, Farrah caught the capitalist fever and began pitching his ideas like he was Nolan Ryan in a pinstriped suit. Before he knew it, he had an endorsement from Oprah and more successful business ventures than he could count on his two well-moisturized hands. At the beginning of the book, he offers the following definition of a reallionaire:

> **Reallionaire:** Someone who has discovered that there is more to money than having money. A person who understands that success is not just about being rich in your pocket; you have to be rich on the inside, too.

While Gray focuses primarily on balancing the power of money with the importance of staying grounded, his message is ultimately one of perspective. The emphasis on internal well-being that transcends traditional definitions of "success" is the key to Farrah's ethos. And, as a recent graduate in a world full of uncertainty, it should be yours, as well.

Do the damn thing, young graduate. You are ready to achieve great things, and we look forward to hearing about them. Remember: whenever you need us, you know where we stay at—Gradspot.com, *the* destination for life after college.